VOICES
FROM A
'PROMISED LAND'

Palestinian and Israeli
Peace Activists
Speak their Hearts

conversations with
Penny Rosenwasser

CURBSTONE PRESS

The publishers thank the following for their support
of this book:
   The Asner Family Foundation
   Carol Bernstein Ferry & W.H. Ferry
   Grandmothers for Peace International
   Neil Ortenberg
   Stephen W. Welch

*to the memory of Albert H. Gaynes who believed strongly
in the need for a just peace in the Middle East*

Front cover photographs:
   left: Suha Hindiyeh © 1990 Susan E. Dorfman
   right: Chaya Shalom © 1989 Sarah Jacobus
        their interviews begin on pages 49, 64, 195 & 253

Printed in the U.S. by BookCrafters

Curbstone Press is a 501(c)(3) nonprofit literary arts
organization whose operations are supported in part
by private donations and by grants from the ADCO
Foundation, the Connecticut Commission on the Arts,
the Andrew W. Mellon Foundation, the National
Endowment for the Arts, and the Plumsock Fund.

ISBN: 0-915306-57-3
Library of Congress number: 91-55411

distributed in the U.S. by
InBook
Box 120470
East Haven, CT 06512

published by
CURBSTONE PRESS
321 Jackson Street
Willimantic, CT 06226

For my Grandaddy, Morris Ness,
who taught me what it means to be a Jew

ACKNOWLEDGMENTS

As I am often reminded through the words and examples of my Palestinian and Israeli friends, it's not one person so much who makes the difference. It's the cadre, the web, all of us together. In that spirit, I want to acknowledge and thank the many, many people without whose support and help these interviews would still be a pile of cassette tapes in the corner of my closet.

Of course without the open hearts of the Palestinian people or the commitment of these Israeli peace activists, none of these conversations could have happened. I especially thank Hani Baidoun, Riyad Malki, Carol Ann, and all the courageous women and men in these pages who welcomed me into their lives. So many of the conversations were not on tape, but helped me understand — with Yvonne Deutsch, Jamal, Hadija, Majda. And I wouldn't have connected with all these people without the help of Barbara Lubin, Sarah Jacobus, Sherna Berger Gluck, Huda Jadallah, Lynn Gottlieb, Ann and Khalil Barhoum, and Larry Harris, among others.

Special thanks for their skills go to photographers Susan Dorfman, Sarah Jacobus, Rick Rocamora and Irene Young and graphic artist/cartographer Jos Sances. I appreciate the use of quotes, charts and resources and thank the Palestinian Human Rights Information Center, the Foundation for Middle East Peace, Alice Walker, Nancy Bereano of Firebrand Books and Patricia Gardiner of the Middle East Cultural and Information Center.

Great gratitude goes to Melanie Kaye/Kantrowitz and Maya Angelou who sent kind and validating words at crucial moments. The sixteen other members of the 1990 U.S. Women's Peace Brigade asked just the right questions at two of the enclosed talks. Thanks to all of you; you know who you are.

And in the beginning . . . there was Professor Al Lever, who taught me to pay attention to what was happening in the world and to do something about it; Sara Gentry, who first introduced me to Palestinians from refugee camps; Amy Horowitz, who helped me early on to love my Jewishness *and* to struggle for justice; Lil Moed, who was "my first interview" about Women Against the Occupation (SHANI) in early 1988. We miss you, Lil.

Krissy Keefer and Nina Fichter of The Dance Brigade were instrumental in opening up my eyes through their performance piece on the Sabra and Shatila refugee camps. Maria Nemuth provided essential guidance and inspiration, and Dulce Argüelles generously donated her multi-media experience.

So many wonderful friends and colleagues provided love and support throughout various stages of this process. Thanks to Barbara Higbie, Elizabeth Fides and Debbie Fier, Lisa Vogel, and Laurie Mattioli for home-cooked meals and massages at vital times, and for being there. Robbie Osman listened while I ranted from a less-enlightened perspective for a few years, and he didn't go away. I am grateful for the love and support of Maria Barron, Cindy Cleary, Robin Flower, Miranda Bergman, Emily Shihadeh, Carrie Koeturius, Carolyn Brandy, Cristi Delgado, Rhiannon, Chris Coyote, Moli Steinert, Donna Canali and Stephaine Marohn. And to Flor Fernandez and Colleen Kelley, who reminded me to keep an open heart, and Gloria Emerson, for her encouragement. The arrival of my brand-new niece Elizabeth kept my spirits up during those grueling final weeks.

Noelle Hanrahan's and Gwen Jones's skillful and creative engineering at KPFA's studios in Berkeley helped me transform these interviews into what I hope was "good radio." I am incredibly grateful for their patience, flexibility and support under great stress. Special thanks also to my radio teachers Ginny Z. Berson, Marci Lockwood, and Asata Iman, as well as the following KPFA family members who helped these programs reach the airwaves: Jim Bennett, Ken Ellis, Sylvia Mullally-Aguirre, Phillip Muldari, Melanie Berzon, Chuy Varela, Tish Valva, Brid Burk, Gerda Daly, and Richard Wolinsky.

The following were part of my human data-gathering bank. Immeasurable thanks and affection to Muna Tamimi, Michel Roublev, Marcia Freedman, Lorene Zarou-Zouzounis, Dolores Taller, Abla Shamiah, Daniel Boyarin, Laurie Hasbrook, and Hilton Obenzinger.

My great gratitude to Sandy Taylor and Judy Ayer Doyle of Curbstone Press who enthusiastically said "Yes!" and keep saying it; to George Evageliou who "made it happen," along with Zeena Tawfik, Dawn Cook, Jim Faris, Irene Glasser, Rana Kardestuncer, Lisa London, and Sevaria Drake.

Heartfelt thanks to: Vivienne Verdon-Roe, who helped me stay healthy; Chela Blitt, who believed in me; Howard Levine, who patiently taught this stubborn Capricorn about computers, and who is a constant source of information, assistance, and support; Claudia Cranston, who teaches me how to love myself; Fran Peavey, for her consistent encouragement, boundless assistance and advice, and chocolate chip cookies; Suha Hindiyeh and Chaya Shalom, for their invaluable perspective, information, time, courage, love, and support; Bob Baldock, who believed enough in this project to literally bring the publishers to my doorstep, who provided overwhelming support and guidance along the way, and who painstakingly created the cover design; Sarah Jacobus, for filling in so many gaps, both emotionally and informationally — for photos, interviewing assistance, data, contacts, taping support — for sharing trust, love and sisterhood in this work; my muse, also known as HP, for guidance and sustenance; and to my Mom and Dad, Dutch and Artie, for always being there.

And especially thanks to Barbara Lubin of the Middle East Children's Alliance, my ever-courageous, ever-outspoken, ever-hilarious, ever-loving mentor and friend, who gave me those first valuable contacts and told me that I *could* travel to Palestine & Israel alone, that I *could* ask "important people" to talk to me — and who taught me to take myself completely seriously, but not *too* seriously.

To all who have been doing this work and fighting this fight long before me, and to all who will continue to seek peace with justice, especially the women — thank you.

Penny Rosenwasser

contents

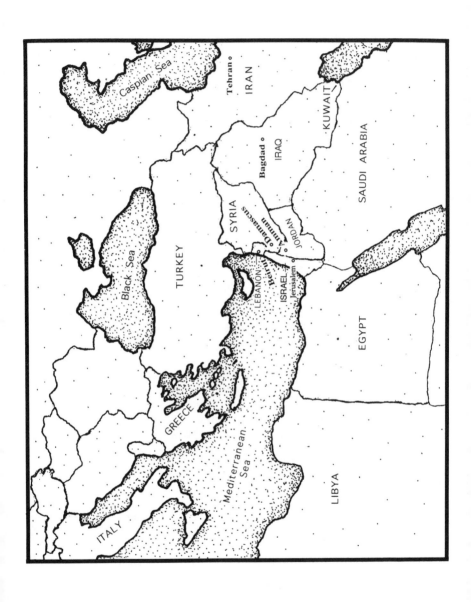

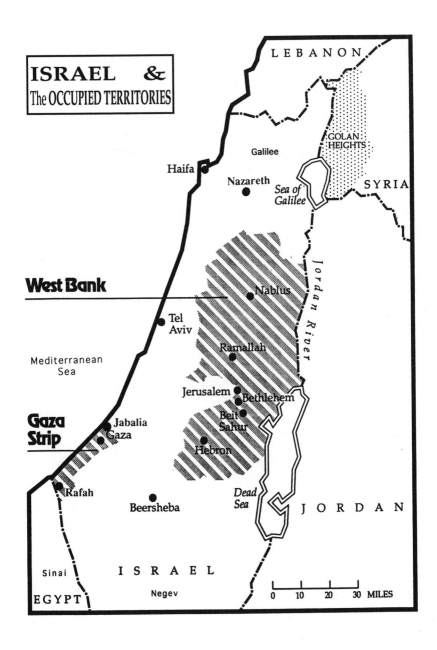

ISRAEL & The OCCUPIED TERRITORIES

LEBANON

GOLAN HEIGHTS

SYRIA

Galilee

Haifa

Nazareth

Sea of Galilee

West Bank

Nablus

Tel Aviv

Ramallah

Jordan River

Mediterranean Sea

Jerusalem
Bethlehem
Beit Sahur

Gaza Strip

Jabalia
Gaza

Hebron

Rafah

Dead Sea

JORDAN

Beersheba

Sinai

ISRAEL

EGYPT

Negev

0   10   20   30   MILES

I fall in love with the beauty
of people in struggle.
The beauty of resistance, especially
when it is non-violent . . .
It is always a magnificent sight
when great masses of people
are able to collectively harmonize
on extremely high moral frequencies.
It is comparable to a sunrise.
— Alice Walker

INTRODUCTION

And Rabbi Tarfon said: "You are not required to finish the job, but neither are you free to desist from embarking on it."
— *The Talmud*

Maybe I'll tell you a little story, a few little stories — no, more than a few. Not so little, either. And not my stories at all.

Here are the voices of Veronika and Qassem, Suha and Tikva, Michel, Nabila, and Rihab. Let them tell you, in a way that newspaper headlines or thirty-second 'sound bites' cannot, how it feels to celebrate Shabbat (Jewish Sabbath) in a West Bank town . . . to survive torture in an Israeli prison and discover a deeper sense of self . . . to march with 5000 other Palestinian and Israeli women from West to East Jerusalem, singing and chanting together for peace . . . to lose loved ones . . . to build trust across differences . . . to hear air raid sirens and run for the sealed room and gas mask — or perhaps there *is* no gas mask . . .

These are voices from a "promised land" — a homeland of promise for *two* peoples, *two* tribes, *all* human beings yearning for a future as well as a present — a present of security, of freedom, of justice and peace. Listen as their stories tell of dreams and realities, tragedies and hopes, frustrations and fears. Stories of roots. Stories of courage, of resilience, of triumph over adversity — and of adversity hurling herself into each new morning.

My story is interwoven now with theirs. These people opened up their homes and their hearts to me, revealing their experiences as well as bits of their souls, over endless cups of thick Arabic coffee on low tables in West Bank villages and Gazan refugee camps. Or perhaps, as in the case of Beit Sahour, there was no table. The Israeli soldiers had taken it away when my hosts refused to pay their taxes to support an Occupation which provides them no services.

The Israeli stories usually came during momentary interludes in their relentless battle for peace: advocating for Palestinian families outside the Russian Compound Detention Center, standing with Women in Black against the

Occupation, grabbing a cigarette during a conference break or in between phone calls.

• • •

And what is my story? Growing up in a Northern Virginia suburb in the 50s and 60s, weaned on dreams of possibility and potential in the Kennedy era, I was a flower-child activist. I picked coffee in Nicaragua, marched for women's and gay rights in Washington, DC, and spent time inside a jail cell for attempts to close down nuclear plants and missile sites. I've co-written organizing manuals on health care and prison reform, produced women's festivals and concert tours, facilitated workshops on fighting racism, and broadcast radio programs on women cultural heroes. Although I was car pooled to Jewish Reform 'Sunday School' for twelve years by Orthodox-bred parents (whose own forebears had fled poverty in Eastern Europe), this was an uncomfortable chunk of my identity. I just wanted to fit in.

Reading Evelyn Torton Beck's *Nice Jewish Girls* (circa 1982) was the catalyst which awakened me to my own internalized anti-Semitism and infused me with a new curiosity about "my people," my heritage, and Jewish women in particular. Soon identifying as an ardent Zionist — based on my new grasp of what had been done to Jews, not just during the Holocaust, but through the centuries — I felt Jews definitely needed a "safe place."

It was only several *years* after the Israeli army wreaked massive death and destruction in the Sabra and Shatila refugee camps in Lebanon in 1982 that I finally acknowledged two distinct realities: worldwide anti-Semitism is thriving, and as a Jew I had to speak out persistently against that and find allies who would stand with me. *And* the Israeli government's treatment of the Palestinian people is inhumane and reprehensible to me — as a woman, as a Jew, as a human being.

Without knowing much about the Palestinian/Israeli conflict, I felt my freedom, in terms of a secure homeland, couldn't be built on the displacement of another people. For me, part of Judaism is *tikkun olam*, or "repair of the world," not adding to its ills. So in December 1989, I traveled to Palestine and Israel, burning with a need to witness, to document, to understand, to listen. That first trip I had only myself, my microphone and tape recorder, and many contacts. And a strong will to create an experience that could help me effectively work for change.

I fell in love with the ancient land, the golden afternoon light, the vast expanses of stone and sky. My heart broke at Yad Vashem — the Holocaust Museum. I bobbed in the Dead Sea, hugged a burro's back in the Judean Desert, prayed for peace at the Western Wall, and days later ran from the clubs and water cannons of teen-aged Israeli soldiers who attacked our exuberant 20,000-strong human chain for peace around Jerusalem's Old City walls . . .

But especially, I was moved by the women. The Palestinian women's unself-conscious vitality, strength, determination, humor, and expansiveness of spirit shone through, from East Jerusalem to Ramallah to Jabalia Camp in Gaza. It shone through whether leading a peace march to Shepherds' Field on Christmas Eve, drawing blood from patients at a mountain clinic, organizing a press conference, or fixing me a huge pot of stuffed grape leaves. They taught me why "intifada" — the Palestinian people's organized resistance to the Israeli occupation (begun spontaneously in December 1987) — means "awakening," or "changing things from the roots." Their struggle for their state, to protect their children from Israeli soldiers, to walk bareheaded through Gaza streets, to learn production skills, to be treated as equals in all their relationships — melded into a dissonant, wobbly-legged but vibrant battle for self-respect and human dignity.

I felt a bond, a kinship, a surge of connection. As Rihab Essawi expresses it: "We are the same; we have the same hearts."

These women told me of the one out of three Palestinian children killed, wounded, or imprisoned since the beginning of the intifada. Of the nearly 1,000 Palestinians killed by Israeli soldiers or settlers. Of the 100,000 Palestinians wounded, including over 50,000 children, 12% of whom are incapacitated for life. Of the 1,700 families' homes demolished and the 800 women who miscarried in accidents provoked by Israeli repression. Of the universities closed since 1988 and the schools open only intermittently, this in a society which values education as much as my own Jewish culture does.

It was with another kind of intensity, a special joy of discovery, that I tapped into the great and earnest hearts of Israeli women activists: committed to change, to movement, to visibility, to cooperation with each other and with Palestinian women, to a persistent push for peace. I saw these women, considered the "heart of the Israeli peace movement," experience the deep pain of being part of an occupying society, with the increased violence this occupation has brought back into their homes and the conflicting emotions which erupt as they take stands against their own tightly-knit Israeli "family."

• • •

When I asked Palestinian women how we, as Americans, could support them, Randa replied, "Bring American women back to work with us." In December 1990, our U.S. Women's Peace Brigade spent two weeks working with Palestinian women's committees and networking with Israeli women peace activists. At Nuseurat refugee camp in Gaza, trapped indoors with "our" families by the nightly eight p.m. curfew, we spent several evenings together — adults and children, Arabs and Jews, women and men, Palestinians and Americans — eating, playing with the kids, struggling with impromptu Arabic/English lessons, discussing politics, looking through each other's family photos. It seemed that if all of us in the world could break bread together like that, then *anything* could be resolved.

We ended our trip by demonstrating at the U.S. Consulate in East Jerusalem against both the Occupation and the U.S. presence in the Gulf. And when Israeli police officer Moshe told us we couldn't chant, we started singing.

Our plane landed in New York City on December 30th, 1990; seventeen days later our country was at war: a war which victimized both Palestinians and Israelis, but not symmetrically. As a result of the twenty-four-hour-a-day, forty-five-day "shoot-on-sight" blanket curfew imposed on the West Bank and Gaza during the war, the economy of the Occupied Territories was devastated, and nearly 20% of its entire gross national product was lost. The "quiet war" continues, with a dramatic escalation of repression and brutality by the occupying forces. Palestinians say they are living under the worst conditions since the beginning of the Israeli occupation — that there is no comparison between conditions before the war and now.

The Israeli government's recent measures, aimed at increased control, have drastically restricted Palestinians' movement and travel. 50% of the Palestinians who worked inside Israel have been refused permits to cross the Green Line and return to their jobs, resulting in an unemployment rate throughout the West Bank and Gaza ranging from 40% to 75%. Cash flow is currently almost nonexistent, food supplies are meager, and 80% of the entire population is living below the poverty line. Gaza is hardest hit, where the economy lost over one hundred million dollars from the war, where we hear reports of women selling their last piece of jewelry for food for their children. A worker told one Israeli reporter: "You are killing us without guns."

The Israeli peace movement not only lost its momentum of 1989 but diminished substantially in response to the Gulf Crisis and war; it is just beginning to rebuild. Yet government polls consistently show that over 50% of Israelis favor negotiation with the Palestine Liberation Organization (PLO) and trading "land for peace" (relinquishing the West Bank and Gaza to the Palestinians). Israeli peace activist Chaya Shalom explained: "People want peace, but they don't know how to input it."

In the midst of the turmoil, new Israeli settlements abound, gobbling up over 70% of the West Bank and 50% of Gaza. According to U.S. State Department figures, Jewish settlers comprise over 13% of the total population of the Occupied Territories, an average of fifty new settlers a day. Over 100,000 olive and fruit trees have been uprooted to create these settlements. Many Israeli peace activists see Shamir's initial grudging agreement to participate in peace talks as a strategy to gain time, while Cabinet Minister Ariel Sharon's bulldozers try to erase the Green Line border between Israel and the West Bank. The plan is to isolate and surround Palestinian population centers, "in the hope of making any discussion of Israeli withdrawal absurd." This occurs despite the illegality of such settlements, according to Article 49 of the 1949 Fourth Geneva Convention on Protection of Civilian Persons in Time of War, which bars an occupying power from transferring "parts of its own civilian population into territory it occupies." Israel claims the land has always been her own and so these conditions are not applicable.

Peace Now spokesperson Galia Golan, who chairs the Political Science Department at Hebrew University, maintains that over 50% of Israelis consider these settlements to be obstacles to the peace process; some Israeli polls place this figure as high as 70%. President Bush has voiced these same words, yet continues to annually send Israel nearly four billion in "no strings attached" foreign aid.

Meanwhile, Israeli Prime Minister Shamir's continued intransigence towards negotiating with the PLO — the Palestinian people's chosen representatives — prevents a real solution to the conflict from becoming more than a distant dream. I hear my Israeli friend Chaya's imaginary imperative to Shamir: "Wake *up*, man!" And a Likud (Israel's ruling party) voter said in a May '91 interview printed in the Israeli daily *Hadashot*, "We have to talk to the PLO. With whom else can we make peace? . . . And of course we will have to give up territories. If we really want peace, there is no other choice."

What do the Palestinian people want? Specifically, the implementation of UN resolutions 242 and 338, which call for the withdrawal of Israeli troops from the Occupied Territories and the establishment of a Palestinian state alongside Israel, building "neighborly relations and co-existence" between the two states. "There is a predisposition among the Palestinians to make peace, but there is not a willingness to give up our basic rights," explains Dr. Hanan Ashrawi, who has met with Secretary of State James Baker on his visits, is Dean of the Faculty of Arts at Bir Zeit University on the West Bank, and emerged as a leading spokesperson for the Palestinian people at the Middle East Peace Conference in Madrid.

And despite the very real complexities of meeting Israeli Jewish needs for security, after 2,000 years of worldwide anti-Semitism — isn't making friends with one's neighbors a much firmer grounding than trying to build stronger fortifications? The motto of the Israeli organization of Arabs and Jews, Shutafut (Partnership), echoes in my ears: "A hero is someone who makes a friend out of an enemy."

• • •

So back to the voices, the stories — the stories without endings. Of what use are these stories to those of us so many miles away? Michel Warschawski gently reminds me that "a society which is unable to grasp its past cannot understand who it is and what to do next." Are there any lessons for *us* here?

Some say this is a phase in the struggle. A long, hard phase. Almost two years ago Veronika Cohen smiled sadly when she said, "I'm not optimistic or pessimistic — I'm working."

And I see Palestinian-Israeli Nabila Espanioli's eyes burning somewhere in Haifa: "I want to live; I love this life. To be able to live in this situation, I have to be active, I have to change things, *try* to change things."

But I am especially reminded of Alya Shawa, in Gaza, gazing at the tree stumps in her front yard — trees destroyed by tear gas. "The trees will grow back. It's good that they didn't burn the roots . . ."

Penny Rosenwasser
Middle East Children's Alliance
Berkeley, California

Statistical information derived from the following sources:
B'Tselem (Israeli Information Center for Human Rights in the Occupied Territories); Coordinating Committee for International NGO's (Non-Governmental Organizations) in Jerusalem; *Jerusalem*, No. 72, May 1991; Middle East Justice Network Newsletter, June 1991; *Middle East Labor Bulletin*, Summer 1991, Vol. 3, No. 2 (Labor Committee on the Middle East); "News from Within," Vol. VII, No. 7, July 1991, and No. 11, November 1991 (Alternative Information Center); "Report on Israeli Settlements in the Occupied Territories," July 1991, Vol. 1, No. 4 (Foundation for Middle East Peace); "The Other Israel," No. 47, May-June 1991 (Israeli Council for Israeli-Palestinian Peace); *The Status of Palestinian Children During the Uprising in the Occupied Territories*, Swedish Save the Children Report, January 1990.

VOICES FROM
A 'PROMISED LAND'

Veronika Cohen
January 1990

Veronika is a Halachicly Observant, or Orthodox Jew, who works in her spare time as a musicologist at Hebrew University in Jerusalem. Since mid-1988, she has spent most of her time organizing dialogue groups to bring Israelis and Palestinians together to try to understand each other's points of view. At the time we spoke, over ten of these dialogue groups were meeting every other week. Originally, members would alternate meetings between Israeli homes and Palestinian homes on the West Bank. Since the Gulf War, however, and the increased travel restrictions barring many Palestinians from crossing the Green Line into Israel, most of these meetings must now be held on the West Bank. While some groups are ongoing, others meet on a short-term basis. Participants average fifteen to thirty per group. How are people attracted to these groups? Essentially by word of mouth, Veronika says — in her own synagogue and in a circle of interested Palestinians.

Veronika's demeanor is almost "grandmotherly" — gentle, yet alert. Her round shoulders carry wisdom, kindness and hard work — and from deep within her bubbles forth the humor of the ages . . .

I spoke with Veronika shortly after the December 1989 international peace actions in Jerusalem.

Veronika: I became very active about a year before the intifada. I read a newspaper story about how we were treating Palestinian prisoners, and I had this unbearable feeling that I either had to leave the country or I had to work day and night to change the situation. I didn't see leaving the country as a solution. You can take the Israeli out of Israel, but you can't take Israel out of the Israeli.

• *What did you hope to accomplish by organizing the dialogue groups?*

Veronika: I thought that even those small-scale contacts between a number of Israelis and a number of Palestinians were crucially important.

• *Because?*

Veronika: I think it contributes to change, in both the minds of Israelis and the minds of Palestinians. To me, the long-term dialogue groups are the important ones because there you really have a chance to grow, to develop, to change. I feel deep within myself that I have changed, I have grown. And I see it among my friends, both Palestinians and Israelis. I think I still have the same political opinions or views that I had before, but I have completely different emotional reasons for having those same views.

• *Can you give me an example?*

Veronika: A lot of us in the peace camp felt, and still feel, that the Palestinians deserve to have a state of their own for both moral and security reasons. A lot of people feel that basically we would be more secure if they had their own state and we had our own state, and it would protect ourselves from within, not being intermingled as we are. Yet a lot of people feel that once they have their state, we really don't care what happens to the Palestinians. They would like to put up an iron curtain between us and them and say, "All right, now you have your country, we have our country and now we don't need to have anything to do with each other any more."

Now that I've gotten to know Palestinian people, it seems to me both impossible and undesirable to have to try to separate our fates. Whatever the solution will be in terms of politics, I think it will have to include at least open borders or some kind of a confederation, in which we will continue to have very close contact with each other. You begin to realize that our fates are intertwined: that we need them and they need us. Whereas, in the beginning, a lot of us felt that what we needed was separation.

A lot of it is simply personal. We feel that these people have become very close friends, so the idea that we wouldn't see each other anymore if there was peace is something that's really unthinkable. I think this kind of close personal contact is missing for a lot of Israelis who are very afraid of Palestinians. Who don't trust them. I think it's possible not to trust a sort of faceless mass of people, but it's something else to sit across from a friend at the table and say to him, "I don't trust you." And I think the kinds of things that happen in the dialogue are because we have an opportunity to say this to each other and then listen to the answer. And teach them why we don't trust them, and let them teach us why we *could* trust them.

They give us very good, rational reasons why it is also in their interest to live with us in peace. Not because they are morally committed to peace, but because it is in their practical interest.

The topic that has come up in every group is the topic of fears. To Palestinians, at first it is shocking and unthinkable that Israelis are afraid. We have very good historical reasons for being afraid. And as time went on and they began to understand our fears, I think it really changed their relationship to us. So they learned about Jewish history. They learn about our traumas that we carry around with us. And we learn about their traumas. It's something very, very different from reading it in a book.

• *Given what they experience in the Occupation, they are still willing to learn about Jewish history?*

Veronika: They are very well informed about Jewish history. I think they are much better informed, by and large, than we are. But together with that they are also willing not only to learn but to become engaged emotionally. Like they learned about the Holocaust *from* us. Not learning about history, but learning about our personal experiences, as each person in the group talked about their family, where they came from, how their family survived the Holocaust.

And so they become very, very careful even in the language that they use. They were once trying to think of an expression, and they said, "Well, this is a solution that we're looking for, but this is not the *ultimate* solution — they were very careful not to say *final* solution, because they realized that that word is not a word that we can put up with.[1]

• *In terms of both the Israelis and the Palestinians in the groups, are the people that are involved from different classes and different educational backgrounds?*

Veronika: By and large, it's better-educated people in the long-term dialogue groups. But there have been a lot of shorter-term dialogues. For example, in Dheisheh Refugee Camp we organized a press conference once for the people of Dheisheh to come and tell their message to the Israelis. Workers and very simple people came. There was a family whose thirteen-year-old daughter had been killed. And the girl's parents came to talk about the fact that they're still willing to live with us in peace. Or families whose houses had been blown up recently. And they came to talk about the fact that they're still willing to live with us in peace. In Jericho a lot of farmers came. But really *everybody* comes to the more open, one-time meetings.

• *Does it ever get really angry?*

Veronika: We try to keep a respectful tone. I think some of the unwritten rules are that every topic is acceptable, but everything has to be treated in a respectful tone. There have been very hot moments talking about violence, because a lot of Israelis look at the Palestinians as being the violent ones in

[1]"Final Solution" was Hitler's term for the mass murder of six million Jews during WWII.

26

this intifada. And so there are discussions about stones versus guns, and the Palestinians get very angry when Israelis talk about stone-throwing as a violent activity. They feel that basically their kids are facing Israeli soldiers with their bare hands. On the other hand, rocks can kill.

Maybe I'll tell you a story. One of my students once approached me and said that he would like to meet Palestinians. He told me that in the Reserves he held a very high position in the army. But he said that he basically considers himself a member of the peace camp, and he would like to meet Palestinians. I told him that there was a group meeting in a few days' time in one of the Palestinian villages and I would be delighted if he came. He said, "*Me*, go *there*? You must be joking. I'm afraid to go there." So I said, "But you just told me that you came back from such and such a place and you were doing such and such, weren't you afraid then?" And he said, "No, then I had my gun, I had my jeep, I had my soldiers. But to think that I would walk in there without my gun — I would never do it."

So I think that that's something that maybe is difficult for you, when you're looking at the soldier blindly beating everybody in sight, to think that this person is terrified out of his mind.

• *Do people cry?*

Veronika: There have been times when I had a hard time not crying. I remember when one of our friends was telling us that the army had instituted a new practice of beating children in front of their parents. Then I think of how I would feel if my children were severely beaten in front of me.

There was a dialogue I wasn't at, I was just told about it. One of the Israelis who came said that he was in favor of "transfer." And I understand that one of my Palestinian friends dealt with it in a very sensitive way.

• *Can you just explain what "transfer" is?*

27

Veronika: Believing that the Palestinians should be forcibly removed from Israel to some other country. And apparently this Palestinian friend responded by saying that he found it so hurtful to listen to that, that his first impulse was to get up and leave the room. But he realized that that doesn't solve the problem, and that in a way he's glad that he had the opportunity to meet somebody like that. To understand that even a person who believes in transfer is in fact a human being, a misguided human being, but a human being.

I think the other important thing that comes out of it is that once you become involved in a dialogue group, you feel a commitment to the people with whom you are dialoguing. So that if something happens to them it's very natural that you rush there and you try to help them. When friends are arrested, you start calling your member of Knesset, and the press, and the lawyer, and you try to appear at their trial as witness and do your best to get them out of jail.[1]

We were called last year the night before Passover. We got a phone call that the Israeli authorities were arresting our friends in Jabal Mukaber [a town on the West Bank]. The night before Passover is the night to stay home and clean your oven. But we just dropped everything and ran. And in fact it really helped. They had rounded up all these people, and they were sitting in a field with their hands behind their backs. And we just walked very close and started yelling over the fence, saying, "We are here, and we hope that you are all right." They said that the minute we appeared the Israelis stopped beating them.

When the massacre happened in Nahalin, they called us immediately and said that no ambulances were allowed through. So we started calling the Red Cross and the journalists and the embassies, and eventually the ambulances got through. And in Beit Sahour, where we have our closest ties, we really try to keep in touch with them, so whenever

[1] *Knesset* — the Israeli Parliament

something happens we try to be a bridge between them and the outside world.

• *Are you ever able to get people out of jail or get charges dropped?*

Veronika: We've been able to have sentences reduced. By the way, I want to correct an impression. It's not a kind of charitable organization. We don't look at it as "Those poor Palestinians. Let's see if we can help them." But it's the way you would behave towards your *friends*. If your friends are in trouble, you help. And unfortunately in the present situation, they're more likely to be in trouble. But I think it's that kind of a feeling, that if there was a real situation in which I would need *their* help, they would rush to my aid.

• *Are there any risks for you in doing this work?*

Veronika: A group of five of us were nearly run over last summer. A settler [a member of a Jewish-Israeli settlement on the West Bank] tried to run us down with his truck. The case is still in the courts. So there is violence, there definitely is violence. A lot of people have been getting threats in the mail or by phone.

One of the larger events that we had planned in Beit Sahour was a Shabbat [Jewish Sabbath] that about twenty-five families, about seventy-five people all together, spent at Beit Sahour. Most of us were religious Orthodox Jews. We came with families and babies, we brought kosher foods from Jerusalem, and the people in Beit Sahour gave us an empty house to use as our synagogue.

Friday night we had dinner together for all the children. The Israeli and the Palestinian children ate together, and then they went out to play. They immediately became friends and somehow managed to communicate. Then the adults sat down to dinner together.

I think the very fact that Israeli parents could just let their kids go outside to play — they just disappeared into the evening somewhere in a Palestinian town, and nobody was particularly worried about what was happening to their child — was maybe one of the most important achievements. We were hoping that the Israeli public would understand that it's possible to go into a Palestinian town, it's possible to sleep there at night. Nobody will slit your throat in the middle of the night. Nobody will drink your baby's blood. You could go there alive and you could come home alive, and really, it felt like a taste of the world to come.

The army didn't know that we were there until the next morning when they heard it on the radio, and then they began to look for us. When they found us they immediately declared the area a "closed military area." Which, unfortunately, is one of the tools that the army uses against the peace camp to really keep Israelis from meeting Palestinians. The minute you appear somewhere, it becomes a "closed military area." But fortunately, a member of the Knesset who was with us argued with the commander and said, "Most of these people are religious; they can't travel on Shabbat." So they decreed that we could stay until the end of Shabbat. Really, the only disaster was that our hosts spoiled the children. Everything else was perfect.

• *Have you ever thought of doing the dialogue groups with young people?*

Veronika: Yes. We have three groups of young people meeting young people. It's much more difficult. I feel much less satisfied with these meetings. We have tried to let them run it without any interference from adults, and I'm not convinced that this was successful. The Palestinian teenagers were much more open, much more conciliatory, and it was very unpleasant for me to listen to the Israeli kids, who were extremely aggressive. They kept saying over and over, "But why do you still throw stones at us?" And basically refused to listen to the answers.

• *Boys and girls?*

Veronika: Yes. I really feel that this has to be rethought. They have a lot of misconceptions. And somebody just really needs to fill in facts, at least historical facts. I was very disappointed that the Israeli kids, for example, just weren't really interested in hearing from the Palestinian kids about what their daily lives are like and what it is like to live under occupation.

They said, "Well, I'm sure it's awful, but it doesn't matter. That's not what we're here for, you know." They wanted to discuss politics and territorial settlements. And these are all kids who started out from a point of view believing that there should be a Palestinian state, but refused to let themselves become emotionally involved with the Palestinian kids.

For myself, I would say that my religious beliefs are basically behind my work. I see it as part of the ethical Jewish tradition. I see no contradiction between what I'm doing and what I believe. I find it heartbreaking that a lot of so-called religious Jews feel that land and power and strict observance of the letter of the law is of a higher priority than ethical behavior towards fellow human beings.

It also makes peace work a little more difficult. I have to rush home on Friday afternoon to be home for Shabbat. I can't participate in a lot of activities on Shabbat, although anything that's within walking distance I can take part in.[1] Like last Saturday's Human Chain around the wall.[2]

I think the situation is changing. More and more peace groups are aware that there are enough religious people

[1]Orthodox Jews cannot drive on Shabbat.
[2]On December 30, 1989, 20,000 people — Palestinians, Israelis, Europeans, Americans — formed a human chain for peace around the wall of Jerusalem's Old City.

involved so that they have to make provisions for that. I know that a lot of groups that I'm involved in have now made adjustments because I'm involved, and know that you can do things Friday morning as opposed to Friday afternoon.

• *Since we've brought up these events which happened last weekend — the women's events and the Human Chain — I'd love to know your reaction to those events, and if you think they will have any effect.*

Veronika: I think that what happened with the Human Chain and other similar events gave me a feeling of dejection, of sort of crying in the wilderness. Because you participate in an event, in a wonderful, beautiful event. And then you look at how it is reflected in the press, and you suffer cognitive dissonance. You don't understand; you think, "What did the press see that was so different from what I saw?" Because what I saw was an incredibly uplifting, wonderful moment. Really a moment of such hope. And then you turn around and all you see are pictures of violence, which apparently was provoked more by the police than by anybody else.

So this kind of reporting makes you wonder, *"How do you reach the Israeli mind?"* I think that is the most important task for the Israeli peace camp, to try to reach the average Israeli who is terrified of Palestinians. And what better medicine for their fear than to see them linking hands with Israelis and saying, "We want peace." But if you can't make your voice heard in the press, if the Israelis are somehow kept from hearing this message, then only the convinced are taking this medicine that might cure them of their fear.

Last Sunday we participated in the event in Beit Sahour where Desmond Tutu came to the Shepherds' Field on Christmas Eve. Both myself and a friend of mine spoke as part of the event. My friend turned to the Palestinians and said, "This is your chance to tell the Israeli people if you want peace." And thousands of them yelled, "Yes!" So we were wondering what kind of effect it would have on the

Israelis. And it was simply *not reported* in a *single* Israeli paper. It was not on the radio. It was not on television. It's as if it didn't happen. So I wonder how the Israeli mind is going to be reached.

- *What do you think?*

Veronika: I have no idea. I really have no idea. The average Israeli is not going to go to the Palestinians to ask him, because he's afraid of him. The Palestinian is not *allowed* to come to the Israeli to tell him what he thinks. And the press does not report our meetings, which are crucial for the average Israeli to know. So that when Teddy Kollek [Mayor of Jerusalem] says, "We are not like Romania [where thousands of protesters were shot by government troops] because we are a democratic country," I wonder what he means by a democracy. Because in a democracy, it's not just a question of people voting for their leadership; it's also a question of having the information on which you can base a reasonable judgment. And I feel that the press, the government, is basically keeping the Israelis from hearing what they need to hear.

- *So what keeps you going?*

Veronika: *Panic.* I really have the sense of a unique moment in history. And if we miss it there could be decades, if not hundreds of years, of bloodshed, to pay for this missed opportunity to make peace. And I have this terrible feeling that the Palestinians are moving, and the Israelis are moving, and that we're moving towards each other. But the pace isn't right, and somehow we're going to miss each other and not meet. That by the time the Israelis are going to be ready to make peace, the Palestinians will have lost their patience, and they will be looking for a violent solution. So I am trying to push Israelis to not miss the moment.

• *Any message of hope?*

Veronika: A message of hope . . . I'm always hopeful. I think the spirit, the Palestinian desire for freedom is an inspiring desire. The same desire that we had in '48.

• *Do you have any message for the people in the United States? Anything else you would want to say to us, or ways that we can support you?*

Veronika: What's very important for us is balanced support from Americans. Americans who go overboard supporting Palestinians only make Israelis more frightened and more entrenched in their views. On the other hand, blind support of the Israeli government's position is probably the worst thing that can happen to us. So some kind of a *balanced* understanding of the complexity of the problem and gentle pressure to keep us moving towards some kind of political solution.

• *In this work you've been doing, what are the main things you feel that you've learned? Especially if you think there are lessons to be passed on from your experiences.*

Veronika: That's a difficult question. One of the things I'm very aware of is that I've been very fortunate in the way that I've been involved in peace work — I've been very aware of the humanity of everybody. Not only Palestinians but also the Israelis that I disagree with. And sometimes I feel that a Jew or an Israeli who feels as embittered about Israeli policy as I do really has to live here, and has to have the daily contact with Israelis, so that you don't demonize your enemy.

You know, I'm aware of the fact that the same person who can break the arms of a Palestinian can turn around and be a very compassionate doctor or a very compassionate teacher. In other words, there is such *complexity* to the situation. There are no angels and no devils. The woman who works in the grocery store in our neighborhood is a very, very lovely woman. She employs a Palestinian in her store and treats him like her own son. She's a kindergarten teacher. Once when I was ill she asked my daughter, "Who is going to cook for you for Shabbat?" She was ready to close up her shop and come cook for me. Then when the intifada started, I heard her say to one of her kindergarten children who said her father was in the army, "Well, you tell your father for me to break the arms and legs of every Palestinian."

You have to realize that we're not dealing here with angels or devils. There's no black and white. Nothing is simple. And all the people who are involved in the situation are suffering. The Left and the Right and the Palestinians. I think maybe that's one of the most important things that I've learned. Because it's very, very important to keep the perspective of the people who disagree with you, to keep that in mind as well.

Their perspective is that they're fighting for their survival. And that I'm pitting ethics against survival. And they're basically arguing that suicide is unethical. I have to argue with them and say that the solution that I am proposing is not suicidal. And I have to force myself on them to make them see this viewpoint. But I think that that's a very important lesson to remember: that it's not that these people are "bad," although some of them probably are — there is always that percentage who are simply evil, and they are really enjoying this — but that's really a very small percentage. The vast majority are people who feel that they would endanger our survival if they would even allow themselves to feel for the Palestinians. And so they refuse to feel. They refuse to see Palestinians as human beings because it's easier for them if they don't.

Maybe the other important thing to realize, that keeps me going, is that human beings can change. Even if I look at somebody whose viewpoint is completely opposite from mine, I don't think it's a waste of time to talk to him. Because his ideas can change as well as my ideas can change. I think maybe that's the greatest cause for optimism. So when people ask me, "Are you optimistic or pessimistic?" my answer is, "I'm neither, I'm working." Because if I meet somebody or something that I don't like, I think maybe I can change it.

Qassem Izzat
December 1989

"They are killing us without guns."
— Gazan worker

I met Qassem somewhat by accident. I was stranded in Gaza, hoping to find a Palestinian family in Jabalia Camp with whom I could spend a few nights. Sure enough, Qassem drove me through the dusty mud-rutted "streets" of Jabalia, waving and chatting to many as we passed, while stones occasionally struck his battered car. Just at dusk we reached Jamal's door, barely in time for Qassem to make it back to his family in Gaza City before the nightly 8 p.m. curfew.

But it was in his cramped journalist's office, bedecked with maps and supplied with a stash of dried beans for munching, that he unfolded his story, as shouts rang out from the street below. Held by eyes so intensely open, I felt his silent tension, his soft and heavy heart, his burning spirit.

• *So you said the intifada started here in Jabalia?*

Qassem: Yes, the intifada started on the ninth of December, 1987, from Jabalia Camp, and then it spread to all of the Gaza Strip, and so continued more than a month just in the Gaza Strip. It was at that time horrible, everywhere massive demonstrations, thousands of people outside in the streets. The intifada still has daily clashes in the Gaza Strip, people are wounded daily. Now, if today ten are wounded, we say it is quiet. Sometimes 200 are wounded. The hospitals frequently get very crowded, you know.

• *And I heard that they want to build a new hospital, but the authorities won't let you?*

37

Qassem: The problem is that we have here in the Gaza Strip just three hospitals. The main hospital is Shifa Hospital, a government hospital, a terrible hospital. I'd prefer to die in my home rather than go to this hospital. But then, we don't have an alternative.

• *Can you tell me why? What's the problem with it?*

Qassem: The problem with the hospitals is that the military government doesn't care and doesn't give money. The hospitals are not clean. There are not enough doctors and nurses. The surgery department has about 100 beds with two nurses taking care of the wounded. Imagine, how can two nurses take care of 100 wounded people at the same time? A lot of different national associations here are trying to build private hospitals, and the authorities prevent them.

You couldn't compare this condition to the West Bank. In the West Bank there are international hospitals, private hospitals. Here, the health conditions are really terrible. Just enter Shifa hospital and you will see. I don't think you will find a hospital like this anywhere else in the world. I believe they will have to destroy it and build another hospital.

• *So tell me about the difference between Gaza and the West Bank, in terms of what's happening with the intifada.*

Qassem: Gaza is a very crowded place, I think the most crowded place in all of the world, and people here are very poor. Two thirds of the population here are refugees from Palestine since '48.[1] So these refugees are just living in the camps and they haven't any land, they have nothing. In the West Bank the conditions are different. Most of the people there are citizens or from the West Bank, so they have better

---

[1] When the Israeli state was formed many Arabs fled or were driven from their homes, hoping to return soon to their own state.

land. They also have some economic advantages, better than in the Gaza Strip.

The main difference with the Gaza Strip is it is isolated from international association, neglected by the media, neglected by everything. Before the intifada you didn't find any agencies here from the TV or newspapers. They haven't any correspondent or stringer in Gaza Strip. Because this is the Gaza Strip. The authorities know this, so there is more brutality here than in the West Bank.

We are famous for oranges here. So sometimes if I want to take some gift for my friends in the West Bank, maybe some oranges, I have to get permission from the authorities, you know. Imagine this! Some fish, because we are beside the sea and our friends in the West Bank, they have no sea there. So, if we take fish from the Gaza Strip to the West Bank, we have to have permission!

This is, I call it, a life of permissions from the authorities. In every detail of life, you need permission. To travel, you need a *lot* of permission. This is the meaning of occupation, not just shooting and arresting. More difficult than the shooting is the daily life of the people here. It is difficult, boring — the authorities control everything and you have always to get permission.

• *When we were looking at the map and I was looking at the settlements, you said two thirds I think . . .*

Qassem: One third of the land of the Gaza Strip has been confiscated for military purposes and for settlements.[1] This is incredible. This is the most crowded place in all of the world, and they bring 2,000 Israeli settlers to live on one third of the land, and two thirds, which is 200 square kilometers, for 700,000 Palestinian people to live on.[2] Imagine! You go to Jabalia Camp and you see how it is. One square kilometer, one-and-a-half square kilometers, and 60,000 people living in

[1] As of July 1991 it's over 50%.
[2] Now 750,000 Palestinians live in Gaza.

it. It is easier in New York City; there they have several-story buildings, you know, but here it is forbidden for people to have a second floor.

• *Why do they have the settlements here?*

Qassem: They haven't any connection to the Gaza Strip. They just want to prove that Palestine is part of Israel. Who will come to live in conditions like this? They can't do anything. They can't work so they take the money from the government, and they build hotels and no one comes. Who's crazy enough to want to take a vacation in the Gaza Strip? They wanted money from the United States, and they spent the money for the settlements while other Israelis need it more.

• *Are the Palestinians in Gaza, especially from the camps, the same culturally as the Palestinians on the West Bank?*

Qassem: The main thing is they are from the same people, the same culture. But, in fact, there are always some details in specific areas like the South. People in the West Bank are living in the mountains and far away from the sea. Here the people do traditional things; the culture is more connected to the sea and agriculture. The West Bank is more open to the world — they can travel, they can go outside. This gives them a more open mind for what's going on all over the world.

In Gaza it is more closed to international people. But in fact they are always speaking some things that are not true about Gaza — that they are more fundamentalist and religious or something like this. Well, this I'm not sure about. Gaza's got religious people, traditional people, like any nation from the third world, you know? Sometimes people make a comparison with Khomeni or Islamic tradition in Iran, but this is just propaganda from the Israeli media about the Gaza Strip.

In the West Bank there are universities, there are institutions, a lot of things that help the people to be more educated, to have more culture. Here in Gaza you couldn't find something like this. Everything here is connected with the authorities. Nowhere are there private associations or national associations. In the West Bank it is different. This has also affected the culture of the people, their way of life. Here it is difficult to boycott a lot of Israeli products because there is no alternative. In the West Bank you have alternatives.

• *When you said you had been detained or imprisoned, what did they do to you?*

Qassem: I was detained. I was arrested as an administrative detainee.[1] I know the main reason is that I am working with a foreign agency. The military government told me, "If you don't stop, we are going to arrest you in six months." In fact, when they arrested me, they didn't give any reason. After a time, after my appeal, they wanted to justify their arrest, so they said that I was a leader of the intifada. This is the accusation against any administrative detainee — "leader of the intifada."

They are banishing all of my family, preventing them from traveling. Because my wife is from the United States, my son is not registered on my ID card; legally he's not my son. This is true! Because they refuse to give my wife an ID card to live here, she is living like a tourist and my son is living like a tourist. The Israeli authorities can deport them at any time, because they have a law that if the mother doesn't have an Israeli ID card that means you have to live outside. So if you stay here, you stay illegally. A lot of things like this exist under the occupation.

• *Harassment.*

---

[1] Administrative detention, a common practice of the occupation, means that a person can be held for months without a trial or even being charged.

Qassem: Harassment. And you feel insecure for your family, so you are always worried. I am always worried about my son, where he will go. The intifada is happening for these reasons. It's not just for national reasons. Even if the Palestinians didn't have any national aspirations, the intifada would come from the daily harassment by the authorities.

• *What do you think is going to happen?*

Qassem: I am a journalist, and I go everywhere, and I see the feelings of the people and how they are thinking. They will not stop the intifada until they have their own independent state. This you can hear from everyone: from kids, from elders, from *shebab* [the boys], from everyone. But the problem is there are no changes in the Israeli government's mentality. Also in the U.S. government's mentality. Palestinians before didn't want to recognize Israel, but Palestinians changed their mentality. The main thing the intifada did was to give Palestinians a peaceful mind; they want to have their own state next to Israel. Even now, the Israeli and American governments don't accept this lesson; they don't change their policy.

I wish what's happened in Romania would happen in Palestine, and then we'd have our own state, and this is better for us.[1] Because to stay two years under this daily pressure and the daily life of the intifada, is worse than thousands being killed. *Really.* Because if thousands of Palestinians died, maybe this would shock the whole world into looking again at the Palestinian people. The Palestinian people are neglected by people on the outside. People are looking at what happened in other places and they forget the intifada, forget the Palestinian people because it has become boring — one or two die, fifteen wounded. If I'm wounded, who is going to take care of my family? We become

[1] when thousands of protesting Romanians were murdered by Ceausescu's troops.

like numbers, and this is the most horrible thing for a human being — to become like a number. Continuing like this is horrible. It's horrible for the children who are living this life daily.

Now, I can give you an example. My son is four years old. He's not living in the camps. He's in better conditions. But still, what's the story he wants from me before he sleeps? Daily, he asks me: "Speak to me about the jail, papa, how someone is arrested and what he eats in jail." What he hears is people are shooting, people are wounded, people are arrested for throwing stones. This he heard from kids in the neighborhood, from the radio, from the TV, from any conversation going on. So the kids are growing up in this condition, and they have this mentality. Imagine how the kids will grow in the future. They are no longer kids. They have lost their childhood. This is the most difficult angle of the life of the intifada which the people outside don't know about: how dangerous it will be if it continues, in terms of how the nation is affected.

For two years now, there is education, but in reality there is no education. Children don't learn anything. They learn how to throw stones, they learn how to protect themselves from the soldiers. So that's why I told you that it is better for the Palestinian nation to lose thousands of lives, and then to have their own state. And the future? Psychologically it's better too, because it will be too difficult to repair the damage from the intifada after we have our freedom, if it continues for another fifty years. It's very difficult. Especially for the kids. A few days ago, we were just speaking to some kids. We want to film a story about them. So, they are sitting with me and we are speaking with them. They looked like men, they were speaking like men. They forget how to be kids, you know.

People need their own freedom . . . their own freedom is coming with the state. That's it. It's not complicated; it's what is happening all over the world. Now, the peace mentality exists everywhere. Eastern bloc and Western bloc.

The problems are solved by negotiations, and Palestinians are willing to do this in order to have their own state. Not to have better houses; they don't need better houses, they don't need better hospitals. They need only freedom, and then they will build what they want. They have the ability. They have the energy. They have the money. They have everything they need to start building. But the main thing they need is their freedom. All of the people support what is going on in the Eastern bloc because the people are asking for more freedom, and they are not occupied. Why not support a nation that has lost all its freedom?

• *So what do you think people in the United States should do? What would be your message to them?*

Qassem: Not to give money to shoot kids. Not to kill people. If they want to give money, give money to help insure peace. The only state that can pressure Israel is the United States, because they get billions of dollars from the United States.

And the main thing is, Israel is not South Africa. South Africa can survive without help from western countries. But Israel cannot live without the money from the United States. If the U.S. takes a stand, they can pressure Israel. It can change the policy of the Israeli government, because they're supporting inhumane behavior with American bullets, with American tear gas. The deportations, why did they stop? Because the U.S. spoke to Israel and said, "No deportations," and now for one year, no one is deported. So it can do something. During the two years of the intifada, 273 people have died in the Gaza Strip. Of those 273, 120 were children, 16 of whom were under six years old.[1]

And just yesterday I was filming a kid, eight years old, from Jabalia Camp. He had three bullets in his abdomen. Three bullets in his abdomen, you know. Eight years old. And this is a thing I see daily.

---

[1] See appendix for updated statistics on intifada casualties.

43,000 Palestinians have been wounded by live ammunition, beatings, and tear-gas inhalation in Gaza. 627 women have miscarried from tear-gas inhalation. And this is just what is registered in the hospital. Sometimes people who are wounded or beaten do not go to the hospital. Imagine 43,000 people from a population of 700,000! Among the beaten you find pregnant women, you find kids, you find the elderly. To be beaten up is really more humiliating than to be shot — more suffering, you know.

And about the curfew. What's the meaning of the curfew? The meaning is, it stops life — *completely* stops life — social life, economic life. Everything is stopped, because you are stuck inside your home and you can't do anything. Every day in the Gaza Strip there is a curfew from eight p.m. to four a.m. So I can't move after eight o'clock. This is daily — from the beginning of the intifada until now. Life is horrible for the people living here. You're awaiting arrest, for soldiers to break into the house to beat you or to beat your family. The mothers worry about their kids. The kids are afraid of the soldiers.

What does the night come to mean? Something that people dislike — hate, not just dislike. Imagine how this changes the mentality of people. Something that should bring rest and comfort has become horrible for them, and this is the daily life of the intifada.

When I leave my house in the morning, I never feel I will come back safely. Something will happen to me. For example, fifteen days ago I was with my friend who was working for ABC. He was filming small clashes, and I was in front of him. Suddenly a bullet hit his abdomen. And he is still in the hospital. He was lucky because he is fat. If it had been me, I'd be paralyzed.

Since the intifada started, eighty-eight houses have been completely demolished as well as parts of other houses, leaving 3,000 people homeless. If one member of the family does some activity, the whole family is punished — it's collective punishment. They punish the kids and the

45

families and the mothers. Of course in Gaza, they can't find a house to rent because there is no house to rent. So they have to live in tents.

• *Do you feel like talking about what it was like in jail?*

Qassem: Before I went to jail for the first time, I was a student at Bir Zeit University, and I was smoking a lot of cigarettes and drinking a lot of coffee. Suddenly in jail you find yourself with no cigarettes, no coffee. It really was very horrible. They'd make coffee for us once a week. They'd make it in the kitchen, which was very far away from where we were, but I could smell it and I'd become very happy that I would drink coffee that day. For days after, I'm happy. The good thing inside the jail is that you become like a kid, because life is very simple. Outside I *measure* myself — I don't find anything to make me happy. But in jail, something like cigarettes or coffee could make me very happy. It's strange — I had my best times in jail and my worst times in jail. Because of the things, you know, which outside you couldn't do — you couldn't have some moments of happiness over simple things like cigarettes or a cup of coffee.

But when they interrogate you they take you to a place called "the butcher shop" — because that's what it looks like. You feel it when you enter. Crying. Shouting. Beating. Imagine for a human being to live in a butcher shop. You're looking for death, because it's comfortable, but it's difficult to find it. You feel it under interrogation. You look for death and you don't find it. Because the life there is more difficult than death. Your physical powers are completely destroyed. You are fighting with your spiritual power. Sometimes you can't, because not every human being has the spiritual powers to fight in this condition.

• *How do you keep going?*

Qassem: For us we haven't any alternative. When I was a student, I was on the student council in Bir Zeit, and I was active in a lot of social activities; of course, this gave me a lot of problems with the authorities — this was before I worked in politics. And then I became a journalist. I like my work. I like journalism, I do my best work in this. I have chosen it for all my life, but still I feel I have to fight. I have to fight a lot just to continue like this. I feel I spent eight months just to be a journalist, eight months inside the jail. They were thinking that I would stop. They raided my office, they confiscated my fax machine and computer, but still I choose it. I believe in it. I am not going to stop.

You can imagine, the last time I was in Ansar prison, I had some problems. The details are not important. But the administration punished me. They put me in an isolated cell. I was alone. They sentenced me to fifteen days in solitary. Imagine! Sometimes even staying one hour alone in your house, you feel bored. But I stayed fifteen days and managed by myself, and I made it useful. I started to think about my life — what's wrong, what's bad — you know, to evaluate your life. You discover yourself, and you discover things you never knew. When you are alone, you start to think about all your friends. I could see them inside my cell, you know. I felt I was becoming crazy. I thought, I am thinking like this because I have nothing — no mattress, just a blanket. This is all I had. No cigarettes. No books. Nothing. Seeing my friends in front of me, but a dream . . . Am I crazy? But I *saw* them, I *spoke* with them. In the beginning I was afraid of something happening in my mind. Then you discover this is another aspect of your life, you can deal with it, and you are not crazy. It is good that you can see your friends when you are that isolated. They are thinking they are punishing you, but still you find some human aspect to help you survive.

I feel the humanity in people everywhere. For me, I don't believe in differences in nationalities or something like this. The main thing is they are human. They can have some traditional practices and beliefs that are different from yours; but the main aspect of human beings is the same. I feel as human beings we all have something inside ourselves which I call potential energy. It comes in its own time, when you need it, but the difference between people is that you use it or you don't use it.

So you have something inside you, you don't know it, as I didn't know it. Before I entered the jail, I didn't feel I could stand up for seven days without sleeping. I never thought about it. But in fact, I find that, yes, I can. I didn't feel that I could stand cold water torture, you know. I dislike cold water. But then I find that I *can*. You don't know it, but it's coming from inside the human being. So this is the way everyone can continue, can go on. *Everywhere*. In a difficult life or a simple life. With a simple life, an ordinary life, maybe you don't have to use it, but in difficult times, you use it.

Suha Hindiyeh
December 1989

The Palestinian Women's Resource Center (recently renamed the Women's Research and Training Society) has just become an institution officially licensed by the Israeli government. Originally part of the Palestinian Federation of Women's Action Committees, the Center is now an independent organization and works with all the Palestinian Women's Committees in the Occupied Territories to document and compile information on the Palestinian and other Arab women's movements, as well as other international women's movements.

Suha Hindiyeh is the lively and versatile co-founder and current director of the Center, managing a myriad of projects in-between her teaching duties as professor of sociology at Bethlehem University. Currently, the Center is focused on developing a women's library, publishing a women's magazine, organizing marketing for cottage industries, and working on pressing social/domestic issues such as assistance for battered women.

When I first spoke with Suha in December of 1989, the Center was situated in a modest house just outside Jerusalem (it has since moved to a sunny five-room flat in central East Jerusalem). It had the usual desks, file cabinets, and typewriters, and hummed with the bustle of women running in and out.

I caught Suha just before she was to escort Archbishop Desmond Tutu on part of his tour of the Occupied Territories. In contrast to the Palestinian women I'd seen in shawls and embroidered dresses, peddling pungent tangerines and figs near the Old City's Damascus Gate, Suha wore a simple western-cut blouse and skirt. I was engaged by her unabashedly direct style, her vast knowledge of the subject matter, her deep sensitivity — and her quick and ready smile.

• *Suha, can you give me some background information on the formation of the Women's Action Committees?*

Suha: The Palestinian Federation of Women's Action Committees was established in 1978 — the first grass-roots women's committee to be established in the Occupied Territories, the West Bank, and the Gaza Strip. When they started the Women's Action Committees, it was about eight to ten women largely from cities, who were educated, well let's say, petty-bourgeois. They found out that large numbers of our women are still socially oppressed, and there are many social problems they're facing, in addition to the national oppression that we are going through as a whole.

Given that, they started going into villages, refugee camps, and cities, undertaking house-to-house visits, talking to the women to see what their needs are. Also, not only talking to women, but to the family as a whole. Because we cannot deny the fact that we are a traditional society or, let's say, semitraditional society, and probably 90% if not more of our women living in villages and refugee camps are socially oppressed, illiterate, and so forth.

Why did we talk with the family as a whole? Because when a woman wants to make a decision to join a committee of her own, the family should know about it — the father, the husband, the brother — and the idea should be accepted. Of course, it wasn't easy at the beginning to recruit women into units and committees of their own, because there were objections from their male partners. It took some time until they understood that when a woman is recruited into a committee in a unit of her own, undertaking different activities and programs, it will benefit her as a person, and it will benefit her family as a whole.

When we asked women, "What are your needs?" they said, "If you want us to be recruited into committees, we have to find somewhere to put our children." The need for kindergartens and nurseries was raised, and then they started establishing kindergartens and nurseries all over. The other need was that a large number of our women are illiterate, so literacy classes started to open. It has taken us some time, but now there are over 220 units of women's action committees, consisting of fifteen to thirty women each. You find them in every village, in every refugee camp, and in the cities. The total number now exceeds eight thousand women members all over the West Bank and the Gaza Strip.

• *In addition to the kindergartens, nurseries, and literacy classes, don't these committees have economic projects as well?*

Suha: Other projects were going ahead — projects such as sewing and knitting, because women used to ask about these skills; they wanted to learn them. We know that large numbers of women, not only in our country, but all over the world, do knitting and sewing — it's part of their domestic work. We went ahead with training in these skills for the women and eventually found out that indirectly we were reinforcing the traditional role of women. Given that, we've started thinking of new projects that won't be as traditional.

For example, we started food-processing projects. Somebody might argue that food-processing projects are also domestic, women's work. But actually when women undertake a food-processing project on premises of their own, in a small factory, it won't be considered a traditional role — because they have to come in contact with merchants to sell the product which they are producing and to go into the market to buy the raw materials. They are getting involved with the society as a whole.

One of these projects, in fact, is the Abasan Biscuit Factory. It's an especially interesting project, and we're really proud of it. Why? Because in Abasan Village, in the Khan Yunis area and the Gaza Strip, we have a kindergarten. Women there used to make biscuits in a small oven for the children, and eventually some of these women came up to the executive committee here and said, "We want to expand biscuit-making to be able to start marketing it in the village, in the Khan Yunis and Gaza, and eventually to sell all over the Occupied Territories."

Of course, as a grass-roots organization, we cannot afford to buy them high-technology machinery. We gave them as much money as we could, and then they put in some money from their own pockets. They went on their own to the market to buy a large oven, which is, for the Abasan women, a big step — to go into the market here in the West Bank or in Jerusalem, to buy a large oven and transfer it to Abasan. And they have rented premises, and now, after about four to five years, the project is going on very well. They've started to be an income-generating project, being able to pay the salaries of the women workers, pay for the rent, electricity, raw materials, whatever is needed for this project. Now, I would say that it's one of our best projects, and they've started marketing in the Gaza Strip as a whole.

Another project that we have is the Isawiya village project. It is a brass-engraving and enamel-work project, which is considered a big step forward for women, because brass-engraving and enamel-work have never been within the realm of women's work. Not only, I would say, here in Palestine, but in general it's considered male work.

• *So how did that get started?*

In one of our exhibitions, a male artist was exhibiting some of his works. Women members of the Women's Action Committees from the Isawiya village in the suburbs of East Jerusalem got interested in this skill, and they asked us if they can be trained to undertake such a project. We asked this male artist, and he's now training them. Now, I can say that they are really trained, and the enamel and brass-engraving work is being sold here and even exported abroad.

Another project which has been established during the intifada is a baby food project, which is a pioneer work among grass-roots organizations. A nutritionist working with

52

us found out that in villages and refugee camps, among low-income people, children are either malnourished or underweight. All the baby food that we have here is either imported from abroad or is Israeli-made, and it's very expensive for these families to buy.

The nutritionist started thinking of legumes and similar foods that we do have here in abundance. She found out that chickpeas and whole wheat mixed together have a protein that is almost like meat protein. This baby food is now being sold in the clinics and childcare centers and has been sent abroad for testing so it can be marketed internationally. Another project involves raising goats and making *lebena*, strained yogurt.

And of course all our projects are run and managed by women. At the moment, women workers and women coordinators of production for the Women's Action Committees are taking a course in management, accounting, and bookkeeping to be able to run these projects efficiently. And these production projects do have a simultaneous aim: to bring women into the production sphere, to earn a living, because we believe that women are equal to their male partners and our program activities are going in that direction.

The other aim of these projects is to be able to boycott Israeli products and, at the same time, to help build our Palestinian infrastructure for the coming state, because our infrastructure has been destroyed during the years of Israeli occupation.

As a nation, we're approaching, hopefully very soon, having our own independent state. Given that, we have to start thinking of laying the basis for a strong women's movement. That's why we're planning to undertake the search and attempt to put forth women's legislation in every aspect — family law, women workers, and many other issues related to women — drafting these legislations and discussing them with the other Women's Committees, with the

Palestinian women's movement as a whole, so as to present it to our government when it comes, hopefully soon.

As Women's Action Committees, we have a simultaneous aim — to raise the socio-economic consciousness of women on a feminist level and to make women aware of our national problem.

• *So a woman is trained, for example, not just how to do the brass-engraving, she'd also have courses in* . . .

Suha: We train them to become leaders in the community, to be able to ask for their rights, to go to school. From a feminist point of view as well, we want our women to be decision-makers in every aspect. On a social and political level.

• *Do the men want that?*

Suha: Well (laughs). . . no doubt there is a change in men's mentality. But still, you do understand that it's not only *our* men who do not want women to be equal to them; it's the case all over the world, and we have to fight for equality, as women.

Our offices here coordinate work with the different units all over, and I should here mention strongly that just because there is a director, it doesn't mean that our work is not done collectively. We *do work collectively* — it's not one person's decision. It's eight thousand women's decision.

In terms of structure, several women are elected from every unit as representatives of each of the eleven districts in the cities, villages, and refugee camps of the West Bank and the Gaza Strip. These representatives participate in the Executive Committee, which then sends representatives to the Higher Committee, composed of about 150 women. Along with the collective structure, there is a president and vice-president of the Women's Action Committees.

• *And then does each unit decide what project they're going to do?*

Suha: Yes, according to the needs of their community. And that's why we say that we do not impose on them what we want, because they live in this village, in this area, and they know what their needs are. They come up and say, "Look, we need this project, if possible, to be implemented." We ask, "Why do you need it?" We discuss it, and then if there is a possibility, the project will be implemented.

• *What effect have the Women's Action Committees had on the intifada, and what effect has the intifada had on the Women's Action Committees?*

Suha: If it weren't for the structure and the organization of the Women's Action Committees and the other women's grass-root organizations — organizations working for the last ten to twelve years among women, in the field, in the city, in the village, in the refugee camps — women might not have been able to be as effective in the intifada as they are now.

We do not deny the fact that Palestinian women have been involved in politics and in the general national movement since '48, if not pre-'48, in military actions, in demonstrations, and so on, but now it's taking a different perspective, a different vision. It's not only that they are going out into the streets demonstrating, it's not only that they're going into the Red Cross or any other institution doing sit-ins. It's not only that they are going to hospitals visiting the wounded, or distributing contributions, food, whatever is needed if a village or refugee camp is under siege. It's more than that. They are *participating in the struggle as equal to men,* which no doubt, indirectly and directly as well, is bringing social change.

But, as we know, social change does not come out of the blue moon, just in a minute or two. It has to take time . . . and we can feel it now, among our women, that social changes are taking root. In addition to demanding their national political rights, they are demanding as well their social rights. But it's all mixed together.

• *In the United States, during the second World War, the U.S. needed women to work in the munitions factories. And then as soon as the men returned, they sent the women back home and the men got their jobs back. I know that in Algeria, women during the liberation struggle were very active and then (laughs) . . . so you understand what I'm asking — how do you keep that from happening here?*

Suha: Well, a nation, *any* nation, should learn from the experience of other nations, and we do say we do not want another Algeria, in respect to women's issues. We do not want another America during the second World War. We're not ready to go back home after the independence, and we know that the struggle is going to be harder when we're going to have our state. Okay, it was said in the Palestinian Charter for the Palestinian State that men and women are equal, but it's an elastic word. We have to work hard for it, to attain this equality.

Here I would like to say that there is a difference between Algeria and Palestine. Why? Because — this is my own personal analysis — in Algeria during the revolution, there was not a strong women's movement. Here in Palestine we do have a strong women's movement, but it still has to work even harder in respect to women's rights, women as decision-makers, as equal to their male partners.

• *Does this movement cross class lines, and does it include women who — I've seen women who appear to be more traditional, maybe in their dress — does it include those women as well?*

Suha: Among the members of the Women's Action Committees, you'll find women who might wear the Islamic dress — long dresses or shawls on their heads — but it doesn't mean that they are traditional in their mentality. Okay, it takes time for them to be able to put aside the Islamic dress, maybe, but through our program we try to make them understand that it's not the way you're *dressed* that shows whether you're decent or not.

And at the same time, it's a sensitive issue that we're going through at this stage of the national and the women's movements. When these women are socially aware, they come to understand, "As long as I'm wearing decent clothes, this is what counts." We are trying to talk with our women from within the social context in which we're living. We should not impose on them western values. We have our *own* values. Given that, we have to be aware of all these issues — how to bring women into understanding how to attain their rights. This is the most important thing to us at this stage.

• *Right now in this period, what are the two or three biggest problems that you're trying to deal with in the Women's Action Committees?*

Suha: On a national and a political level — that we are under occupation. As Women's Action Committees, or any other grass-roots organization, whether it's women's or not, we are facing harassment and brutality from the occupiers. This is the biggest problem, that we're working on. We're struggling to attain our freedom.

The other problem is making women *aware* of the social problems that they are experiencing. And this is what we're trying to do through our different projects and programs, and our discussions with them: to see what their problems are — whether social or psychological — and to train them in different fields. In this respect, it's not only our women, but the nation as a whole.

Because for the last twenty-two years, education has deteriorated, health has deteriorated — all aspects of life have deteriorated as a result of the occupation. It's not easy when you come to think of building up a state after having been under occupation for so many years, and at the same time, as a nation, we've been going through this problem for the last forty years as well.

• *Some of the Israeli women I've spoken with who are active in the peace movement have said to me that they're realizing the priorities for them in their work are to be working with Palestinian women, to be building those relationships. Is that anything that's important to the women that you're working with?*

Suha: Now and then we do have meetings with Israeli women from different organizations, and we're attempting to discuss issues frankly with each other. It's not an easy situation, but we have to work on it as hard as possible, and not in one meeting or two meetings. It takes time to be able to open our hearts freely, but it's going on.

• *Could you tell me some of the lessons that you've learned about what's worked, what hasn't worked, and what's important right now?*

Suha: In any field you work in, you learn a lot. But maybe, as a woman myself, I've learned even more: how to struggle for our rights as women and for my rights as an individual in the society, and how to be able to work with women. It's not easy going into villages and refugee camps to be able to talk and convince them, myself being a Jerusalemite living in the city and having been brought up in a western way. They've taught me a lot.

I recall an incident with a village woman, talking to her about farming. And I asked about the male farmer. She said "Look at my hands; *I'm* the farmer." You come to know that our women — 90% of them, if not more — are working in agriculture. They are the supporters of the family, especially during the intifada, when their husbands, brothers, fathers are being hunted or are in prison. The women are the main breadwinners of the family. Having myself not gone through being on my own, I realized you can learn a lot from them. You learn how to be strong and struggle for life.

• *Who are your heroes, your heroines?*

Suha: All Palestinian women. I don't believe in one hero, because you learn from the people more than you learn from one person. The Palestinian nation as a whole and Palestinian women are the heroes that I look for. And not for an individual. I don't believe in charismatic leaders.

• *Why not?*

Suha: Because nothing is done by one person. He or she might be good in one thing, or several things, but not in everything. I believe in collective work, and collective work brings success — more than one person's work.

• *What do you feel has been your greatest victory so far, either for yourself or as the Women's Action Committees — the greatest achievement, the happiest moment?*

Suha: When I work among Palestinian women, in the village, in the refugee camp, when I see their sufferings, and in spite of these sufferings they still do have hope and yearn for peace.

• *What message do you have for the women in the United States?*

Suha: That we Palestinians are a nation that have suffered a lot. As women, all over the world, we've suffered a lot and we're still suffering, and women of the world should work hand in hand for a better universe. And we are a nation who do have rights, and we should attain our rights. We do not ask for pity, we ask for real work — among all the nations of the world.

• *How can we support your struggle?*

Suha: When you understand our suffering, I think you can find the way to help.

Women Go for Peace
December 1989

"Shalom [Peace] — Yes! Kibush [Occupation] — No!" *The chants rang out through the clear Jerusalem air, reverberating among the ancient hills, heralding — everyone hoped — a time of change, a Time for Peace . . . It was December 29, 1989 — a historic day of international women's peace activities in East and West Jerusalem. Beginning with an international women's peace conference, the day culminated in what's being called the largest women's peace march ever in this region, from West to East Jerusalem, involving over 5,000 Palestinian, Israeli, European, and American women. Remarkably, for the first time the march included Palestinians from the West Bank and Gaza.*

Sandwiched in between the two events was the traditional Women In Black vigil, situated at the large square outside the King's Hotel, a major intersection in downtown West Jerusalem.[1] Everyone was dressed in black for the occasion, and Chamtzah *or handshaped signs were rapidly distributed for each woman to hold; the signs read, in Hebrew or Arabic, "Enough of the Occupation."*

The air was festive, noisy, full of chatter, as I squeezed through the crowd with my microphone. I was anxious to hear what motivated all these different women to put aside the rest of their lives to be here today.

• *I'm a journalist from California. Can you tell me why you're here today?*

I'm an Israeli from Nazareth, and I'm here because I want to demonstrate against the occupation. Now we feel that it's time for peace. We want to end this year in telling all the

---

[1] The one to two p.m. weekly Friday vigil was initiated by ten Jerusalem women in January 1988, one month after the intifada started. The vigils eventually spread to thirty Israeli cities, involving both Jewish and Arab Israeli women, and to other cities around the world. By June 1990, the Jerusalem vigil was drawing approximately 150 women each week.

world, "Enough bloodshed, enough occupation, enough killing and imprisoning and deporting people. Let the Palestinian people be free, living in their state beside Israel." That's why I'm demonstrating.

• • •

I noticed a small woman with a somewhat tentative expression.

• *Why are you standing here today?*

I want to see some movement. We all represent various political opinions, mostly from the Left to the far Left. And I'm one who's afraid of a state, a Palestinian state — some are *for* that. But I want to see some negotiations begin. I'm from Boston originally.

• *And how long have you been here?*

Five and half years, because my children are here, and they want me here.

• *So you're going to stay here?*

Yes.

• *So what do you think needs to happen?*

We have to get together. I'm afraid that we might have to *talk* anyway to the PLO.

• *Do you stand here every Friday?*

Every Friday.

• *And what is it like standing here?*

We hope it's making an impact. We have many people who pass by and are afraid, and they spit at us, but I see more and more people giving us the positive signs than two years ago.

• *And what does your sign say?*

In Hebrew, it says, "Enough of the occupation."

• • •

My eye was suddenly caught by a woman with thick white hair and strong stature, whose deep lines of sadness connected her eyes and mouth.

• *Can I talk to you for a minute? Why are you up here?*

I am here because all my family was in Auschwitz.

• *Your family was in Auschwitz?*

Yes, and I don't want the Palestinians to suffer what I have suffered. I am from Italy. I was okay there, but all my family was in Auschwitz . . .

• • •

I then found myself before several shy and lovely young women.

• *I'm with a radio station in California. Can you tell me why you are here?*

Because I want to give the Arabs their country — to stop the occupation.

• *Do you come here every Friday?*

Almost always. When we can.

• *How old are you?*

I'm thirteen.

Me, too.

• *And what do your parents think about the fact that you come here?*

My mother is here.

I'm here alone.

• *So they don't like it that you're here?*

They do like it. They're *proud* of me.

• • •

Just prior to the Women in Black Vigil was the actual "Women Go for Peace" Conference, organized by the Israeli Women and Peace Coalition.[1] When I spoke with one of the coordinators, Chaya Shalom, I asked what some of the problems had been in organizing the event.

Chaya Shalom: The hardest part was coordinating all three groups — Europeans, Palestinians, and us, and not only technically but to know that we have the same concepts and ideas. In the organizing itself, the most difficult thing was just to be able to meet together, because women come from différent organizations all over. We have this concept that it has to be open to each woman who wants to be an activist, so sometimes it's not easy because, as I say, they are really big groups, and it's hard to organize. But, to my surprise, we

[1] The Women and Peace Coalition is an umbrella for seven groups: Women Against the Occupation, Women for Women Political Prisoners, Peace Quilt, Bridge for Peace, Haifa Women's Group, Women in Black, and Women's International League for Peace and Freedom.

overcame it, and now I can say that we can do it. We made it after all.

• *Why wasn't the major Israeli peace group, Peace Now [Shalom Achshav], involved in the organizing?*

Chaya: Peace Now is such a big movement, and I think they have their own concept of how a movement has to be. They don't have any consciousness of women — only of activities, only as mixed, even though there are feminists there, including a few of the leaders.

• *What were the goals of the conference?*

Chaya: To push towards activities of *doing* the peace, not just talking. Our slogans were "Two States for Two Peoples" and "Negotiation with the PLO." We want the people who are in the government not only to talk, but to *do* something on the one hand, and on the other hand to show that we the women are not just an emerging part of this peace movement but we are quite big. We have our own opinion and our own statement, and we want to speak out, and they have to listen to us because we are at least 50% of the population. We want to change, we want the situation to change, and we are not passive anymore. Now we are into action.

The conference itself was held inside West Jerusalem's Migdal Knesset Hotel, whose yard was jammed with booths of women's peace groups selling their calendars, buttons, posters, T-shirts, and literature. As over 1,500 Israelis, Palestinians, Europeans, and Americans swarmed together for the event, the air grew rich with excited greetings in Arabic, Hebrew, Italian, and English. Eventually women streamed into the crammed meeting room where the international press were setting up their video cameras.

The first to speak was Nabila Espanioli, a Palestinian psychologist who lives inside Israel and so is also Israeli. She spoke first about Israeli women who see the Palestinians struggling against the occupation and relate this to their own battle against social oppression in Israeli society. Then she talked more about the effect of the intifada on Israeli society, such as a growing machismo and the resulting popular new children's game of "street roulette."

Nabila Espanioli: ". . . Especially after the intifada, women in Israel began to be more active than ever, and we ask, "Why?" Women went to the streets, to Women in Black, to the Peace Quilt, to the demonstrations, and began to realize the effect of the occupation on their own society. I'm not speaking about the economic and political effect; I'm not speaking about inflation and about unemployment. I'm speaking about more *specific* effects which women began to see in their own families, effects on their roles and image, effects on their partners and sons. The Israeli society began to appreciate more and more the ideal of machismo. Israeli children wanted to be heroes, too. They began acting like heroes. They began to play "intifada computer games" and "street roulette," where children try to dart out as fast as possible in front of moving cars, acting like heroes, to experience their power."

Nabila continued speaking about the increasing attitude of Israeli soldiers that "I can solve the problem with my power."

Nabila: ". . . Women were concerned about this development and joined the women's peace movement, needing to express their fears here, feeling the support and understanding from other women. When machismo became the norm in Israel, women could feel the dangerous effect, because they just have to go out on the street or watch a TV program to feel it. Women had to make a move in such conditions, and they did.

"Some other women understood the peaceful message of the intifada. This is the only peace program which can provide peace in the Middle East. The intifada demands Israeli withdrawal from the Occupied Territories, a Palestinian State in these Territories, and an international peace conference to reach peace: these are the peace programs of the intifada. And women understood this message —

women who changed from being passive, oppressed women to being active, emancipated women — understood and believed in the change. Because if I realize my personal change and believe in the possibilities of change within myself, then why not in others? And why not in organizations such as the PLO?

"The intifada encourages us and supports our hope for change. The intifada supports our cultural wisdom which says: 'No one can scratch your own skin except your own nails.' Watching the breakdown of the old system of leadership, which is being replaced by young and dynamic leadership, gives women the hope that we will succeed too. We will succeed in destroying the patriarchal system, and we will succeed in our struggle for equality within our own society. Our Palestinian sisters are giving us, in their continuous fight, this strength. When Palestinian and Israeli women struggle together against occupation, they are struggling for their own liberation, for their own emancipation — and I believe that after having peace we will have more common issues to struggle for. So let's bring peace so that we can begin. Thank you."

The largest delegation of European women at the conference was the Italians, who in 1988 initiated several projects with Palestinian women, including their Adopt-a-Child Program for children in the refugee camps. The Italian speaker described how they put these transformative experiences together into a book about bridging the gaps between Italian women, Palestinian women, and Israeli women in the peace movement. They called it Women In Jerusalem.

I learned that the chairwoman of the Palestinian Federation of Women's Action Committees, Zahira Kamal, taught herself English by studying books while she was in prison. With striking dignity, she spoke about the major aspirations and concerns of the Palestinian people. Drawing a parallel between the Palestinian quest for a homeland and what she called the recent "intifada of nations of Eastern Europe," Zahira emphasized self-determination as the most significant right for the Palestinians.

Zahira Kamal: ". . . The Palestinian people are being severely and brutally punished for seeking a right which is theirs by human and national law. By denying us our right to self-determination, Israel is trying to negate the very basis of our nationhood and identity. I would like to state clearly that our national integrity is not subject to Israeli definitions or priorities, but is the self-determination of the Palestinian people themselves, including the right to designate our legitimate leadership — the PLO — and to establish our own independent state. The whole essence of gender politics, as well as national politics, can be encapsulated in our right to control our own lives and future without oppression, discrimination, and subjugation.

"Israeli society can never be free so long as Israel occupies other people's land and denies them their freedom. Israel can never claim to be a genuine democracy so long as it denies the Palestinians their most basic democratic rights. Neither freedom nor democracy can be selective or fragmented in a double standard system of values. Nevertheless, Israel cannot enslave our spirit, or capture our will."

Lastly, Zahira talked about the need for symmetry and equilibrium between Palestinians and Israelis as the proper conditions for just peace.

Zahira: " . . . That imbalance between occupier and occupied, oppressors and oppressed, military might and human determination has to be redressed on the basis of mutuality leading to mutual recognition, which is the basis of the two-state solution. For real negotiations to take place, one side cannot choose the negotiators of the other nor veto its participants. Nor can one side impose a closed and politically deadlocked agenda on the other as a means of dominating and restricting the peace process. For peace is not the result of fear or interrogation or insecurity but must be embraced wholeheartedly with confidence and determination. Let us all — Europeans, Israelis, and Palestinians — embark on this joint quest for peace in all sincerity and in sisterhood, and in striving together we shall demonstrate the true substance of peace."

The Jewish Women's Committee to End the Occupation of the West Bank and Gaza has been holding weekly vigils in New York City since April 1988. Represented at the conference by their co-founder and political writer, Irena Klepfisz, their aim is to make public the Jewish dissent in the U.S. to Israeli government policy and to clarify that, "The actions of the Shamir government are not to be justified in our name."

Irena Klepfisz: " . . . Some Jews in the United States accuse us of being disloyal to the State of Israel. We certainly do not view ourselves that way. Instead we see ourselves as loyal to all those Israelis who are struggling for peace, who want to begin negotiations with the PLO so that a Palestinian state can be established alongside Israel, so the two peoples can live in peace.

"But if these were the only tenets of our beliefs, I would probably not be speaking at this conference today. Those of us who first started the Committee were clear that it had to be a Jewish *women's* committee. As Jewish feminists we wanted to join with those Jewish and Palestinian women in Israel, and in the West Bank and Gaza, who also perceived that there was a need to step outside of the existing structures, a need to create a new women's avenue of action — that there was a need to be part of a peace process that would not simply abolish military violence but would be instrumental in forging a different kind of society. We understood the relationship between military power and sexism and violence, and we understood that only a feminist perspective could make our vision a reality.

"During our vigils in New York City we experience a variety of responses. We are frequently accused of being traitors, Nazis — and other times the responses are not so ugly. We sometimes hear, 'Your aims are good and I wish you luck. Peace is good, but you're dreamers.'

"I'm sure many of you have heard similar reactions. I do not believe there is a single woman here today who is not aware of the continued killings of Palestinians, of the increase in expulsions, of continued illegal detentions. We could despair, but those of us who are here today refuse to do so. We know that just to dream is useless, but to dream and work for that dream is the only reality any of us can accept, the only choice we have.

"We feminists believe that peace *will* be achieved — that there *will* be two states — Israel and Palestine. The certainty comes from the strength that emanates from the Israeli and Palestinian women, each of whom faces very different obstacles, very different struggles. It is these women, bypassing existing social and political structures, who were and remain the spur and inspiration that made Jewish women and other women in North America begin organizing to help the peace process here.

"Jewish and Palestinian women here are our models. They challenge us to think about a subject that feminists are deeply concerned with — history. We believe that common, ordinary women are not passive participants in historical events. How each of us shapes our life, shapes history; how each of us *resists*, shapes history; how we interact with each other, with other groups, shapes history. It is this view of history that the women in Israel and in the West Bank and Gaza have adopted, and it is this view that the international women's community must support."

Naomi Chazan is a well-known Israeli peace activist and political science professor at Hebrew University.

Naomi Chazan: "What a tremendous display and demonstration of women's power in this room today! I believe fully that women are the mediators of peace, and in order to mediate that peace, we have to develop a women's political strategy that will be heard throughout this land. We believe, and we have said so all morning, that we understand the necessity of mutual recognition and mutual self determination, that we wish to bring an end to the Occupation and to the violence, that we believe in the right of each people to determine their own representatives — *yes, we believe in two states for two peoples!*

"We have many different women's organizations. The most impressive element of peace work since the beginning of the intifada is the creation of this women's political power, and it is constantly expanding. But our strength lies in our diversity, in the differences among us, in the fact that we are here for different reasons, different motives, and we reflect different political opinions. The more diverse we are the more forceful we are, and let me suggest that one of our key challenges is that we expand our base and diversify our base and incorporate new and different elements that respect each other."

And from the Greenham Common women's peace camp of Great Britain, Rebecca Johnson roused us with her passionate determination.

Rebecca Johnson: "When 35,000 women encircled the USAF Greenham Common Nuclear Missile Base in 1982, Mrs. Thatcher told us to go and form a circle around the Berlin Wall. And we told her that that's exactly what we were doing, in our own way and in our own country! We women know we have to start at home. We're not going to follow the leader anymore. We have the right, and moreover we have the *responsibility*, to resist oppression and violence. We are angry at the futile misery and slaughter, and we want *change*. We want freedom, justice, and peace. Not one without the others, but *all three* — and we want them *now*.

71

"It will be the Palestinian and Israeli peoples who bring peace and a just settlement of two countries for two peoples to this beautiful land, and especially the women — not only as mothers and grandmothers, but as sisters, as lesbians, as daughters, as granddaughters. And women from the rest of the world can participate. We must give support and help to argue and explain and publicize the people's power of the intifada to the stubborn and arrogant politicians of our own countries. After all, Europeans bear a very heavy and grave responsibility for this conflict. We can join with you and support your demonstrations, knowing also that when the international spotlight shifts the brutality intensifies.

"Every struggle is different, and we face different levels of brutality and oppression, and only women directly involved in their own struggle can decide what is possible to do. That is the point of self-determination, and that is why I was so excited when I heard about your movement of Palestinian and Israeli women and about the Women in Black. There *will* be peace, because this movement has reached an unstoppable momentum. But there will also be terrible hardship and suffering before that time comes. And we must be prepared, and we must be strong and loving, determined and ready."

One of the final speakers was Sandra Rivers of the U.S., representing the Women's Democratic Delegation.

Sandra Rivers: "This conference has provided us with the opportunity to tell Israel that the world is watching and that their efforts to blank out the intifada and other initiatives are failing. Our obligation is to return to our respective countries, especially the U.S., and pressure for comprehensive, fair, objective, and honest media coverage of the intifada and of the Palestinian people's right to self-determination."

These excerpts are only from the women who spoke in English. A Palestinian woman from Gaza explained in Arabic how her husband had been deported just before their baby was born. Now Israeli authorities are denying her an exit visa to visit him. We learned that this is a common harassment tactic used by the Israeli government to split up Palestinian families.

An Israeli woman spoke in Hebrew about the transformation she went through when she learned the house and courtyard she loves were originally loved and owned by an Arab family who had been driven out. These were only a few of the narrated stories.

When I asked organizer Chaya Shalom why she felt the conference was so successful, she replied:

Chaya Shalom: I think the matter of having a *women's* peace movement is what makes the difference — that yes, we are in power, and that we will move things. Also, of course, it's the long work and collaboration that we had with the Palestinians, and it is after our first conference a year ago, so it's progressive. I think the Palestinians can see more and more that we can have something in common in working together. But very slow, I'm not jumping now and saying, "Well now we're going to do this, that, and the other thing." It's a very slow process, but maybe this will push more.

• *And what can you tell me about lesbian involvement, either openly or not openly, both in the leadership and in what you think might have been the participation in the conference?*

Chaya: Well, lesbians are still quite in the closet here. The Jewish state is not yet a good place for lesbians to be out. But I can say personally, of the women I know, that the organizers are at least 50% lesbians, and participants, like Women in Black in Jerusalem, around 30%. There are some that don't talk about it, or people just know.

• *Do you have any sense about the Palestinian women?*

Chaya: Nobody talks about it, so I don't know.

• *Were the goals for this year the same as the goals for the conference last year?*

Chaya: Last year the goal was to establish this movement. So we made it. Here we have after a year a women's peace movement, a national movement. So, now we have to move on. And this is the other purpose: to bring more women to the movement, make more women active, have more women talk, and not only be in their homes and talk to their friends, but be on the streets and voice their own opinions. Because I know, and we all know, that they are there. So we are moving on, and really we will be everywhere; everybody will hear us, so they cannot ignore us anymore.

With the conference and vigil behind them, it was now time for the feature event of the day, the women's peace march to East Jerusalem. Still mainly dressed in black, but adorned with bright scarves and sashes, women wound their way from fashionable downtown West Jerusalem along the walls of the Old City and finally up the hills of East Jerusalem towards the Arab Cultural Center. Many others cheered them on, especially in the eastern part of the city, waving olive branches and wearing traditional Arab dress. March monitors whispered to the women to remove their conference buttons with the Palestinian and Israeli flags, since the Palestinian flag is illegal in the state of Israel, in any form.

About halfway through the march, the women raised the banners they'd been carrying low to the ground — obviously an arrangement worked out with the authorities. While Israeli helicopters hovered overhead, the soldiers and police, many of them barely eighteen years old, flanked the route of these thousands of women — Palestinians, Israelis, Europeans, and Americans — marching together with hope, for justice and peace. Again I wandered through the crowd, searching for answers.

• *Many of you have on green scarves today. What do they mean?*

It symbolizes the Green Line between Israel and Palestine. It is the border between the two states on the map of Israel; it separates two lands.

• *You mean to signify a state for Palestinians and a state for Israelis?*

Yes.

• *Where are you all from?*

We are from Acre, from the Organization of Democratic Women. We are Arabs, Palestinians living in Israel.

• *Were you at the conference this morning? What did you think of it?*

It was very good and very interesting because many women from all over the world gathered to say, "Stop the occupation — we want to live together and establish a Palestinian state, we want to live together! We are women, we are mothers, we want to live in peace."

• *Were there any things said today that you disagreed with?*

I don't think so. In general we have the same ideas and the same struggle. You can find certain differences between us, but in general we have a common position.

• *Is it new that Israeli Jews and Arabs, as well as Palestinians living in the West Bank, can come together and have a common view?*

For our organization it's not new. We have always had relations between Israeli and Palestinian women. But in general it's new. And it's very good and very useful for our struggle.

• • •

• *And you said that you're Jewish Israeli? How long have you been here?*

Twenty years.

• *Why are you in this women's march today?*

Because I sympathize with them. Of course I want us to have peace, I want the intifada to stop, I want the Occupation to stop. I want people to live peacefully.

• *You said that you weren't really very active in the peace movement?*

That's true. I'm not doing the work. I'm not working hard actively.

• *So from that perspective, what do you think of the Israeli people in general? Are attitudes changing at all as far as the Occupation and the intifada and rights for the Palestinians are concerned?*

I can't say. We are divided into two groups. One group thinks that we should give back the West Bank and develop Israel *within* the Green Line and that we should let the Palestinians develop their country. But some people think it's better to keep the occupation. We are divided in half.

• *You said that you think the occupation should stop?*

I think there has to be a Palestinian state. I would like there to be one.

• *So what do you say to your friends and neighbors who disagree with that?*

I don't say anything. They are sure of themselves, and they are more talkative than I am, so I usually don't discuss it with them.

• *So if people don't change their minds, how are things going to change?*

Well, they do because when the sons grow up and go into the army, the mothers and fathers start to react, and the young people themselves start to react. Slowly, slowly there is a reaction.

• *You mean that by sons going into the army, that can change their mothers' opinions?*

It does. It affects people when it comes to them having to serve in the territories, them having to kill people, or them having to be killed — then it's very serious. Then they don't want to serve anymore; some of them refuse and are put into prison, and that eventually affects them and their friends and their neighbors.[1]

• *So what do you think is going to happen?*

I don't know. Basically I would like them, the Americans or whoever, to force a beginning to negotiations. I think that's the only possibility. I don't think it will start from the inside.

---

[1] Y'esh G'vul (meaning, literally, "there is a limit") is the name of the organization of Israeli reservists who refuse to serve in the Occupied Territories. To date, approximately 160 have been jailed for refusing to serve in the Territories, though others have chosen to leave the country before being sent there, while over 1000 others have managed to avoid assignments in the Territories.

• • •

Marwha is a twenty-year-old Palestinian arrested with eighteen other women and ten men — Palestinians and Jews — for demonstrating against the Israeli army's demolition of Palestinian homes in Kalkalia.

• *Where are you from?*

Marwha: I am from Taipe. It's an Arab village in Israel. I have been in jail with a Jewish group because we were in a demonstration against the demolition of houses in Kalkalia. We were in jail for one week, and this Sunday we will go to court. The lawyer said that we may be in jail for six months and maybe we will pay money. I don't know.

• • •

• *And where are you from?*

I am here from the Women's International League for Peace and Freedom in Israel. We are here, together, in this coalition movement.

• *And how do you feel about what's been happening today?*

Wonderful! It's beautiful! We never thought there would be so many women! I think we have hit the right feeling of very many women, and they've come. *Look* at them!

• *How many do you think there are?*

Thousands, thousands. I don't know exactly. . . Have you heard anything about the cooperation between the Jewish women and the Palestinian women? We have a peace movement which is called "Bridge to Peace." We are working together — Jewish and Arab women — for peace, for two states for two nations.

78

• *So everyone agrees on two states?*

In our group — yes, most of them. It's a big group, and we have all sorts of people in it. The special thing is that it's in Tel Aviv, in the center of Israel, where you don't have so many Arabs or Palestinians. So when we bring Palestinian and Jewish people together in homes in the middle of Israel; it's a very great thing we are doing. We have a dialogue of peace between the people.

• *So the women are really willing to listen to each other?*

Those who come to us come to listen, yes. They are coming to find themselves, to find Jews and Arabs, Israelis and Palestinians in the same home.

• *You said there were lots of different kinds of women. What do you mean by different kinds?*

Some come because they just want to *start* the dialogue; they are not yet prepared. But the majority of us agree. That's why we are here today.

• *What do you think is going to happen?*

That's a very good question. In the end there must be peace of course. I don't see any other solution. I am sorry that lately we are not so much in the news. People say that they are tired of our problem. I am sorry about that because the help from abroad can be very helpful to us. I do believe we here have to do the main job, like what we are doing today.

• *What do you think American women can do to support the peace between Palestine and Israel?*

To voice their opinions, to send telegrams to the President and government. To do what they can to bring the Israelis and the Palestinians together — *and I mean the PLO*. To speak together and to find a solution. We cannot go on killing and being killed, wounding and being wounded. It's terrible to live like this. We just can't go on living like this.

• *Do you think it's possible for Israelis and Palestinians to live peacefully together, side by side?*

Yes, I do. I am sorry you don't have time to come to one of our meetings. You would see how we love each other. We are very good friends, Jews and Arabs together. I'll tell you a little story. There was a Congress for Women's International League for Peace and Freedom in Sydney, Australia, this summer. I went with a Palestinian woman. We didn't have enough money so we ordered one room on the way. The woman in the travel agency called me and said, "Look, there is something I have to ask you privately. There is only one bed. Are you prepared to sleep with this Palestinian woman in one bed?" And I said, "Don't worry, we are prepared to do it. We are good friends, and we *trust* each other." And if we can do it, there is hope.

As the golden late-afternoon Jerusalem light cast ever-longer shadows on the jubilant marchers, they trudged up the last hill and around the bend towards the Arab Cultural Center. Suddenly, amidst the whir of the helicopters, shouts and sirens were heard — it was hard to tell which came first — but the atmosphere quickly changed. Instantly, the air became thick with tear gas, tension, and anger. Word was quickly passed that children in the march had just raised their Palestinian flag, and police had charged in with batons and gas, beating children, women, and men, and ultimately arresting sixteen. I asked one of the marchers what she had seen:

As we turned the corner up to the theater, some of the children who were in the front of the march started changing the chants. As soon as the kids started chanting, "PLO, PLO!"

you could feel the tension rising in the soldiers; the whole quality of the area changed. Around both corners were about five to ten police trucks, and trucks full of soldiers. An Italian woman standing next to me said, "Here comes the tear gas." We both ran, and as we ran we felt the gas.

As the melee subsided, women jammed into the first floor and balcony of the former El Hakawati Theatre for the final presentations of the day. Many were still blinking from the tear gas as a Palestinian speaker summed up what had just happened, saying, "We came talking for peace, and the police came to break the demonstration." But, amazingly, the spirit of the day remained undaunted as the strains of "Biladi, Biladi," the Palestinian national anthem, resounded through the theater: "We love our country, Palestine must be free."

As everyone spilled out into the cool Jerusalem night, I wondered if the day's actions would have any effect? Once again, I asked Chaya Shalom:

Chaya Shalom: The only way I can protest, or the only way that I feel I can live in this world, is by being an activist, by trying to change. Maybe it won't change, I don't know. It's such a slow process. But being active is the only way I can deal with this patriarchal and aggressive world.

• *And how can the women in America best support you?*

Chaya: It's nice to know that we have this networking and that we know each other, as organizations and personally. It gives us strength and hope. Women can do it across countries, and across oceans.

• *So there is room for hope?*

Chaya: Yes, otherwise I don't think I could do what I'm doing.

Rana Nashashibi
with Amal Kresheh
January 1990

It's a rainy Jerusalem night in early January 1990, as Amal Kresheh and I wind our way along narrow streets to the headquarters of the Union of Palestinian Working Women's Committees. Inside it's bright and busy — women bustling about, greeting and laughing with each other. My eye is caught by a nearby display of hand-embroidered bags and wall hangings and pictures by children of their experience in the intifada. Soon we find Rana Nashashibi, who's on the Executive Committee of the Union and also works providing psychological counseling to Palestinian children.

I'm ushered into a room off the main entrance, but close enough to hear the phone and central enough that we're frequently interrupted by women running in to speak with Rana. Initially, Amal fills in with information, but soon she joins the conversation in earnest.

I'm struck by the blend of intensity and humor these women share. They clearly care deeply about their work, their lives, and each other — and they carry a long-range perspective which eases their daily load.

• *On the way over here, Amal was saying something to me about the intifada being the "women's intifada." Do you feel that the men you work with see you as an equal?*

Rana: Not always, not always. It's a struggle to really make the men take you seriously and look at you as equal. They have been so used to undermining your abilities, because that makes it so much easier. There is less competition when you are undermining a whole population. On the other hand, *our* fear of really imposing ourselves, really forcing ourselves in, played an important role in our not being really perceived as equals. So this process is a dual one: it's the process of how men perceive you as women and how you perceive yourself as a person and as a woman. These two things are interdependent, and sometimes your perception of yourself can be more dramatized and more cruel than men's perception of you. I think basically when we're talking about re-education, we have to talk about these two aspects of re-education: how you re-educate the women to perceive themselves and also how you educate men to look at women.

• *I guess what you're saying is self-esteem?*

Rana: Yes, self-esteem and self-confidence. What I mean by that is that we feel in many cases women accept certain attitudes toward themselves beyond even the societal expectations of them. This is seen, for example, in issues that relate to the Shariá — Islamic law. Even the rights of the woman in the Shariá are sometimes given up by the woman. Sometimes they give up their rights voluntarily because they do not want to face up to the men. Because sometimes the way they perceive themselves is that they're incapable of running their own affairs, so they need a male guardian. This is the socialization process which affects the women in such a manner that their confidence in their own abilities begin to be sometimes shaky. The fear of taking the risk and the fear of making a mistake sometimes stop the women from really being forceful and assertive.

• *How are the men responding when you're being forceful and aggressive and taking a strong kind of leadership?*

Amal: How do you think they act? I am a mother of two boys, and I was shocked when I saw in my son's schoolbook that he learned from the beginning, in kindergarten, how his father holds the power and how his mother is a "weak" woman. In this reading book, there's a dialogue between two children, the girl Rabab, the boy Basem. Basem always says to his sister, "Father is working, Mama is cooking. I, Basem, help my mother put out the fire." So his mother can't put out that fire, she's so weak. And this is only the beginning. From this age, the society begins to give awareness to children that there is a difference between women and men. Men means the power, the leadership, the mind. And women — the "lovely wives, lovely mothers."

But during intifada the distinguished new role of the Palestinian woman has brought up the question: how does the Palestinian women's movement employ this role to make essential changes in the position of the Palestinian woman as a human being in this society? As Palestinian women we want and we struggle for a democratic state. We are very happy that the Declaration of an Independent State[1] talks about the equality of the Palestinian women to men. But from our experience, from the other women in the national struggle's experience, we are afraid that *in practice* we will lose this. And because of that, we want a democratic state: women in the Parliament. We get nervous about what happened in the Gaza Strip, how some reactionary people put pressure on the Palestinian woman to wear the Islamic cover — the veils that women are expected to wear covering their hair. When we went to the Gaza Strip, we had a very wide discussion with women, how to face this undemocratic behavior.

• *How did they respond to you?*

Amal: The young girls rejected this behavior. They want to begin, but they told us they are afraid. And we gave them some solutions: they could go together in the streets without being covered. And it needs a lot of effort. It is not easy, really, it is not easy.

• *I know when I spent a couple of nights and days in Jabalia refugee camp in Gaza, the family I stayed with gave me a*

[1] November 1988 when the Palestine National Council declared the West Bank and Gaza to be the independent State of Palestine.

scarf to wear on my head outdoors. I hadn't realized that was something I needed to do.

Amal: Rana and I used to not wear the cover, and they asked, "Why? Are you foreigners?" We said, "No, we are Palestinian, we are from a village, but we are not convinced about wearing Islamic dress." The Islamic religious leaders asked the women to wear it because that's the convention. But if you're not convinced about wearing it, we say it's hypocritical to wear this headcover. We are not convinced that this is the way that we should express either our feelings about what's happening or our feelings about our social status. Our social role and social status should not be related to headcovers, but to what we do or what we're capable of doing, and not by the way that we are dressed.

• *How did they respond to you?*

Rana: It was really a very interesting discussion. We held the discussion in a taxi as we were going on a trip to Rafah in Gaza. In the taxi there were only four men and both of us without the headcover. And when they didn't know how to really convince us, they said, "It's the Islamic law which tells us that you have to wear your headcover." And then we said, "Okay, but the Islamic law does not force us. It says that it has to come after conviction — you have to be convinced."

So they didn't know how to proceed with this conversation, and they insisted that the Gazans are different from the West Bankers. They said that the difference is that in Gaza there are more people from refugee camps, people who were forced to emigrate from their original homes and were then forced into the camps, and because of that they were required to pick up certain attitudes which were different.

But we kept up the conversation, and we said that we have women in the refugee camps also. Their attitude is different also. And the men could not proceed with the discussion. Because I'm sure also they themselves are not convinced of it. But like Amal said, when men stop knowing how to proceed with the conversation, they bring up the rights that are in the legislative and the *legal* aspects of it.

• *This actually relates to something I was wondering about when you were speaking earlier. How are you reaching women who come from more traditional ways of thought?*

Rana: With women who have a more conservative attitude, you have to work more on a concrete basis about how to make changes happen. This is done by basically involving them in actions and activities that will get them to slowly but steadily understand that it is not the *appearance* that makes the woman assertive or gives her a good position in the society. It is actually *what she does* and how *productive* she can be and how *forceful* she can be within the society.

This is the learning experience that we do through our cooperatives. We involve women in our cooperatives, we involve them in production, and somehow in that process, through having skills and going through the experience, they learn that they can do it *by themselves*. And they can do it with their own strength and their own power; they don't have to be subordinated, and they don't have to be going through the traditional ways to make it happen. They can make it happen by themselves and by their belief in their own abilities.

• *Was this level of activity going on before the intifada?*

Rana: I'll tell you the difference, the way I personally see it and the union sees it. Basically, before the intifada, one of our major problems was really to be able to *reach* women, to mobilize women. To find women who are not only capable but willing to participate actively. That was a major problem in the beginning because the whole situation was more stagnant.

Along with that was the position of women, which was also reflected in being less active.

But with the intifada — its meaning in Arabic is "to change things from the roots," you know — it also changed the *attitude* of women about themselves, about what they are capable of doing. From their involvement, which began spontaneously in the beginning, they learned that this action should not be limited to being spontaneous, but it can be *organized*.

Amal: During intifada, the Palestinian women discovered their power, their ability, to do the same things as the men. In cities like Ramallah, Beit Sahour, and Nablus, intifada began with women's demonstrations. In many cases, during intifada women stand behind the barricades for the first time, throwing stones, facing the Israeli soldiers. So this participation gives them more self-confidence, and we can see this reflected in family relations. Like the youth, especially among the very young women — they refuse to do everything that the elders do, the things their fathers and brothers wanted them to do before. There is a *new dialogue* in the family. Women participate in this dialogue actively.

At the beginning of the intifada, in 1987, our union made a program for Palestinian women from all sectors. We appealed to the Palestinian women to boycott an Israeli wool company because this company had dismissed Palestinian and Arab workers from Gaza and Hebron when they participated in the general strike on December 21, 1987. So when a woman boycotts the products of this company, she feels that she is a part of the intifada. We appeal to the Palestinian women to knit a sweater for every detainee: five thousand Palestinian women are involved in this project. So the woman who has a large number of kids also finds the chance to participate in the intifada.

Rana: To add to that, I think that the intifada has, to a certain extent, made women more assertive. One of the major problems that we used to face before was that we were not taken seriously because we were not active participants in the struggle itself. Women were always looked on as being less active, and it was mostly men who were in jail. Mostly men were active in the struggle, and women were less active.

But in the intifada, like Amal said, women found for themselves the different roles that they played. And these different roles were very important in the confrontation, in the struggle itself. Women became more assertive and more confident that they are capable of being parallel to men in their work. So that made them think that, "Okay, we have learned this issue of resistance. We have learned confrontation. So why should we only apply this to the soldiers in the streets? Why should we only apply it to Occupation, when there is another struggle that we have to face, which is our struggle for a better social status as women?"

Amal: For the first time we began to make division in the work inside homes, to have enough time to participate in the political and the social life. And now many men begin to ask about *their* liberation, not only from Occupation but also from women (laughter).

Rana: For example, take our Union in these peace march activities.[1] I don't know the exact number, but a number of women were completely involved in the work here. Many of them put this priority above their homes and their children, because this is something that they believed in, and they wanted very badly to force it through. They came into confrontation with the families who did not want them to spend so much time on this, who did not want them to spend their nights in Jerusalem because they are from other areas. But we wanted them in Jerusalem so that they could be always available in times of need. This was one example of

[1] Rana is referring to the international women's actions and Human Chain around Jerusalem on December 29 and 30, 1989.

the confidence that our members felt, and it pushed them into action. Not only talk, but action.

• *I don't know if this is an inappropriate question. If it is, I apologize. I'm wondering if women are part of the Unified Leadership of the intifada?*

Rana: It's very obvious that women are involved in the political decision-making within the leadership in the Occupied Territories.[1] Now the structure itself of the Unified Leadership of the intifada is not known to anybody, because this is an underground structure and nobody knows who is part of it. And it's better that people don't know. But from what is apparent from the grass-root popular movement, you see how much women have influence in these circles, how much political influence they have.

Amal: The United Leadership of the intifada respects the role of the Palestinian woman, and they reflect that respect through their statements. In March they congratulated the Palestinian woman on International Women's Day and asked women and the society in general to hold activities on this day.

• *So were you all — I guess personally, and your groups — involved in the women's actions last Friday: the conference, the march?*

Rana: You can see this on our faces. (Laughter) Believe me, we didn't sound or look this way before this past week. We really put a lot of effort as individuals and as a union into the organization of these activities. We were there from the beginning in the organization, the decision-making, and in the implementation of Women's Day, the Human Chain, and

[1] It is significant that when Secretary of State James Baker first met with Palestinian leadership from the Territories in March 1991, two of the ten members of the Palestinian delegation were women.

in the programming for the different international delegations. It also involved preparing ourselves in publicity terms and in public relations terms to be able to talk to the groups, to be able to express our opinion, to open certain channels of cooperation with them. So in all these aspects we were very active.

Amal: Also we took initiative. We published a petition asking Rabin to stop the deportation of women, the Palestinian women who haven't an identity card even though their husbands have. More than 218 women have been deported to Jordan. We asked more than 600 foreigners who participated in the peace march to sign this petition, and today we sent it to a friend from the Democratic Front to discuss this in the Israeli Knesset.

• *How was it for you all to work with the women in the Israeli peace movement, organizing those events and marches?*

Rana: For our Union, working with Israeli women is not distinctive at this stage. We have relations with them that run for many years in the past. We don't have a problem working with people who share our attitude toward our rights and who believe in our right to live freely as people in our independent state. We are more than willing to work together with partners that share with us in the struggle.

• *What did you think of the women's peace march and the Human Chain around Jerusalem? What effect do you think it will have on the Israeli people, the Israeli government?*

Rana: I think it had a a tremendous media effect, publicity effect, to show very clearly to the world that Palestinians are stretching their hands out for peace and that peace *can* happen if there are efforts made for that purpose. Because the activities of these two days have shown that stretching their hands out for peace is what the Palestinians really want. They're willing to live with the Israelis if peace can prevail, and each side has their rights within their own territory.

And I think these activities were a very important symbolic message that we sent to show that this could happen — and that the Israeli authorities and the Israeli government are the only ones who are not allowing it to happen. That was reflected very clearly by the way the police reacted to these issues: that we as Palestinians are mobilizing so many people, and the peace movement in Israel is mobilizing many people who *want* peace, but it is only the *government's position* which is not allowing it to happen. They're not really listening to the voices expressing a desire for peace. But if they would, then peace could happen. We are stretching out our hands for peace, but we are not finding ears that will listen.

Vignettes:
Beyond the Green Line

Randa works with the women's cooperatives in Ramallah, on the West Bank. Her mind is keen, her smile wide . . .

Randa: As long as women started taking a more active part in the struggle, men would respect that, especially in the intifada, and they would try to help them in their household work. I know a person who has been in prison for six months. Before his imprisonment, his wife was not active and she was not working. After he was imprisoned, she started to get active in society, to go to demonstrations, although she has kids, and she was coping with all this nicely. When he came back from prison, he found that a lot of things had changed. But he has to adapt to it. Before he went to prison, he wouldn't get a glass of water on his own. Now he is helping her take care of the children and the household and everything.

• *Randa, I had heard that when a Palestinian woman has a child, what she wants is a boy. Is that still true?*

As a matter of fact, it's still true, although we try to change the mentality of the people around us on this issue. Still the reactionary attitude is not only from the man himself; it's also from the woman. This is a feudal idea, because of how the men were more productive on the land or whatever. In the intifada, this idea has been emphasized as well, because a lot of the martyrs have been men. A lot of people said "No, we want to bring back the men again who will fight." Some of the progressive people, of course, think, "No, men or women, I want them both."

• *I don't know if this is fair to ask, but you're going to have a a baby any day. How do you feel about whether it's a boy or a girl?*

I want it to be a girl (laughter). And I wanted the first one to be a girl.

• • •

Leah Tzemel is a Jewish Israeli lawyer who has been representing Palestinians for over twenty years. She's rarely won a case. In a compelling voice, husky from endless cigarettes, she describes a major issue for Palestinians, that of "family reunion." . . .

Leah Tzemel: Many Palestinians marry women from abroad, from other countries, many of them relatives. Those wives, and the children that are born later, cannot live with the fathers who are inhabitants of the West Bank or Gaza and they are not. A spouse doesn't have the right to live with the other spouse, and marriage makes no difference here. So we have many cases of women who are actually deported, children who are deported, because the wives are considered to be staying "illegally" here with their husbands. I try to fight back. Not very successfully. I try to fight to say it's in contradiction with international law, with human rights, with any other essential principle of humanity. But, as I say, it doesn't help very much.

• *So why are you doing it?*

Leah: Someone *has to* do it. And secondly, if we don't do it, it will seem as if we agree to the situation. We don't. That's the way to fight back.
   There is no democracy in the Occupied Territories, and nobody expects there to be democracy. Because it's occupation;

it's an outside regime *against* the wish of the population. Democracy means that people have the right to choose their own leadership. They are denied that right.

• *What's the hardest part of your job?*

When, after working so hard for so long, I start to think what good does it do? What benefit does it bring? Those are hard moments.

• *So what keeps you going?*

I can't stop — probably that. The *necessity*. The rightfulness of doing it.

• • •

Jameila lives in Ramallah and is an administrator with the Popular Health Committees. She describes two recent incidents with Israeli soldiers.

Jameila: Of course, they didn't have a search warrant, but they could raid any houses any time they wanted to. Most of the people in camps sleep on mattresses on the floor, because of economic hardship. So when the soldiers went into the house, they walked on and smashed the baby and killed her. And after they killed her, the soldier said, "Oh-oh, no, we didn't kill her. We'll prove that to you." And they took her for an autopsy in Abu Kabir, which is the official center for autopsy for the Israelis. After the autopsy results, they announced on the official radio: "We have done the autopsy on the baby and the results show that she was killed by suffocation and exposure to cold; there were no signs of torture or of walking on the baby. We didn't kill her. She died by herself."

In our neighborhood, they blew up a house. And the reason for blowing up the house? There are two brothers, and one brother has a family of fourteen. The bachelor brother does not live in this house and doesn't own this house that was blown up. The Israelis alleged that this man had killed a settler. He had not been tried yet nor sentenced. They decided they wanted to blow up his house. They went looking for his house, and they found that he doesn't have a house because he is a bachelor, and he stays at different places. So they said, "Okay, fine, he doesn't have a house. We'll blow up his brother's house."

And the brother protested, of course, and said, "I own this house. I have the papers. My brother doesn't live with me. You have all the evidence that he doesn't live with me. You cannot blow up my house." They said, "Well, too bad, we're blowing the house up." And so they came at eleven o'clock at night: "We've got an order to blow up the house. You have half an hour to evacuate or we'll blow it up on your head." Okay, they have no choice. The soldiers are going to blow up the house. And they did.

Alya Shawa
December 1989

*It's the day after Christmas, a warm and sunny day in the Gaza Strip,
which is currently the most densely populated area in the world. I
can almost smell the sea a mile or two away.*

*My friends Sarah Jacobus, Deena Hurwitz, and I are in the
comfortably furnished living room of the local guest house, Marna
House, having Arabic coffee and cakes with the hotel's owner, Alya
Shawa.[1] A haven for visiting journalists and delegations, Marna
House offers its guests sumptuous meals, beds and bathtubs, a
telephone and veranda for general use, and lush gardens. This
contrasts sharply with the hot dusty streets jammed with taxis,
Israeli soldiers, donkey-drawn carts of fruits and vegetables, and the
teeming poverty of nearby Gaza City. Marna House is a small oasis
in the midst of a twenty-eight-mile-long, five-mile-wide strip of sand,
dotted with refugee camps.*

*Alya herself is widely known and respected throughout the
region. A traditional long dress hugging her small frame, she's the
first Palestinian woman I've seen in Gaza without the headscarf; her
graying hair is tightly pulled back into a bun above her neck. Alya
speaks with a slow and quiet authority. Her lined face is both
appraising and astute, welcoming yet maintaining distance. As
everywhere, I realize trust must be earned and is not exchanged
simply for good intention.*

• *Alya, can you tell us what changes have happened in Gaza
since the intifada started?*

Alya: We feel much more proud of ourselves, of what we are
doing, really. And it's a very good thing that, with all that's
happening (of course, there are some small mistakes), the
Palestinians are unified very well. Sometimes the press

---

[1] Both Sarah and Deena participated in conducting this interview.

comes here and they concentrate on the Hamas [a major Islamic fundamentalist political organization with a large presence in Gaza], "Ah, they're becoming bigger." And this is something I hate, because we don't want to have splits and fight each other now. We need more and more to be unified.

• *What are some of the biggest problems in Gaza right now?*

Alya: To continue the intifada as it is: clean. And not to have misunderstandings between each other. You know, it's very difficult, and the Israelis are trying very hard to split us up. Sometimes they bring the leaflets of Hamas. They even bring leaflets themselves which are not true. But the boys are aware of this. The Israelis are putting more and more pressure, shooting with live ammunition. It's not like before, when they shot at the legs. Now most of the shooting is at the head and the stomach, and many boys have been killed or paralyzed. If you go round to the schools now or to any house, you see that any minute the soldiers will destroy the walls of any house that they suspect stones were thrown from. These things the outside world can't see; it's underground pressure on the people.

• *How are women, especially, being affected in Gaza?*

Alya: During the intifada, the women *found* themselves, you see, in Gaza. They found that they are needed now. At the beginning a girl couldn't go out to the street. Maybe she had to ask permission from her father. But now when she sees her brother or her neighbor, and the soldiers are taking him by his hair and beating him against the wall, all the women come out, and they try to attack the soldier and save the boy. And this is how it started. Because other boys can't come, they'll be beaten and shot too. So the girls come out and try to protect the boys, and after that they see that they have a role.

97

When there's a strike, even in a curfew, elderly women can go out and because of their age they are protected, to see if their neighbors need food, or something. And they help each other in everything.

I have a film about one of the girls who teaches at a school. She was saying that before she couldn't go out, but now her father is proud of her, that she's teaching children, trying to save boys. It's not that they were not there before the intifada, as people think — it's not that. But most of the refugees used to be farmers. And they used to have children to help their families. With more children they can cultivate the land more, and the woman can help side by side with her husband. Sometimes they send one or two of their boys to college and the others work on the farm. But since the Occupation, there is not much land, so they have started to educate their kids. The time of Nasser was the best time for Palestinians — he opened all the universities to Palestinians for free, so most of them were educated in Egypt.

And we have so many now. I think the Palestinians are the best-educated people in the Arab world. But now the Israelis will not give us permission to have any university or polytechnic school or even a hospital. They don't give permission to build a hospital in Gaza, or private schools, or anything. If you go to the refugee camps you can see that all the girls are trying to teach the children in the houses, in the mosques, wherever. They bring them books and give them work to do. Of course, it's not like daily school, but better than nothing.

They also set up clinics twice every week, I think. They go to a home, and they put up sheets as curtains, and you see the doctors treating people. They are learning how to deal with things.

• *And what is the response to this increasing activity by women?*

Alya: When a girl used to go to a shop to try on a dress, the Israeli authorities had some people — collaborators — take her picture when she was without clothes, and then combine the picture with a boy's picture to make something out of it — that she was with a boy. They threatened the girl, "if you don't do this or do that, we'll send the picture to your family, and you'll be killed." It worked for a month, during the beginning of the intifada, but then many leaflets came out saying that we know these things are false, and you don't have to worry about them. The people are aware of what Israelis are putting out as rumors, sometimes leaflets — whatever you want, they're trying all the ways. But never the right ways: to be honest and to be as real soldiers or as real human beings.

Because you can't imagine. I've seen a soldier here beating a boy of three years old because he was throwing a stone. The boy doesn't know the meaning of it. The soldier was putting him in a corner and beating him. I called the Red Cross, and they came. I can't understand these soldiers. And I pity them, I really pity them. Because I can't imagine that I could beat a boy of five or six — if he is a Palestinian, or a Christian, or a Jew, or whatever he is, he is a *child*. Once I told one of the soldiers, "Aren't you ashamed of yourself doing this? Don't you have children?" There were three of them. One of them looked at me and said, "I have two kids." And he was trying . . . he wanted to talk, but the others took him by the shoulder and moved him on.

Once I told the people from the American Embassy, where I saw some soldiers, "Come and see the people you are protecting, and you give them money . . . see what they do with it." And one of them said, "I'll see about it." After that I didn't see them. But, I don't know, they say that there is a bit of change in the American policy. I didn't see anything yet. But we will see. Time is with us.

Once General Shiffman asked me, "What do you think your boys will do now that they're used to throwing stones?" I said, "They'll be all right if they have a good home and a good school and a playground and, above all, an identity. And if they don't see soldiers going round with their sticks, there's no need to throw stones. But," I told them, "You have to be worried about your teenagers, who are shooting and beating women and kids. What will happen to them after everything is finished? How can they live with it when they have children and families?" He did not answer.

I'd just like the outside world to see that we are not terrorists, and to see who the real terrorists are, who have been for three years now killing the boys and beating kids and women. They are the terrorists. We are not.

Once Alya, my granddaughter, came here, and she was drawing. And she said, "Come, *Tata* [grandmother], see." And I said, "What's this?" I saw an ambulance — it was an ambulance and a stretcher. I said, "What's this?" She said, "Yes, I saw it in front of our school today."

And you know that the soldiers, they always go around the schools when the boys get out. If the soldiers get out of the way, at whom are the boys going to throw stones? I told the general when I met him, "Just let the army stay out of the way when the boys get out."

Once I went to bring Alya with her father, and I saw two jeeps going round and round, looking at the children and the kids. And of course one of the boys might be irritated because his father might have been killed or in jail or beaten, and he might try to do something. And throwing stones is what he can do.

• *I've heard that in the intifada schools children are being taught anti-Jewish songs. What do you know about this?*

Alya: Not hatred of the Jews but nationalist songs, you see. That you have to be strong, you have to have your state, you have to have your identity. But no, I've never heard the song that says kill the Jews or do something like the stupid things that used to be before. No.

• *What are some of the differences between the situation in Gaza and that of the West Bank?*

Alya: Here in Gaza they can close the area and there's no way for anyone to get anything. But in Beit Sahour [on the West Bank] you see what happened: there are many areas where the boys could get food or go in or go out. Here, if they close the area, there's no way to get out. When they close Rafah or Khan Yunis or Beach Camp, it's from one side of the sea to the other side that they close it. It is *closed*.

• *In Gaza, do you also use the tactic of boycotting Israeli goods?*

Alya: You know, we don't have as many of our own products as the West Bank. Like dairy products — we don't have those here. So we buy the Israeli milk and cheese. We don't buy their sweets because there are some products from the West Bank, and biscuits and bread. We don't buy the bread that's baked in Israel any more. We try to stick to the fruits that we have. The same thing with vegetables — what we have. And clothes, the same thing, you see, because there are many factories here that make clothes, that used to make them for the factories in Israel, and they still, I think, send them to Israel.

So, as much as we can, we try, because if we ask for permission to start a factory for clothes or something for dairy products, it's forbidden. And we have the vegetables; we need to open a market for them. Because everybody's growing tomatoes and eggplant. We try to find our way slowly and peacefully.

• *Well, how do you feel about the Israeli peace movement? Do you think they are accomplishing much?*

Alya: They're not working hard enough. I know they want peace, but they're not putting on enough pressure. Especially the intellectual ones. They know that the situation is bad, and it's bad for everybody. They can make more demonstrations, they can even refuse to pay taxes. They must do something to put real pressure — the Israelis and the American Jews also. You must increase the pressure from outside.

I wish we'd see some of the Israeli activists for peace come and visit the families. It will make the people here understand that there are some good people there. But we don't see them in Gaza at all. They never come here. I'd like to arrange for them to meet with people, because this is very important — for our children to understand that there are good people there. What they think, I'm sorry to say, is that all Jews are bad, and all Jews want to kill Palestinians. And they don't differentiate.

But now they are beginning to understand because we are having many groups of Americans. Many of them are Jews, and they go and they help. And the people here know that some of the lawyers in Israel are doing a very good job. But it's not enough. They need to see some of the *people,* you see, to come and talk to them and tell them that they understand the situation and that they do not agree with what the soldiers are doing. It would have a very good effect on the people here.

• *What is your perspective on U.S. foreign policy right now?*

Alya: They talk of democracy in one place, and they do something else in another place. Their democracy and the Israelis' democracy are different from anything right. Nobody likes Noriega — he's a smuggler, he's everything. But what did they do in Panama? It's not the right thing, you see, to invade their country. Why? And everywhere, when it suits them, they say it's for democracy.

Ah . . . I don't know. All I know is that the Palestinians, and I'm one of them, we never had hope except when the intifada started. Now we think that things *have* to change and there is no way of going back.

And believe me, Palestinians are good-hearted. If Israel would recognize the rights of Palestinians now, and we could have two states, we'd live in peace together. It's not as people think, that there will never be peace. There *will* be peace. And we'll forget everything. Although they are making it more difficult every day because more people are shot and injured, and, of course, this brings hatred. But if there is peace, there will be *real* peace. I can see it: everything quiet and nice, and we are living together in peace, and maybe we visit each other. Not the first year maybe, until we organize things (laughs). And we make schools for our boys, and let them turn the page, to think of their future, their education, their health. There are so many things to do.

Life is for everybody and it's beautiful, if they know how to enjoy it. You sit under a tree and look at the birds — they don't attack each other. Even the tigers don't attack each other unless they're hungry, and then they go and find themselves something to eat. What happened to this world? I don't know.

Of course, the people are getting impatient. Some of the people. But thank God that they are still controlled. They know that they will lose if the weapons come out, that if one Israeli is shot, maybe a thousand Palestinians will be. This is what the Israelis are waiting for. For the weapons to come out so that they can shoot whoever they like and they can deport whoever they like. I hope it will never reach this point.

And the process is going on very, very slowly. But the world must be aware of it, that they can't stay like this forever, you see. There must be something *moving* and something right, not the five points of Shamir, five points of this, five points of that.

Unless they recognize the rights of Palestinians, that they are a *nation* and they have the right to choose their own representatives. Not Shamir to choose them, nor Mubarak, nor Baker. No. We are a nation and we are *people.* We can't choose for the Israelis whom to send, so they can't choose for us.

And I don't believe at all in this thing of election. "Election under Occupation" — what kind of election? Who's going to be elected? No, I don't believe in this. I believe in starting the negotiations, and after that having an international conference. It's good for us and for the Israelis. They have to have more confidence in peace, and to know that peace is good for everyone.

We cut our trees. Now we have fewer birds — but the trees will grow and the birds will come back. But that tree there was affected by the tear-gas bomb — that's why we had to cut it. I brought many gardeners to see it, and they said many trees were affected. So we cut both of them — they'll grow back. It's good that they didn't burn the roots.

Women For Women Political Prisoners: Dalia Kerstein
December 1989

There's nothing Russian anymore about the Russian Compound except its name. This century-old stone guest house for pilgrims is in fact most inhospitable. This is where Palestinian political prisoners — women, men, and children from age twelve and up — are detained by Israeli authorities while they're waiting to be charged for their alleged crimes. Squatting in the middle of downtown West Jerusalem, it's frequented by Arab families from all over the West Bank who are anxiously hoping for that weekly ten-minute visit with a daughter, son, or other loved one.

This is where Women for Women Political Prisoners, an Israeli peace group, does much of its advocacy work, interfacing between the Arab families and the Israeli authorities. They assist families in finding out if their children are even being held here, and if so, getting them legal help, arranging a family visit, or getting in clothing or toiletries. Dalia Kerstein works here every Friday, sometimes with another volunteer from the group, sometimes alone.

On this Friday, late morning, the sun beats down on the Russian Compound yard jammed with families waiting for their visits. Police vans barge in and out; I am cautioned to hide my camera. There's a constant barrage of shouting from the authorities. Dalia and Rachel from Women For Women Political Prisoners weave through the crowd as many people tug at them for assistance. With strands of dark hair slipping over her glasses, Dalia's face shows me the strain of this work. I guess that she's in her early thirties. Looking serious and pressured, yet quite down-to-earth, she feels as familiar somehow as my friends at home.

• *So, Dalia, when you come here every week, you're essentially talking to the families and talking to the authorities?*

Dalia: Yes, we are trying to be go-betweens, and, of course, it depends on the policemen, because some of them just call us "Arab-lovers," and that's about all the dialogue we can have with them. During the weekdays, we bring the parcels in which are sent by the families — that includes soap, shampoo, sheets, towels, sanitary napkins, because they don't get these things from the authorities. Also, we look for new women detainees whom we don't know about yet. This is the best place to find information on families, or hear stories. For example, someone heard that in the next village someone was arrested. Then we can make some phone calls to that village trying to locate anyone who could give us more information about it. This is the best place to find these people, to get all the information they can give us about the women, how old they are, who's the lawyer. Then we contact the lawyer and go to the court room to see what's happening.

We have a lawyer who goes in twice a week. She doesn't represent these women in court. She is working for us in the sense of getting all the information from inside about what's happening: who was beaten, who's under punishment, who's sick. With the information she brings, we are doing all sorts of things, whether it's to contact the jail doctor, or to make a lot of public noise about certain treatment that was given to a woman.

One woman, Fahima, is forty years old, and was brought here recently with her nineteen-year-old daughter. Fahima was suspected of being a member of an illegal organization and was kept in what is called "zinzana," or isolation — total isolation for fourteen days. The first ten days she got hardly any food, which is a thing we keep hearing about, getting hardly any food for the first days. The food they are getting is just a piece of bread with all the soft part taken out, and in the hole they just stuffed whatever there is — you can get the most disgusting mixture in there. And it's just thrown into that little zinzana cell, that isolation cell, which is usually very filthy. There is no water or the water doesn't work, the sewage is running all over. And on top of that they put a sack on her head which is extremely filthy. There is a string on the neck area which they can tie. You don't see a thing, you can hardly breathe through that thing, and they just keep you this way, and whenever they march you to the interrogation room or back they put it on. Sometimes they just leave you in the cell itself alone with that sack, so you can see who's the boss around there. We think it's pure humiliation.

• *But the families can't go and get the same information you can get?*

Dalia: No, because they have only a ten-minute visit after thirty days. Sometimes they can get it from the lawyer, though.

We hardly ask *why* she was arrested because we are not interested actually to know. Or if we are interested, it's only for formalities, so we'll know once she's being sentenced what was the proportion of the "crime" to the punishment. Our lawyer doesn't have to take care of the legal case as far as the trial goes, so she has a lot of time to come in here and get an affidavit on how this woman was treated from the moment she was arrested, how many times she was beaten and by whom. And she can file complaints in our name.

So most of the time, as far as the conditions here in the Russian Compound Detention Center are concerned, we're much better informed than anyone else because we're aiming for exactly this information. The reason we can give such personal attention to each one is because women are the smallest in number, the smallest sector in here.

There is another group here, women who take care of youth detainees. But there are hundreds of youth detainees. There is no way they can give them personal treatment. So they take what's called test cases and follow them.

• *And where do the women go from here?*

Dalia: Usually to Tel Mond Prison. Sometimes even before they're sentenced. It depends on how crowded it is. There's only one cell for Palestinian political prisoners here, and they keep them together, younger ladies together with elderly ladies. Sometimes there can be as many as twenty-three women in one cell. There is hardly room to move. There are only four cement things stuck to the wall which they put mattresses on, so when there are more than four women in there they just lay the mattresses on the floor. They're given blankets, if they have enough blankets. Many times there are *no blankets*. The winter is coming. It's cold. This place was built in the last century as a guest house for Russian pilgrims. Not too much has improved since the last century as far as the conditions inside are concerned.

This is the most problematical place because women from all over the West Bank (not from the Gaza Strip) are being transferred here. And from here they can be transferred all over. If the authorities want the interrogation to go without too much interference, then they don't allow the lawyer to see the client, of course. But if they want even to prevent any *request* about that, they might transfer them to Jelamin Prison near Haifa for a few days, or to Petach Tikva near Tel Aviv for a few days, so they can interrogate them without having any "harassment" from outsiders or lawyers or anything like that.

Political prisoners, sorry, *detainees* — political detainees have no rights. There is not even a status that is called political prisoners. As far as the authorities are concerned, once they deal with detainees, they only have to give them three meals a day, a place to sleep, a mattress, a blanket, and an outside walk for half an hour. Which they don't really keep to. The walk could be five minutes, it could be "not today," but the authorities feel no other obligation.

No one's allowed to bring food in from the outside. If the woman is pregnant she usually informs the doctor, and then she is immediately brought to the hospital to check if the pregnancy is okay. We achieved this only after several cases of women who lost their babies because of very hard conditions. This has improved slightly, but they can still be treated very badly during interrogation, pregnant or not. We put pressure on the doctor in order for the kitchen to give these women a double portion of food. Because it doesn't include everything they need anyhow; there's always a lack of fresh vegetables and fresh fruits.

They have nothing to do in the cell. *Nothing*. All they can do is smoke there. They are not being given newspapers, they are not being given paper to write on, nor pencils, nor games. If the walk outside is taking place, that's their only activity for the day. The rest of the time they just sit in that cell, very crowded with women. And the punishments are not to have a visit from the family, not to have parcels in, and not to go out for the walk. A lot of times the women all decide not to take that walk outside as a form of protest.

Of course, anytime they sing songs, national songs or not, the punishment is there. When we blame the authorities for having collective punishments, of course they come and say, "We don't have anything like collective punishment." But in practice, in reality, it's *always* collective punishment — they *all* have to share not having visits, not having this, not having that.

Sometimes they're being arrested with their children, on the Allenby Bridge, for example, going to Amman, Jordan, for a family visit, or coming back. The children will be put somewhere else while the authorities contact someone in the village or town she is from to come and take the babies. They're not allowed to have their kids with them.

• *Why would she be arrested coming across the bridge?*

Dalia: It varies. They could suspect that she carries letters. Then they search her. Whether they find letters or not, once they arrest her it's very hard for them to let her free. So they bring her here. There is a very popular arrest as far as

109

they're concerned: they arrest women because their husbands are wanted — whether the husband has been wanted for a long time and this is a way to put pressure on him to give himself up, or whether the husband is here, and they want information from him.

We had a case of a woman, twenty years old, eight months pregnant. Her husband had been wanted for quite some time. But they had him when she was arrested on the bridge. She was interrogated for ten days. Her husband was brought into the cell, and they threatened him — if he didn't give them all the information they wanted from him, they would cause her such pain and such suffering that she'd lose the baby. That was supposed to be their first baby. I have no idea if the husband gave in and informed or not.

• *Why did you start doing this work?*

Dalia: Because what's going on is so awful. I wanted some kind of activity that was not just protesting in the main streets of Jerusalem on Fridays, which is just protesting within the Israeli society. I felt I had to be more involved in terms of really helping, really getting involved, really coming into regular contact with Palestinian families, detainees. And don't forget we're here daily.

• *How many of you are doing this?*

Dalia: We're about fifteen as the hard core. We divide the job, everyone chips in whatever they can.

• *And what effect has it had on you?*

Dalia: I'm so tired. Constantly. It's an emotional exhaustion, if you will. For example, today I came early and I saw the policeman marching the people to one side of the Russian Compound, yelling and screaming at them and then marching them back, just giving them a hard time. And I was alone. A lot of times I am alone here. Today I felt I just couldn't handle it, and I went to the telephone and called Rachel to come and help me.

I just spoke with a woman who asked to see her son and the policeman was, of course, very rude to her and told her, "Oh, you're all animals." She protested and said, "You can't say that to us." He said, "If you add anything to what you say, I'm going to prevent you from seeing your son. You will have a punishment of two weeks." She said, "You can't do that. No one can treat anyone this way." He said, "Well, you're not going to see your son."

So she wants to complain now about this policeman, which I hope she does. I think the more complaints, the harder time the authorities might have, although we all know the results. It won't change anything, but it can put them on the spot, to show them that people there are noticing what's happening. And someone will have to put the time in to investigate every case like that, though nothing will happen in the long run. But maybe that ongoing pressure, if we keep it up by filing complaints, maybe it will do *something*.

I want to talk a little about the woman lawyer we have. We decided we need a woman lawyer. We had a man lawyer at first, very political, very devoted. But we realized that because of the women who were inside, the detainees, there is certain information a man will never get from these women. Any sexual harassment will never, *never* be told to a man. It doesn't matter if he's Jewish or Palestinian or anything. It just doesn't work this way. So we decided that we're going to have a woman lawyer. Because it's a completely different situation. I don't know if trust is the word, because they trusted the man. But they are more open about it when it's a woman-to-woman situation.

It's our experience that sexual harassment is usually aimed at very young women, from age thirteen to eighteen. There are a lot of sexual curses and humiliation and threats like "We're going to bring your mother, and we're going to rape you in front of her," or situations like that.

There is a story that we heard more than once from different women about men interrogators, always men interrogators. They show the young girls a piece of wire, suggesting they are going to penetrate her body, her genitals, with that. Beatings, of course. Most of the beating is done by women, by policewomen. It's not that policemen do not hit the women, I would never say that. But most of the testimonies we have indicate that policewomen beat the girls.

I told you about women who are what we refer to as hostages. These are women whom there is nothing against but whom they need in order to put pressure on the husbands, whether wanted or not. There was a case of a woman, twenty years old, Sarat, from Idna. She had a girl three years old. Her husband had been wanted for years, and one night there was a clash between the Israeli army and his people, armed Palestinians. An Israeli soldier was killed along with three Palestinian men, including her husband. She was arrested the next morning; she didn't know her husband had been killed, because he didn't live at home. He was wanted and had lived outside in the caves and mountains around Hebron.

They brought her in, and after they arrested her, they demolished the house, which again she didn't know. The information we got is that she is in isolation, in what's called the "hazana." This is not only isolation, it's the *coffin*. It's a tiny little cell where you can either stand up — sometimes they tie your hands back to the wall — or you can sit down, but you cannot stretch your legs because there's is not enough room. It's like 70x70 centimeters, so you have to sit with folded legs. They have held women there for quite some time. She was lucky enough to be there for twenty-four hours only. Of course, no food. Of course, you cannot go to the bathroom, nothing. You are just there until they decide to let you out.

From the "hazana," the coffin, she was brought to isolation. At that point, because we knew the background of the husband being killed, we turned to some Parliament members and asked for one of them to request information — if they suspected her of anything, or if it was just a punishment because of the activity of her husband. They were not willing to so much as stick their nose into it. They said that they got information from Israeli intelligence that the group the husband was involved in was very cruel, and maybe they didn't catch all the members. That's why they need the wife in order to get more information from her.

The point is, which we know — we found out after she was released — they did not begin to interrogate her until three days after the arrest. If they were in such a panic to catch more members, why wasn't she interrogated the first day she was brought in? How come everyone gave her such a hard time, to be spending twenty-four hours in the coffin and then in isolation, with no one asking her one lousy question about the activity of her husband or anything?

• *The other women that you're working with . . . I just wanted to get more of a sense of what their backgrounds were.*

Dalia: Some of the women were never active before and might never have become active. There's a theory, which I don't know if it is backed up or not, that the intifada brought women out of their houses into the streets and into activity — women who had never been active in that sense before. They might have had political opinions of one sort or another, but they didn't spend their days and nights in taking care of what's happening here.

We have two women who have been very political for ages. And some who are very naive, if you will, who are just beginners, and are doing it more from the point of view of human rights. There are all sorts of opinions among the group, and we don't even discuss it. Because the moment we have some kind of ideology set down, it's going to keep a lot of people from participating. And we don't want to be one of these left-wing political groups who keep splitting in two because this one doesn't agree with that idea exactly.

There were so many fights on the Left over the "solution," whether the solution should be one secular state for two nations, or two states for two nations. People were splitting up, movements were splitting up. It's not the case these days because there's sort of a consensus about the solution — two states for two peoples. But we don't want to come to a point where we might split because this one thinks A and that one thinks B. So every decision we make the majority decides upon, and we follow it.

We have a lot of women, young and old, all sorts of ages, all sorts of professions, all sorts of political backgrounds, united in *that* struggle, if you will, but not anything else. We have members of the group who are Israeli Arabs or Israeli Palestinians, which means Palestinian women from the borders of '48, so they carry an Israeli ID just like me. And they have equal rights, too.

One of these Israeli Palestinians was receiving a lot of threats over the telephone, that if she would not leave her political activity, she was going to be murdered. It was a woman's voice on the telephone in Arabic. We think it could be a collaborator. But we don't have Palestinians from the Occupied Territories because they cannot do a thing — they'd be arrested in no time for doing such an activity.

• *What can women in the United States do to support you?*

Dalia: Just put a lot of pressure on senators, the President, anyone. Help us end it the way it should end in order to have two states and live in peace.

I think it's killing both societies. I mean Palestinians are being killed practically speaking, not breathing any longer. But it doesn't do any good to the Israeli society. All the systems are collapsing. Laws are not laws any more. The level of violence is growing, the level of hatred is growing tremendously. Beating little kids. Everyone is shooting these days. Everyone is equipped with weapons. First you shoot, and then you think of what's happened. And even some tragic things here. A terrible incident — the father thought it was terrorists, Palestinians, outside of the car. He was shooting, and the army was shooting, and his little boy was killed. There were no Palestinians in the area. And that happens only because everyone is so threatened and carries guns. It's not a normal way to live.

I don't think we've yet penetrated the other body of right-wing people. The barrier between the two sides is just getting deeper and deeper. The dehumanization of Palestinians is what is happening. What the policeman said today, "You behave like an animal," is just quoting one of the Parliament members, our "respected" Parliament members.

We had about four demonstrations outside the Russian Compound to protest the inhumane treatment. In two of these events, we were "held in," which is before you're arrested — they hold you in until they decide whether they're going to have you there for the night or not. They don't like us; they don't like our activity there. But because we deal with the police over there, they cannot do what other people do, for example, to Women in Black in the main square in Jerusalem, cursing and throwing things at them. Policemen cannot do it.

So they have their own way of telling us what they think about us. For example, every Friday they see me. Saturday is our day of rest. They say, "Hmm, did you cook for your husband and children already? Is the food ready for Saturday?" Which is their way of saying, "You should be in your kitchen and not here."

Beit Sahour: Village of Dignity
December 1989

It's Saturday night just before Christmas in the village of Beit Sahour, a largely Christian town of about 12,000 Palestinians nestled in the hills next to Bethlehem, just outside Jerusalem. All I know about Beit Sahour is its fame for peacefully and persistently resisting taxation by the Israeli authorities. This is one strategy of the Palestinian intifada against the Israeli occupation. In a town like Beit Sahour, I quickly grasp why intifada also means "awakening."

I walk right into an evening's social gathering of several neighboring families. I notice this is a lovely home, but there's an obvious lack of the usual couches and other furniture. My hosts, the family of Issa Tawil, bring out fresh plates of pita bread, hummus, and olives, and uncork a bottle of wine. I unpack my microphone.

• *Can we start by your explaining to me what has been so unusual about Beit Sahour's tax resistance?*

Ellias Rishmawi: Well, Beit Sahour is not the first town to do this. All of the towns of the West Bank and Gaza have their own way of expressing their practice of the intifada. In fact, not paying taxes is a trend existing in all the Palestinian citizen towns. The reason for Beit Sahour's being so famous or special is that 99% of the Beit Sahourians are not paying taxes. They have stuck to their position, and they proved it very strongly and very efficiently during the tax raid against them that was organized by the occupying authorities. The reason for the tax raid was to break the will of the Beit Sahourians, and if things can be measured in the sense of who won and who lost, whose *will* was at last victorious, I think the Beit Sahourians have won.

116

• *And you said they took your washing machine?*

Eiman Rishmawi: We were subject to two confiscations. First they confiscated my husband's business, his pharmacy and drug store. Second, they confiscated our house. In fact, the confiscation of our house affected me very much, because when you have chosen every piece in your house, it affects you emotionally. But the confiscations have made me more determined not to pay taxes. They can confiscate our furniture, they can kill us, they can put us in prison. But they can't confiscate our dignity — they can't kill our spirit and our determination.

• *And Issa, when I first came in, you told me you had lost most of your furniture, including the piano you bought for your daughter Muna when her eye was injured in an accident . . . Muna, how old are you?*

Muna: I'm 13.

• *So tell me about what happened when they came?*

Muna: When I came home from school, I saw the Israelis. I watched while they took all the sofas and the piano. My mother told them "Take everything but the piano. My daughter plays on it." He said, "Don't tell me what to take. I will say what I will take."

I watched and I couldn't believe it. My friends told me, "Don't be afraid, Muna, don't be afraid, don't cry." But I can't help it. They took everything.

• *So how did you feel?*

Muna: Sad. Very sad. And now we don't have sofas to sit on. We have to sit on the floor, you know.

Ellias Rishmawi: According to the Jordanian Law, the act of collecting taxes is subject to a deal.[1] It is a kind of agreement between the people and the government, whoever the government is. They cannot just collect money according to their wishes; there are *conditions* that should be satisfied in the process of tax collection. Now according to this, the Israelis have violated the basics of the Jordanian law of tax collection. And according to the law, any act of violating the law makes the law null and void, and this is one of the basics that the Beit Sahourians are going to depend on in the future courts. Though I am not optimistic enough to say that this will be considered in the military courts, because they can pass a military order, a new one, that can cancel everything.

Whenever we say, as Palestinians, that we are against occupation, it doesn't by any sense mean that we are against Israelis and against Israel. We are against *occupation*, whatever the type of occupation is. But we are not, by any means, against Israel; we are not against Israeli people.

• *Well, in terms of adopting this strategy of tax resistance, did you all sit down and have a meeting?*

Eiman Rishmawi: From the beginning, when the leaders said "Don't pay the tax," we agreed with them and decided together — all the people in Beit Sahour — not to pay the tax.

Millany Nasser: I think one of the articles in the Geneva Convention says that an occupying force can only collect taxes which it then reinvests for the people it occupies. The Israelis say they put the money back into the West Bank, but independent reports have said only about 10% of the tax money collected has actually gone to the West Bank for the support of the schools, streets, hospitals, or whatever. They

---

[1] The law of the West Bank and Gaza is a mixture of Jordanian law, Egyptian law, and old British mandate law.

don't, of course, consider the Geneva Convention as applicable to the West Bank, but we do.

Eiman Rishmawi: We have a point of view, that you are paying taxes for your elected representative government, but for us, to whom should we pay taxes? To our occupation? What for? For more killing? For more injuring? For more handicapped people? For more closures of educational institutions? What for? We pay taxes for our state, our Palestinian state, but not for our occupier.

There has never been a budget given by the Israeli authorities as to how much money they have collected, whether by direct taxation or indirect taxation, from the Palestinian areas. The expenditure they make here are considered as classified material and is only distributed among Knesset members. Even Knesset members, which is the Israeli Parliament, don't know how much tax Israel is collecting from the Occupied Territories. We are paying to the Israeli army part of their expenditures in this war — what kind of sense is this?

Issa Tawil: Four months ago, when they started to confiscate the belongings of the people of Beit Sahour, they announced the reason was a shortage in the budget of the West Bank. They said they needed money, and they were obliged to collect the tax from the people. One month later, inside the Knesset, it was announced that there was an excess in the budget of the West Bank of 160 million shekels![1] So you can see how they are lying.

Ellias Rishmawi: Actually it is considered a very, very fruitful and economical occupation. They have controlled all our resources, they have controlled the tax collection, they have controlled exports and imports to the Palestinian areas.

---

[1] One shekel is worth approximately 50¢ in U.S. currency.

Now speaking of the resources and services we are getting, we are paying for all types of services, like water supply, electric supply, and telephone. So it is not *service*, because we are *paying* for it. Imagine this, for water I am paying one dollar per cubic meter, while in an Israeli settlement just five kilometers east of Beit Sahour, they are paying half a dollar per cubic meter. The residents of Israel are paying sixty cents per cubic meter. Now this is not the end of the story; you must know that they are using 94% of the water resources of the West Bank and transferring it to Israel, which amounts to 20% of the total Israeli consumption of water. They make me pay double the price they are paying, and they call it democracy.

Millany Nasser: I have a brochure from Israel for tourists, and they call this "water-sharing." They say: "One of the benefits of the occupation is water-sharing," so called, "in that the water which is available goes to the persons who need it most." Apparently the Israelis need it more than the Palestinians because they take the water and they leave us with 6% of it. This is "water sharing." This is not stealing.

They don't allow farmers here or in any Palestinian towns to drill new wells for water, to bore water holes. They take the water, and we can still use the holes that exist, but the rest of the water that we need we have to buy from them at their price.

• *Can you tell me how the siege of Beit Sahour a few months ago took place?*

Millany Nasser: Well, it started the nineteenth of September [1989]. The tax cars started coming to Beit Sahour and going to one or two businesses at first, and, of course, immediately all of the other businesses in town closed.

Every day, at the beginning, they went to three or four shops and they emptied out whatever they wanted. They dumped things on the floor, just taking, taking, taking. The word spread around town quickly. They took away the refrigerators and freezers from the grocery stores; they took the machinery from the woodworking shops and from the carpenters, from the people who work in mother-of-pearl and in other small factories — essentially, their means of livelihood.

Some of the machines for heavy work were imbedded in concrete, so they brought cranes and ripped them out of the floors. They ruined them, actually, and every day they threaten they are going to sell them at auction. They threaten and threaten and threaten. If they didn't think they had enough, they went to the houses and they took their furniture. Every day we could see the tax cars coming in with their moving vans in the morning and leaving at 2 o'clock in the afternoon. For the first few days there was a curfew in Beit Sahour, and during the whole time there was a nightly curfew.

• *What happens when there is a curfew?*

Millany Nasser: Well, every day you are confined to your house. That means for twenty-four-hours-a-day you can't leave the house: you can't go on the roof, you can't go in the yard, you can't even be on your balcony. Theoretically this is the case, but practically there are ways to get around it.

• *And if you do that, what do they do?*

Millany Nasser: Well, the worst I've seen them do is yell at people and tell them to go back inside the house, but in other towns they have shot people for being on their balconies. You never know; it depends on the soldier. Sometimes they come to the house and beat people up.

They had about six to ten houses where they posted soldiers on top of the houses twenty-four-hours-a-day. They ate up there, they cooked up there, they took baths in the water which we use for cooking and eating. They would piss

121

in the water. They washed their clothes in this water. After they left, the people had to disinfect the water containers. When the soldiers were on our neighbors' roof, they would call to us, and when they got our attention, they would piss from the roof.

• *It's harassment.*

Millany Nasser: Yes, harassment.

• *So they're doing all these things, and you're still not paying your taxes?*

Millany Nasser: Oh, this is just the beginning. After they saw this didn't work, they started putting up road blocks to block off the city, forbidding people to leave and enter. And they didn't allow diapers and vegetables and things that people need in town, like fresh milk, to get in.

Ellias Rishmawi: And soldiers would stop us on the street and ask to see our ID. Then they would tear up the card and tell us we needed to get a new one by the next day, which cost 130 shekels. We complained to the municipality, and the deputy mayor contacted the military governor. The military governor said, "Listen, we don't give such instructions to the soldiers, and we don't think that our soldiers are doing such a thing." Personally, I don't think a soldier can dare do such a thing without orders, but this is the case.

And if anyone is killed, as they claim, by a "mistake" made by a soldier, that he didn't act according to instructions given to him — what sentence is he getting? He is getting a *suspended* sentence. And what sentence does a stone-thrower get? Years in prison. Sometimes demolishing his house. There are some settlers who have *killed* people, and they have been released, while we are getting very hard sentences and terms for even very mild (what they call) "violence."

Millany Nasser: Fourteen-year-old boys get six-month sentences for throwing stones. I know a boy fifteen years old who they accused of throwing stones, and he has been in prison for four or five months. He hasn't even been accused in court yet, because the court proceedings have been postponed four times.

Ellias Rishmawi: I was in jail myself and have seen horrible things there. Boys my son's age, ten years old, they brought to the detention. They were kids, *children* brought to the detention. It is unbelievable what is going on here. You would never believe it unless you saw it with your own eyes.

Millany Nasser: Something that was very interesting yesterday. I heard President Bush on television commenting about the killing of an American citizen in Panama. He said: "Well, we can't allow a citizen to be killed like this; we have to go in and we have to protect our citizens." But there was an American citizen here, a Palestinian with an American passport, who was tortured and killed. His body was found here in the West Bank. The story was mentioned once, and we never heard anything else about it. This is an American citizen — where is the American army?

Ellias Rishmawi: Another incident took place in Bethlehem some months ago, where a group of Israeli intelligence agents (the Shin Beit) went undercover as tourists. They were wearing shorts and had handbags, cameras, and maps in their hands. They were waiting at the "hot point" in Bethlehem for a demonstration to take place. You can't imagine how they killed Palestinians in cold blood from a distance of two meters. I cannot imagine how any human being can kill in such a way, and not only kill, but to stab on the head, on the chest, on the belly of the killed.

• *Why did they do it?*

Ellias Rishmawi: To liquidate the young people.

Eiman Rishmawi: Now our young men cannot trust the tourists.

• *How long were you in prison?*

Ellias Rishmawi: Well, I was in prison twice. Nobody told me why. I was just taken after midnight and was sent to the prison for eighteen days without any questions, without any charges.

• *And what were the conditions like there?*

Ellias Rishmawi: Don't ask me. I'm trying to forget. They are totally inhuman conditions. I'm really trying to forget that period of my life. Our people are ready to face the hardest measures, but when you are faced with inhuman measures, this poses such great stress on your emotions that you want to retaliate. And believe me, this is the most difficult situation we are facing. We are trying our best not only to forget but to forgive those who give us all this suffering, for the sake of the future of this land.

• *So are you all celebrating Christmas this year?*

Issa Tawil: Yes, we are going to celebrate Christmas in the church — but half of the youth of Beit Sahour are in prison. It is now nine o'clock in the evening; maybe within one hour, or usually at midnight, they come to arrest people. So maybe you will wake up and find one of us arrested.

Millany Nasser: You can imagine how many children have their fathers in prison right now, their brothers as well.

Abla Rishmawi: We feel that the women of America can help us put some pressure on the man who is in the place of responsibility. We hope that they will feel with us as mothers, as sisters, as daughters. How can we celebrate Christmas without our sons? How can the children celebrate without their fathers? This is a land of peace, and I think that Jesus is offended in his cradle. For what is he seeing around? Injustice, bloodshed, killing in his land, in the place where he was born.

Eiman Rishmawi: The soldiers, they come to our street, to our places, and beat and shoot and kill even small kids. This is hard for my kids. Why do they do this with young people? Once they caught a ten-year-old and beat him severely in front of my kids. We have a point of view, that we are suffering to avoid our kids having to suffer again.

Ellias Rishmawi: Palestinians and Israelis each have their dreams about the land of this area. As Palestinians, I think we have dreamt a lot in the past, and now we've stopped dreaming and started to be a realistic nation. Our attitude is based on our knowledge of and acquaintance with the Israelis as a nation in the last twenty-two years under occupation.

I don't think realistically that any Palestinian cannot accept the existence of the Israelis as a nation and as a state. This doesn't mean that we have given up the dreams, but I cannot continue living only on dreams. I can only continue to live on realistic attitudes. Unfortunately, at the time *we* start to be realistic, the other side starts to be dreamers, and this is our tragedy. I hope they won't wait another forty years to stop dreaming.

● ● ●

The next day, Muna and her friend Saliba led me from house to house in Beit Sahour, visiting each neighbor and hearing their stories. At every home, upon my arrival, the entire family was summoned whether or not they spoke English; I was greeted with warmth, curiosity, openness, and always a pot of Arabic coffee.

When they learned I was Jewish, they were often surprised, but their attitude toward me did not change.

Rabeeh Rishmawi and his brother and their families live a few doors from Issa Tawil's home. Their dwelling was clean and pleasant, though small, and it was clear they had little to spare. Still they cooked me a hearty Palestinian dinner.

• *What happened, Rabeeh, when the soldiers came here?*

Rabeeh Rishmawi: They took me to prison at night, and the next day they came to my shop with many, many soldiers and tax men and took everything in the shop — the big Frigidaire and everything. Then they came to the house and took the television, stereo, washing machine, and the sewing machine my wife used to sew trousers and things like that for the children.

• *How many children?*

Rabeeh Rishmawi: We have five children and one on the way. They took everything that is good in the house.

• *And when they came to take it, what did you say? Did you get angry?*

Rabeeh Rishmawi: No. We said, "Take everything and anything you want." We didn't care because we want them to know we won't pay taxes for them. This is one kind of peace struggle, not a struggle with knives or guns, to show them that we want peace, *real* peace.

• *So you think it's possible then for Palestinians and Israelis to live together in peace?*

Rabeeh Rishmawi: Yes, it is very simple to live with them because there are many kind people among the Jewish people. But the Israeli government is not good. If they want us to live with them, we can live with them. I speak alone, but there are many, many Palestinian people who speak like this.

• *They're beating you. They're arresting you, putting you in prison. They're killing you. Aren't you afraid?*

Rabeeh Rishmawi: No. When they take us to prison, and when we come out of prison, we become very strong because there is a school in the prison, a big school. Here, there's a small school, but in the prison there is a big school, a university.

• *What keeps you going? I mean this is a very hard situation. How do you keep resisting?*

Kaldon Rishmawi (fourteen years old): Because we want to be free. We want our land. That's it. We're one hand. One voice. And we are walking in one street. The street of freedom.

• • •

By now it was late afternoon on Christmas Eve, and as the church bells pealed, all of Beit Sahour poured out of their doorways and into the streets. Women and girls led our march through the hills together, while the sun set over Bethlehem in the distance. We were on our way to Shepherds' Field for a Christmas Eve mass with Bishop Desmond Tutu from South Africa.

The site itself was overflowing with tour buses, press, and soldiers. As Saliba and I pushed through, we saw that the entrance to the actual "field" area was tightly restricted to what appeared to be dignitaries, the media, some tourists, Israelis, and a few Palestinians. With mixed feelings, I showed my press card and was shoved in by the guard, leaving behind my young companion and guide. It was difficult to be separated — this is his country — shouldn't he be the one allowed inside the fence?

I squeezed through the crowd to get as close as possible to Bishop Tutu.

Bishop Tutu: ". . . Friends, we come speaking peace, but there can be no peace anywhere in the world without justice. We support the struggle of the Palestinian people for their state. The Jews have a right to their independent state as well."

Amidst Christmas carols, prayers, and greetings, the mass ended with a plea from an Israeli peace activist.

Hillel Bardine: ". . . You should know that most Israelis are opposed to the occupation and would like to see it ended. They want real peace with the Palestinians. So why don't we Israelis accept the idea of an independent Palestinian state? Many Israelis do not yet believe that you really are willing to live with us in peace. My friends in Israel need to hear from you that you're prepared to live with us in peace. And I ask the thousands of Palestinians that are here, Will you make your voices heard now? Can we live together in peace?"

The crowd responded by roaring: "Yes!"*

---

* In 1989 Beit Sahour was nominated for a Nobel Peace Prize.

top: Rana Nashashibi speaking in West Jerusalem at the 1990 Women's Peace Conference. © Susan E. Dorfman

bottom: Tamar Gozansky, member of the Israeli Knesset. (December 1990) © Susan E. Dorfman

top: Veronika Cohen who organizes dialogue groups of Israelis and Palestinians. (January 1990) © Penny Rosenwasser

bottom: Tikva Honig Parnas at the Alternative Information Center in Jerusalem. (December 1989) © Penny Rosenwasser

top: "Women Go for Peace" march on December 29, 1989. © Penny Rosenwasser

bottom: Women and children of Beit Sahour preparing for the peace march to Christmas Eve mass at Shepherds' Field with Bishop Desmond Tutu. (December 1989) © Penny Rosenwasser

top: Palestinian women waving olive branches during the women's peace march, December 2 1989. © Penny Rosenwasser

bottom: Over 20,000 Palestinians, Israelis, Europeans and Americans joined hands to form a "Human Chain" around the Old City of Jerusalem, December 30, 1990. © Penny Rosenwasser

top: Palestinian child gives the intifada victory sign in a refugee camp in Gaza.
© Penny Rosenwasser

bottom: Israeli police and army violently disrupt the peaceful "Human Chain" around Jerusalem. © Penny Rosenwasser

top: Palestinian clergyman giving the intifada victory sign during the "Human Chain" around Jerusalem. (December 1989) © Penny Rosenwasser

bottom: Israeli woman at a Women in Black vigil; her sign says, "Enough of the Occupation. Originally from Italy, she said her whole family had died in Auschwitz and she didn't want the same thing to happen to the Palestinians. (December 1989) © Penny Rosenwasser

top: Israeli soldiers in the Old City of Jerusalem. (December 1990) © Susan E. Dorfman

bottom: The Wailing Wall [Western Wall] in the Old City of Jerusalem, sacred to Jews.
In the distance is Dome of the Rock/Al Aqsa Mosque, sacred to Moslems. (December 1990)
© Susan Dorfman

top: In the Jabalia Refugee Camp in Gaza. Ibtisan (left), 17, is a kindergarten teacher. Her brother, Ghassan (right), 15, wants to go to Russia to study medicine and return to help his people. (December 1989) © Penny Rosenwasser

bottom: Palestinian woman waiting to visit her son in the Russian Compound Detention Center in West Jerusalem. (December 1989) © Penny Rosenwasser

top: Palestinian child in Gaza. (December 1990) © Sharon Wallace

bottom: Women mixing dough at the Abasan Biscuit Factory in Gaza, a project of the Palestinian Federation of Women's Action Committees. (December 1990)
© Penny Rosenwasser

top: Palestinian woman at the women's carpet-weaving cooperative in Gaza. (December 1990) © Penny Rosenwasser

bottom: Woman shop-owner in Beit Sahour whose sewing machine and clothing goods were confiscated by the Israeli army when she refused to pay taxes to Israel. (December 1989) © Penny Rosenwasser

Palestinian children in doorway. (December 1990) © Susan E. Dorfman

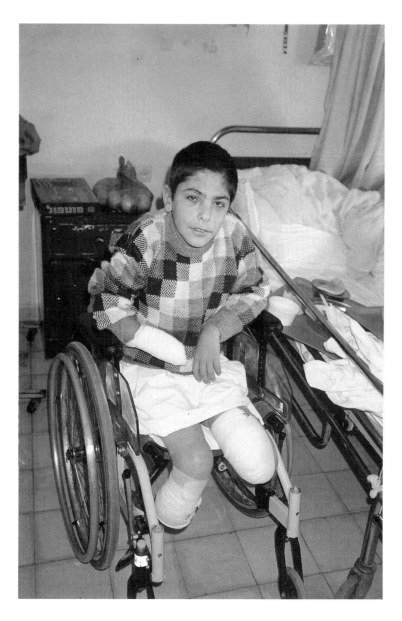

Palestinian boy at al-Muqassed Hospital in East Jerusalem. He lost two legs, one hand, and part of his eyesight when Israeli soldiers threw an explosive into his home. (December 1989) © Penny Rosenwasser

top: Families in Beit Sahour; on the left is Muna, whose piano was confiscated by Israeli authorities after her father, Issa Tawil (at the back), refused to pay taxes to Israel.
© Penny Rosenwasser

bottom: Palestinian kindergarten in Hebron, on the West Bank. (December 1990)
© Sarah Jacobus

top: Young women working with the Palestinian women's committees in Nablus, on the West Bank. (January 1990) © Penny Rosenwasser
bottom: Alya Shawa of Gaza with Penny Rosenwasser. (December 1989) © Sarah Jacobus

Zahira Kamal, president of Palestinian Federation of Women's Action Committees, who has participated in Palestinian delegation meetings with Secretary of State James Baker. (Dec. 1990) © Susan E. Dorfman

Michel "Mikado" Warschawski, director of Alternative Information Center, speaking in Berkeley, CA during a speaking tour in the U.S. (July 1991) © Rick Rocamora

Tikva Honig Parnas
December 1989

Tikva Parnas is an outspoken Israeli peace activist, both in the women's peace camp (working with Women for Women Political Prisoners and the Women and Peace Coalition) and in the Israeli peace movement as a whole.

An army officer in the 1948 war, Tikva now works with the Alternative Information Center, which collects and disseminates information from both the Occupied Territories and from within Israel itself. Established in 1985 as a joint project of Israelis and Palestinians, the Center also serves as a meeting place for cooperation and discussion between Palestinians and Israelis.

Whether editing leaflets or juggling phone calls and appointments at the Center, leading a women's protest march for international protection of Palestinians, giving a workshop, standing with Women in Black, or relaxing over dinner, Tikva's articulate and uncompromising integrity shines through. To be with Tikva, even for a few moments, is to feel a constant, scarcely containable surge of energy — to see the ever-present cigarette embellishing the words from her uniquely expressive yet tightly shaped mouth — to know the pain, the required patience, the passion of caring so deeply for justice.

I first spoke with Tikva in December 1989. She begins by describing an action taken against the Center.

Tikva: At the peak of its success in February 1987, the Alternative Information Center was suddenly raided by more than twenty police from the Shabak [the Israeli equivalent of the FBI]. It was closed down by an administrative order, without any trial, without anything. But because the protest within Israel was so great against the closing of the Center, the Israeli security police retreated and allowed it to reopen after six months. The Center's director, Michel "Mikado" Warschawski, was detained and accused of typesetting a booklet for an illegal Palestinian organization, and of refusing to reveal the names of the persons or organizations who brought him the booklet. The Center, as part of its budget, used to give typesetting services to peace activists and to progressive organizations in the West Bank. The content of this booklet was about how to withstand torture and interrogation from the Israeli security police. Warschawski was released on very high bail on condition that he not return to the Center.

In November 1989, Warschawski was sentenced to twenty months in prison. Now the protest against the sentence in Israel was wide — you can't imagine how. Because everyone felt that this was a political decision with a warning finger at the peace camp to stop any cooperation and solidarity between Israelis and Palestinians. You see, it's using the anti-terrorist laws which are the emergency laws. According to these laws, for any type of cooperation you can be put to trial for supporting illegal organizations.

You can see already the beginnings of a new trend of tens of groups — what *moves* them, like the women who support political prisoners, is the willingness to cooperate with the Palestinians. And when you say "cooperate with Palestinians," it's not *individual* Palestinians, because all the civil life in the West Bank, all the cultural life, all the economic life is now organized under recognized organizations which are led by the Unified Leadership. So any connection with Palestinians can now be defined as helping illegal organizations.

• *So, you're saying that it's getting worse, not better.*

Tikva: Oh, of course, it's getting worse. Various groups of Israeli peace activists have met with the PLO in Romania and elsewhere — people such as the infamous Abie Nathan, who met with Arafat.[1] This is one level of cooperation which is prohibited. But now they are turning to prosecute the lower level of cooperation of activists for both sides. For instance, things have been changing so fast, Yesh G'vul [Israeli soldiers refusing to serve in the Occupied Territories] went to Beit Sahour, and they made a joint leaflet, a joint declaration of the council of Beit Sahour with Yesh G'vul. Once you say a joint declaration, you mean a *joint struggle*. This couldn't have happened two years ago — the whole idea of solidarity, of coordination of the struggle. When I say it's a turning point now, I don't mean it in terms of numbers. These are not yet very large numbers, but you can see the beginning of a new trend. And this is what the authorities are so concerned about.

People are not moved by slogans. People are mobilized and politicized by being active. For instance, the women who support political prisoners. These are women who, many of them, were never in a demonstration before. They didn't even articulate or say in words to themselves, what the solution is, the political solution they are for. They know they feel *furious*, they feel *solidarity*, they want to *act*. And by acting, they are politicized.

They don't even say we are for the common struggle, but basically what we are doing *is* the common struggle. Because when we picketed in the Russian Compound against torture and against bad conditions there, there were at least two hundred Palestinians waiting for their visits — it was on a Friday. A police officer came over and said, "As long as you picket here, the Palestinians won't get their visits." So of course we wanted to leave. But the families came to us and said, "We don't care about our visits, you go on protesting." What happened there, as a matter of fact, was a common struggle of Israelis and Palestinians against a certain faction of the Occupation.

[1] As recently as the summer of 1991, Abie Nathan went on a prolonged, highly visible hunger strike in an unsuccessful attempt to pressure for the legalization of Israeli groups and individuals to meet with the PLO.

So the very bitter and long argument within the peace camp becomes, "Does the protest movement have to be an educational group?" which I objected to and my friends objected to. "Or shall we leave it open and only concentrate on objecting to the occupation accompanied by activities of solidarity?" This last approach has proved to be right, because you can now see that more and more groups are working in solidarity.

• *What you're saying is that the Israeli government is getting more repressive. How will you fight this?*

Tikva: First of all, I'll tell you an example. We have here a worker, an Israeli Palestinian worker, who comes three times a week and does the typing in Arabic. One night I received a phone call from a friend in Tel Aviv asking, "When is Fatima coming tomorrow? I need her to translate a leaflet of support for Beit Sahour, calling for a picket." And I said "She has to be here around 9:30." He called and brought her the leaflet.

The whole next day, she didn't show up. I didn't know where she was. Finally, at five o'clock she came. When she had come to the Center at 9:30, plainclothes police were waiting outside. They took the leaflet and threatened her, saying that it was illegal. And, of course, it *is* legal. They took her to the Russian Compound. She was interrogated for eight hours, slapped in her face, told that the leaflet was illegal, and asked questions about the Center, which is a registered, open, legal place. Not allowing her to call a lawyer or to call us. Just a woman disappeared for eight hours! What is behind it? Warning her: "Don't cooperate with Jews, don't cooperate with Israelis. Not even Israeli Arabs."

• *So your phone must have been tapped?*

Tikva: Of course, it's tapped. Of course.

- *You were in the army?*

Tikva: I was in the army. In 1948. In the struggle for the independence of the Israeli state. And I have many, many new thoughts about it which I didn't understand then.

- *What was your job then?*

Tikva: I was a wireless operator. But I have a letter, you know, written on the Arabic stationery of the manager of the gas station midway between Jerusalem and Tel Aviv. I wrote it on the thirtieth of October in 1948, to my home. And I found it only recently. I was shocked to not recognize myself in this letter. What I can tell you is that this letter shows how the process of the dehumanization of Palestinians was already at its peak with my generation, the generation before 1948.

There is a description in the letter where I am saying how we conquered a place just a few days before. I don't even refer to the stationery — some person's name is on it, and I am writing on his stationery and I don't even refer to it! And I say, "Dear Mom and Dad, You know, there are hundreds of Palestinians, women and children, that our soldiers met on the way. They are starving," (in Hebrew it is even stronger), "starving to death and begging to come back to their villages." I don't refer to it, I don't even say how we answered them. And then I go on and say, "And, you know, in the evening, at night, two American-Jewish volunteers started shouting and saying, 'If this new state can't take care of its citizens, it should not have been established.'"

And then I say to my parents, "Mom and Dad, dear Mom and Dad, you know, I'm sick and tired of these philanthropic American Zionists." I don't even say humanistic, or human. So this gave me a lot of material for thought about what kind of generation my generation was. I was already a Marxist then, and a leftist about everything except Palestinians. And you know my generation, when they are asked if they hated Arabs, used to say, "Of course not." We didn't hate Arabs.

133

Because they were so dehumanized that we didn't need to hate. We just, in a way, we didn't care.

• *What changed you?*

Tikva: As I told you, I was already on the Left then. Then I joined Mapam, you know, the Zionist Left party. I was their secretary in the Knesset. But I considered myself very Leftist. And then the Twentieth Convention in Soviet Russia changed my political ideas about Stalinism and Russian communism. I became more and more anti-Zionist, in terms of seeing that you can't establish a *democratic* Jewish state while the Arab citizens are second rate citizens, while Arabs living in Israel do not have all the rights that Jews have who live there. And this is how I became what I am now. (Laughter)

Still we don't have the right answer to the question, "How come the women's protest movement is much stronger than the men's?"

• *Is that true?*

Tikva: Yes. I'm involved in the Women and Peace Coalition. And I am also a representative in the general peace coalition, made up of men and women. You can't compare the efficiency, the coordination, the organization of the women. Women now have the most organizations with prolonged activity. Not with an occasional demonstration, but with *continuous* activity. On the other hand, if it weren't for the intifada, nothing would have been here, no protest movement. The protest movement had been dormant since the Lebanon war. It's the reaction to the intifada, women protesting and the whole protest movement. So you need a more sophisticated answer to the phenomenon. But it's an agreed-upon phenomenon that women within the protest movement are the strongest in their ability to mobilize their constituency. A hundred women every Friday, in Jerusalem.

I'm not talking about Peace Now, which can mobilize thousands. I'm talking now about the *protest* movement, because Peace Now is only now coming more and more into it. Peace Now was very active during the Lebanon War, and then nothing, because it was part and parcel of the whole Israeli society which didn't pay any price for the Occupation and believed that the status quo could go on forever. And the "three no's" — *no* to the PLO, *no* to an independent state, *no* to negotiations — were part of the national consensus of Israeli society. This national consensus was broken down by the intifada.

• *When you talk about the women involved, does that include women across class lines?*

Tikva: Not yet. Not yet. The protest movement is yet a middle-class phenomenon. But already more and more, you can see an Oriental front.[1] Yamin Swissa [a Moroccan Jew] is not a Leftist person. I mean, he is part of the Labor Party, maybe he is Leftist in the Labor Party. He wrote a letter to Gorbachev asking him not to let Jewish people emigrate to Israel, because the economic situation is so bad that Oriental Jews in the neighborhoods and the developing towns are living in bad conditions. The unemployment is increasing from day to day. So all these are reactions to the intifada — the beginning of the dissolving of the national consensus and the polarizations of the society.

• *So you really see that happening . . . the dissolving of the national consensus?*

Tikva: Of course, with the right-wing becoming stronger and stronger, more and more arrogant, more and more daring. Like burning the door of a university professor because of his liberal ideas. On the other hand, you can see the change in

---

[1] Oriental Jews are those not originally of Eastern European descent, whose secondary language was not Yiddish.

the Labor Party to the Left for recognizing the PLO — not all the Labor Party, let's say the doves, at least a third of them. And of course, Mapam, Ratz, the kibbutzim, and Peace Now.[1] All these are very important changes, and you can't but conclude that it's a reaction to the intifada. Nothing would have moved inside Israel without the intifada.

• *The kibbutzim are changing?*

Tikva: Of course, they are planning to send five hundred kibbutzim members to Egypt to meet Arafat. But on the other hand, I want to say again, the Palestinian state is not waiting around the corner.

• *So in terms of your strategy for change, you'll just keep doing what you're doing, working with Palestinians? How are you going to keep fighting this?*

Tikva: We'll keep mobilizing more and more people against the Occupation, and strengthening our solidarity with the Palestinian people, which means continually being harassed by the Israeli authorities. I'm harassed every time I leave the country, every time I come back into the country, and I'm not the only one. These are everyday harassments against Israeli peace activists, which are becoming more and more harsh. Here and there some people can retreat, but I don't think this is going to change the march towards cooperation which is already there.

• *So what do you think the future's going to bring?*

Tikva: I don't think that our Palestinian friends fighting here believe that the Palestinian state will come about in a short time. The intifada is going to accelerate, not in terms of using force, but in terms of the *real* intifada, the revolution *inside*, the strengthening of the alternative institutions —

[1] Ratz is the Citizen's Rights Party, also a part of the Zionist Left.

medical, educational. And, of course, building towards mass civil disobedience. According to the Israeli press, you can feel that this is the main thing that they are afraid of. They don't care about stones. They care about what's being built every day on the ground, the alternative society.

• *How can U.S. peace groups help?*

Tikva: I really believe that the main thing is calling upon the American public to stop aid to Israel. It's the only thing, the only pressure that can make any impact on this society. I mean not only on the government but on the Israeli public. This, I think, is the most important thing to mobilize all energies for.

• *And you're saying that as an Israeli?*

Tikva: As an Israeli, and as a Jew, and as an Israeli activist who's concerned about Israeli society and the Israeli people. Because according to me and to my friends, the occupation is bad for Israeli society as well as for Palestinians. It's rotting the society. Inevitably this society will become more and more fascist, more and more undemocratic. You can't keep an occupation without illegal and terrorist measures of repression crossing the border into our own society.

• *Could you just tell me a little more about the effect on the Israeli society that you think this is having?*

Tikva: I don't believe that the Israeli society can change just by means of educating. No. The American public didn't start reacting en masse to Vietnam until the *cost* of the war was high. The cost of this war — because even the Israeli military high officials define the intifada as a war — the cost of this war for Israeli society is not yet high enough. Only when the economic and the moral cost — I don't want even to say the *lives*, but there are other costs — are high enough, will

Israelis come in the thousands into the streets. And cutting American aid can be a very high cost which can change people and make them come out against the Israeli policies.

December 1990

The Gulf crisis had such a dramatic effect on the Israeli peace movement that in December 1990 I asked Tikva about her perspective on the changing situation. We were perched on the low patio wall outside the Israeli women's peace conference in West Jerusalem.[1]

Tikva: Recently, especially since the Gulf crisis, I had to rethink the basis for my cooperation with the Zionist peace camp, with which I am very much involved, although I am anti-Zionist. Part of my being involved in it was that I have felt that this peace camp can mobilize more and more of the Israeli public into recognizing Palestinian rights.

But since the Gulf crisis, most of the Zionist camp has begun speaking very arrogantly *against* dialogue with the Palestinians. I think the Zionist Left never was ready to really deal for themselves with the *sources* of the Palestinian-Israeli conflict. They have come to the dialogue as if it's only a question of where the borders of each state will be, as if we have two national movements which can bring the solution by dividing, by partitioning, by each one giving up some of the territories. They haven't taken into consideration the Palestinians' longing to return to their land, their pain about not having the Right of Return.[2]

Now, when it comes to the Gulf crisis, the peace camp in Israel is disappointed, is shocked: "How come you have this Arab identity? How come you are even talking about not going

[1] Noelle Hanrahan assisted me in this portion of the interview with Tikva.
[2] Because Israel is a Jewish state, Jews from other countries can make "aliyah" — they have the automatic right to return and become Israeli citizens. For Palestinians, however, it is much more difficult to return — and it is not automatic — even when their immediate families hold direct claims to specific parts of the land

together with the Americans?" The Zionist Left sees the United States as the force that is going to bring enlightenment to the Third World. They do not see that it's not a question of borders; it's a question of living together in this area.

• *So what do you think needs to happen?*

Tikva: We have to re-educate people about the sources of the conflict. It didn't start between two national movements — it started between a colonialist movement which dispossessed Palestinians, and we don't come as *equal*. The solution can't take place without transforming Israeli society and the whole concept and institutions of the Jewish state.

• *Some of the Palestinian women have said to us that they're disillusioned with the Israeli peace movement — especially the women's peace movement, which has been acknowledged as the heart of the Israeli peace movement — because they say that the women are not taking risks. What's your response to that?*

Tikva: They are right. When most of the Palestinian women withdrew their participation in this year's peace conference, Israeli women came and said, "But our conference and our workshops are so important to us, you have to understand," and "It's your role to help us explain to our people." No, it's not their role! There is misunderstanding of the unequal situation between the Palestinian women and the Israeli women. The Palestinians are in the midst of war, they are the ones who are being killed, they are the ones who are being arrested. And their whole tactic, their whole strategy is different than ours.

Israeli women were disappointed that the Palestinian women didn't want to be involved in this conference — *of course* they didn't! Their priorities are absolutely different right now. But more and more, the "hard core" of the Israeli

Women and Peace Coalition are absolutely ready to go to more illegal, militant actions together. More and more they come to the conclusion that the situation is such that we can't go on with the same means, the same tactics — that even inside Israel, the protesters, even if it's not the masses, must be willing to take more risks, to be arrested.

And more and more, I feel that cooperating with the Reshet, the more middle-of-the-road, or mainstream, of the Israeli women's peace movement, goes against the political aim of mobilizing more women. Because I think you always have to distinguish between a small radical group, which goes forward and pulls along the less militant by its action. And Reshet is pressing us to give up our actions and do the same thing *together* all the time. But I think we need to be a kind of catalyst which pulls along the less militant, which says the things that the others are not willing to.

For instance, to call for "International Protection of Palestinians," we had to negotiate with the Reshet, who wanted to say "Defend Human Lives." I would respect them and their political role if they would say: "Our constituency is not ready yet. *You* go forward, *you* do it, we'll try and educate *our* public." So at least the explicit clear voice would be heard, and others would come after. But instead they are asking us to present a mild formula. This is not a question of formulas; it's a question of expressing and representing the issue truthfully to the public!

• *If you have this marginal Left-wing in the Israeli peace movement, one possibility is that it pulls the rest along, but isn't the other possibility that it isolates itself and alienates the rest of the group? Some of the Israeli women who seem to be doing important work have expressed this conflict in themselves. When I asked, "Why aren't you doing civil disobedience?" they'd say, "Well, personally, I would, but I want to bring a lot more people with me."*

Tikva: No. We have a different public and we have different constituencies. The Women and Peace constituency is already convinced that the political solution is a Palestinian independent state. This is *our* public, so we have to radicalize them more, bring them to more cooperation and solidarity with the intifada, which is a slogan that is not yet mentioned. We have our public and they have their center of the political map. It's very important to work on theirs. But it's a different tactic, different public, different activities.

• *When I first saw you this trip, you said that you'd gone through some significant changes this year — that you'd become more of a feminist . . .*

Tikva: I've always considered myself feminist — I knew the theory, I am a socialist. I thought that the main battle inside Israel is to fight against the Occupation, and that's all. But from my work with the Women and Peace Coalition and Women for Women Political Prisoners, my whole identity as a feminist has become stronger.

Because only now do I understand that the fight against Occupation and the fight for feminism in this country nourish each other. The more you fight against Occupation, the more you alienate women from the Israeli government; the more they are alienated from the Zionist regime, the more they can come forward with *their* values and not feel subdued by and inferior to the values of militarism, of the security of the state, and so forth. And the more you are feminist, the more capability you have for real solidarity with oppression.

So now I also feel at home — as a socialist, as a feminist, as a fighter against Occupation — in frameworks *only* of women, which was only by accident before. By accident I started the Women for Women Political Prisoners. No mixed (women and men) protest movement in Israel could have now gathered this number of women.

• *Was there one thing that happened this year that brought this change about in you?*

Tikva: Oh, it's the intifada. The intifada has stripped off, made naked, in one shot of lightning, the whole heroism of the militaristic culture which is dominant in Israel. These "wonderful wars," and these "heroic men" — these heroic men are now beating children and women. Now women can come and express *their* values, because of how the men's brutality has been revealed.

• *But what was it that changed you personally?*

Tikva: It's the very fact of working with women. You see, so many of us think that, by reading and by thinking, people can reach real politics. It never goes like this. The very fact of *acting* radicalizes. I radicalize, not theoretically, but emotionally.

Israeli Women's Peace Vigil
December 1990

I: Zéhava Mehager

On a wintry afternoon in late December 1990, Israeli women began an all-night vigil in front of Prime Minister Shamir's home in West Jerusalem, scheduled just prior to the women's peace conference being organized for the following morning. Many of those shivering good-humoredly had just walked over from the weekly Women in Black vigil nearby. They started distributing blankets and pinning up banners bearing the slogans "Two States for Two Peoples," "International Peace Conference," "Negotiations with the PLO," and "International Protection for Palestinians."

The vigil site was a wide sidewalk adjoining a major downtown thoroughfare. While some drivers slowed down, peering curiously, others honked, gunned their motors and spat in protest. Flanking the sidewalk was a low cement wall topped by a wrought-iron fence. I guessed Shamir's estate was behind the lawn, off somewhere in the distance.

A woman with a blond punk haircut drew my attention, and I began to speak with Zéhava Mehager, an Oriental Jew who works with East for Peace and the Black Panthers.

• *Zéhava, I'm glad to meet you because Chaya Shalom told me you had a lot to say about what's happening right now. Why are you here today?*

Zéhava: I'm here because I'm protesting the Israeli occupation. I think there are a million and a half people here in Israel who are existing, not actually living. This is very humiliating. Racism is getting stronger and stronger in Israel, and this is only part of it. Actually if the intifada hadn't developed, people would ignore the fact that there are a million and a half Palestinian people pressed down here to a very poor life, not the way people should live.

I think Israel must leave the Occupied Territories, go back to the borders of '67, and declare "Two States for Two Peoples." The Arabs and Jews must live here together. Nobody can disappear, nobody can go away. Meanwhile, we are at war here. We should be clever enough to know how to live in peace because we are both here and that is the final fact.

• *Given the tensions, do you think it's possible realistically for Arabs and Jews to live together in peace?*

Zéhava: Of course! We have the same culture. Israelis have tried very hard to make this a western country but it is not. We are here in the *Middle East.* 60% of the citizens of Israel, besides Arabs, are from Muslim countries. We love the country, we love the smells, we love the Bible culture, and this is how we should live.

The Oriental people who came all this way, like my parents for example, came for a big dream — to live under the Bible spirit with Arabs as they used to live in Morocco, in Iraq, in Kurdistan. We talk the same language, we have the same mentality. The western people here have tried very hard since the minute they built this country, under a very criminal racism, to make this a western country. This is *not* a western country. We can live here in peace with Arab peoples.

• *How long have you been doing this work?*

Zéhava: Ten years, unfortunately, instead of making my life enjoyable. But when you live in Israel, you read papers, and you cannot stay calm after reading the papers. While I was growing up, I never had a thought of being an activist. Yet I was opening my eyes, and I saw pluralism of cultures here. I saw two different main cultures: oriental and western. I connected myself to my roots, and I realized that I love Arab people; I get along with them more easily even than with the westerners.

I made my search — what made this split between me and the Arabs? I realized that it's the westerners that made the split. What is all this for? For me it means that the Zionist people brought the war here. All these peace groups — you probably know, one of the biggest is Shalom Achshav [Peace Now] — they continue this line of making a big split between the Arabs and Jews here, instead of closing the gap.

Peace Now perhaps represents the "bad boys" of the government, of the leadership here. But they are not really working to make the people here come closer together. If they are ignoring the Orientals, how can they speak? The left-wing here was very glad to place the stigma of "right-wing" on the Orientals, and this is not true. This is taking us further from peace than anything else because we are 57% of the citizens here. I don't know what the next generation's statistics will be, but as you know we have more children than the Ashkenazi.[1] The left-wing is, in my opinion, doing nothing. Sometimes they protest, but aside from that, they don't use their talents, their knowledge, their studies to make a big change here.

• *What do you think they should be doing?*

Zéhava: I think first they have to work with the citizens of Israel who are against Arabs, to understand exactly what it means when you say "I'm against Arabs" or "Death to the Arabs." The situation now is that whatever this Shalom Achshav person will think, the Oriental neighborhood person will think the opposite, without logic. So they have to work first with these people to bring them closer to peace ideas, which are the Leftist ideas.

[1] Ashkenazi are Jews of Central and Eastern European descent, who originally spoke Yiddish.

Then they must make militant protests. We are not powerful enough. The right is growing bigger and bigger. Only yesterday they tried to murder three Palestinians — a father and his two kids — and on this same day three Israelis from Hebron and Kiryat Arba were freed from jail after serving only seven years for being Jewish underground radical religious fanatics. They had been given life sentences, but after seven years they were released. One of them had entered an Islamic University in Kiryat in Hebron with his shotgun, and killed whoever was in his way, including the Mayor of Ramallah. So the government should stop liking these right-wing Jewish fanatics and give *real* punishment for acts such as murder.

• *Some of the Palestinian women have said to me that they were frustrated with the Israeli peace movement because activists were just "playing it safe."*

Zéhava: This is right. Before we knew we didn't have a permit for this demonstration tomorrow, our plan was to walk towards the American Embassy. Suddenly plenty of women, and I was very surprised, thought this was a very radical step, and unfortunately they could not do it.[1] What are we for if we cannot even do this small symbolic thing? I don't blame the Palestinians. The activists here are not really fighting for the Palestinian struggle and human rights; they are more cultured ladies.

• *Earlier you said that you hadn't planned to be an activist, but you couldn't stay calm. But it seems that so many of the*

[1] Zéhava is referring to the fact that in December 1990 the Israeli High Court refused a permit for a women's peace march, citing increased tensions in the region. The Palestinian women and some of the Women and Peace members wanted to march illegally, while other Israeli women did not want to break the law. In the interests of keeping the coalition together, the march was canceled. However, several days later, on January 3, 1991, approximately thirty-five Palestinian and Israeli women marched peacefully through East Jerusalem to the British consulate. They presented a petition requesting an international peace conference.

Israeli people are staying calm in the midst of this injustice. How do you explain that?

Zéhava: Well this was also a typical question about the Holocaust. There were a lot of questions to the non-Jewish people there: "You knew what was happening and yet you actually continued your life." Many people who are here now came from that same society. How can they stay calm when only twenty kilometers from here young boys aged sixteen, fourteen, ten, are getting killed because they throw stones? And *they* are sitting in their houses having wine. When everything is very bad, and everything is false and not built on a really ethical and humanitarian way of thinking, you must make yourself blind to facts, and this is what happens here, unfortunately.

• *You must feel isolated.*

Zéhava: I don't anymore because I looked inside this kind of society, and I realized they have nothing to offer me. When you want to fight against something, you have to be as strong as it is.

II: Nabila Espanioli

"A hero is someone who makes a friend out of an enemy"
— *Shutafut* (Partnership) slogan

Nabila Espanioli is a Palestinian-Israeli, or a Palestinian living in Haifa, within the borders of Israel. A psychologist, and a professor of Women's Studies at Haifa University, Nabila is co-director of Shutafut, a peace and social welfare organization of Arabs and Jews. She is also an organizer with the Israeli Women and Peace Coalition. Sarah Jacobus and I spoke with Nabila at the Israeli women's all-night peace vigil in front of Prime Minister Shamir's house in downtown West Jerusalem. In spite of the cold and the late hour, at the vigil site we found nearly fifty women chatting and laughing, sprawled on sleeping bags on the sidewalk, or dishing out large pots of steaming soup under a makeshift shelter.

Nabila is a well-respected vivacious leader. Dark curls cascade down her back as she shakes her head to emphasize a point or wave to a new arrival at the vigil. Sarah and I asked Nabila about the Israeli Women's Peace Conference planned for the next day.

• *Nabila, my friend Chaya Shalom was very encouraged earlier in the fall as this conference was being built because she felt it was more of a joint effort between Palestinian and Jewish Israeli women than ever before. From what I can gather right now, that's really broken down. I'd love to get your perspective on that, as a Palestinian-Israeli who's obviously in a leadership role.*

Nabila Espanioli: First of all, I have to say that we worked together for one year — Palestinian women in an all-Palestinian organization and the Israeli Women and Peace organizations. It was a good experience for both Israeli women and Palestinian women. Sitting in between as an Israeli-Palestinian, I can evaluate this as very encouraging. But the political situation is overwhelming us.

I think the main development was the massacre at the Al Aqsa Mosque in Jerusalem, when nineteen Palestinians were killed by Israeli soldiers this past October. That was the breakdown which was prepared beforehand by the Gulf crisis and prepared by a lot of the Israeli peace movement's problems. As the Israeli peace movement, we were *stuck*. We were trying to do something, but we were not moving ahead. This caused a lot of frustration and a lot of problems between us as Israelis, and we found ourselves in fewer and fewer numbers. I think that's the background for the breakdown. I think that it is just a break between dialogue partners, maybe. And each dialogue can break down for a while, but it's going to be continuing for sure.

• *Some of the Palestinians I've spoken with have said maybe this is the time to do civil disobedience?*

Nabila: Personally I believe this is the time, and personally we're trying to engage in other activities which are not within the law. For example, a hundred of us Palestinian and Jewish Israeli women, signed a statement calling on the soldiers not to serve in the West Bank and Gaza, and this is illegal. Not every woman today can face this dangerous consequence of going to jail, but these hundred women were a start.

When we are working in Israel we have to think about the general atmosphere, and the general atmosphere is very, very right-wing. We have to walk between the raindrops and not get wet; we have to be very sensitive to what's going on. We are working from one side with Palestinian women, and from the other side we are working within Israeli society. We want to cause some change inside Israeli society. I'm not sure that doing something against the law helps develop the peace process because it doesn't bring *new* people.

But right now I believe that we have to have the courage to make some efforts, even if they are illegal, but it is only the individual's responsibility. I can't be responsible for telling thousands of men and women, "Come and do this with us." We asked the women, telling them exactly the danger that's standing in front of them, and one hundred women — it's a big number — decided to sign. So we published this petition, and it was against the law. Now, we have do more such activities, but to cook it on a very slow fire.

Sometimes, I believe we really have to push things more. When I think logically, this is my emotion, that I want to *push*. But when I'm thinking politically *and* logically, then I have to decide how to be politically effective. Politically effective means trying to be so wide that we can speak with all the women standing here, because not all the women standing here are thinking the same politically as I do or as other women do or as *Palestinians* from the West Bank and Gaza do. These Palestinians are living in a harder situation, and I understand their demands. I demand them too, but you have to be realistic.

• *I know some of the Palestinian women feel that the Israeli peace movement has not been willing to go far enough to demonstrate its commitment to the creation of an independent Palestinian state. What's your response to that?*

Nabila: I have the same analogy. I don't think that the peace movement is a *Left* movement, it's a *peace* movement, — nothing more. A big part of it is trying to conduct activities just to justify their continuing to be here. I don't think that a lot of them are doing it because they are willing to *pay* for such change. I'm speaking about big movements like Peace Now.

We of Women and Peace are the radicals among the women's movements. We are also working with some people more to the right of us and we have to go *with* them in order to *bring* them. If we want to do nonviolent disobedience, we have to pay. Our jobs in the future will be affected if we are politically active, our income will be affected, we will be not respected enough. We will have to pay with our own "good life." And the Israeli peace movement is not ready to do it. Personally I, and a lot of women here, are ready to do it, but, unfortunately, we are not The Peace Movement. The problem is that the general Israeli peace movement is trying to impose its opinion on the Palestinians, and that's why there is frustration on both sides.

• *You spoke earlier about your identity as a Palestinian-Israeli, and I wonder what kind of tension or feelings that creates for you — being in the middle like that?*

Nabila: It is very hard sometimes, and I have to struggle for this identity. I believe that I'm very clear about my identity: I'm a Palestinian living in Israel, trying to build the Israeli identity that I wish to have in the future. I think what we're building as Women and Peace is an *alternative Israeli feminist identity*. I don't see it right now. I don't have any possibilities to say I am Israeli — *right now*.

But if we succeed in building this alternative, then I will be able to say it. Right now I'm also a Palestinian whose people are oppressed. Even if a political Jewish woman feels my oppression and gets tired of the oppression and gets affected, she is getting affected because her own people are doing that to the "other" people. But I'm getting affected because *my government* is hurting *my own people* and my own blood.

I feel I am building the bridge for the future. I don't see myself in the middle, because then I would have two faces, and I don't have two faces — I have only one very clear face, which is Palestinian-Israeli, which I try to build here and try to build there. I am Palestinian; I am a very proud Palestinian, and I want to fight for our rights as Palestinians. But I am living in Israel, and I want to build in Israel. Because I believe it's not just tactical when I say "two states for two peoples." I *believe* in that. So when I say, "I am a Palestinian in Israel," I believe it in my heart, my soul, my body — so it's part of my life.

I believe that when a Palestinian state is established — and it *will* be established, beside Israel — I'll continue to be a

Palestinian woman inside Israel, fighting for my rights as a woman, fighting for my rights as a Palestinian inside Israel, fighting for a democratic Israel. It's no joke. I really want it. I'm standing in Israel and building the bridge to this future Israel right now.

• *When you mentioned the two states, of course I wanted to ask you: will you choose to stay in Israel, or will you go with the Palestinian state? You said you'll stay in Israel, but my understanding is that when a lot of Jewish-Israelis talk about two states, they think of Israel as a state for Jews. So . . .*

Nabila: Well this is one of the problems of the peace movement, I believe. This is one of the specific problems of the so-called "Left Zionists" — that they are Zionist and they want Israel, right? So I say that if "Zionism" means wanting Israel, then I am Zionist! But it's not just that. It's the problem of being ready to accept the other partners as partners, of accepting the minorities as part of your life, as part of your identity. To be ready to accept the woman as a full partner is also part of it.

And this is the problem. The Zionists see themselves as the "elected" people and they want to dominate the majority. I'm not going to work with that, I'm not going to play this play, I'm not ready to be dominated — not by a Jew, not by a man, not by a woman. I want to be fully a *partner*, and that's what I'm working towards. I know that it sounds like a dream, but feminism is also a dream, and this is *my* dream — to be a Palestinian feminist in this state.

I'm working to build the other alternative. Not every person here, or in Peace Now, or in Women and Peace is working because of this ideological need and motivation to build the alternative. They are working, a lot of them, so that when we go abroad, we can say, "How beautiful Women in Black are!" For me, it's not enough. And that's why, for the Palestinians also on the other side, it's not enough, what the Israeli peace movement is doing.

I've had big discussions with a lot of women here — one of them from Peace Now in Haifa, for example. She's a good friend of mine, but we have difficult discussions when it comes to paternalism and to the Jewish state. It can't be a democratic state when you speak about a Jewish state, because a Jewish state means racism above any other element.[1]

That's why I try always to say that if you want to build a Jewish state, a truly democratic state (not just on paper), then you have also to consider that there are other people living here. Don't speak about the history: if you speak about your suffering, I have hundreds of sufferings. If you speak about your diaspora, I have a diaspora. If you speak about your uprooting from your place, I have an uprooting from my place. If you speak about your political prisoners, I have my own political prisoners. Whatever you speak about, we have it.

So let's begin from this point: our history is good to understand — *both* histories. We have to learn it, but not to *repeat* it, not to use it as justification for what we're doing. Right now, Israel's government is using the history and the suffering of the Jewish people to justify the awful things they do to the Palestinians. And this is a big problem for me, as a Palestinian in Israel, and as an Israeli. *For how long can they use such a suffering, such an awful part of the history, to legitimize what they are doing?* I can't believe how the people allow it, how the people who suffered from the Holocaust don't go to the street and say, "We don't want you to use our suffering to justify this!"

Look at the Iraq/Iran war, how much suffering there was. Look at Europe — I went to East Berlin, I was just crying. I mean, forty years of war — six million people were dead, twenty million people were dead. And still, can't we learn from that? That's very sad.

---

[1] In this context, racism refers to giving rights to the Jewish citizens which are denied the Arab citizens.

• *Since you mention Iraq, we're part of the U.S.Women's Peace Brigade, and today we had a demonstration in front of the U.S. consulate in East Jerusalem against the impending war in the Gulf and linking it with the demand to stop the Occupation. I just wondered what your perspective was on what's happening right now?*

Nabila: I see it as a global problem first of all, and specifically, it is aggression. It's aggression by Iraq against Kuwait, it's aggression by the United States against all the area. I'm against the invasion of Kuwait, I'm against the invasion of the United States in the Gulf. But I see how the United States used such a problem to solve its future problems. I just was thinking about how good the Gulf War is for the United States — just when the Cold War finished, they're creating another place to station their soldiers. And it's better, because it's going to be paid for by the Saudis.

In global terms, I see the problem as the new development of the North/South conflict, which is the division of economic resources. And this is going to be worse and worse. Even the Pope, in his speech for Christmas, said that the Western world has to think about a "new division of resources."

So I wrote something in the newspaper saying, "If Iraq went to the United States and told them, 'We are going to occupy Kuwait, so we will have access to petroleum, and we're going to sell you this petroleum for twenty-five cents instead of the fifty cents that the Kuwaitis are charging you,' then what would happen? *Nothing* — the United States would agree. And they would continue without any problems."

But right now it's a "human violation," it's "Hitler again." And Israel is using that. It's doing a favor for Hitler when they say that Saddam Hussein is Hitler. What did he do to be "Hitler"? Did he kill six million people? Did he have gas ovens where he put the people? He didn't. He *killed* people. He killed the Kurds in Kurdistan, but when he killed using chemical weapons, no one spoke out about it. Thousands of people were killed. What happened? I don't believe how the media can influence the logical thinking of the people. Where were these people? Where was the U.N.? All these declarations from the U.N. against Israel. Nothing happened. Why? Because it's in the U.S. interest to keep Israel as its dog in the Middle East. And now Israel is proving to them that they are a "good dog." They can stay aside when they're asked to be silent, and they can enter and bomb Iraq when they're asked to.

• *You were talking before about some of the limitations of the Israeli peace movement, and I know that within the women's peace movement women have been struggling around the fear of Arabs. I wonder how it feels to you personally to confront that fear among Israelis?*

Nabila: I would say that a lot of fear and ignorance exists in the general population. A lot of people don't even have any idea what a Palestinian is; they see a Palestinian only as a cleaning person on the street or as someone fixing the roof on their apartment.

As a psychologist, I would say that one way of dealing with fear is to avoid the object that you fear. And that's what's happening. The fear that exists in the Israeli society is so strong, and the media is trying to equate it with "Arabs," "Palestinians," and so people are avoiding any contact with Arabs and Palestinians. If you are looking for an apartment, you would look for an apartment where no Arabs lived nearby. If you wanted to sell or rent an apartment, then you wouldn't choose an Arab, you would choose a Jew: "The only good Arab is a dead Arab."

It's easy, it's very easy, and the people who have fear succumb to it. As a women's peace organization, we saw this problem, and we tried to deal with it. We had a special conference last summer in an Arab village, and we consciously chose to have our women stay in Arab houses where they

155

could meet real Arabs, real Palestinians — eat their food, live with them, and speak with them about fears. That was the subject of this conference: fears as obstacles to peace. But, as I said, unfortunately we are not in the media, and though we are strong, we are not effective enough. And this doesn't get on TV — the fact that we are dealing with the fear of the people.

There's my fear as a Palestinian also: I can't leave my car at the station with an Arab newspaper inside it. For the first time, I have to take it out. I can't just walk around with my Arabic newspapers because I have fear, and this is a real fear. I'm not avoiding my fear, I'm very conscious of my fear. That's why I'm taking action also. Because leaving things as they are, it will become only more fascist, more racist, it will be destructive for all of us. I don't want to be destroyed, and that's why I'm dealing with it.

Just last month in Haifa, we had a meeting one evening with Israeli-Palestinian women and Israeli-Jewish women which we called the "minute of reality." We were supposed to speak about this problem, and about our fears. That evening, a Jewish woman was speaking about her fears of Palestinians and their history, and so on. A young Palestinian woman spoke, and she was in tears; she was angry. She said, "I understand your fear, but do you understand *my* fear? Do you understand my fear of going out on the street? Do you understand my fear that I can't have a job? Do you understand my fear that I can't have an apartment, to live alone as a woman?" She was really in tears. And that's why we dealt with it — to learn to cope with the object of the fear.

• *So how do you keep going?*

Nabila: By continuing to act. By continuing to love. By having all this love from all the women around and from all the activists around. I want to live, I love this life. And to be able to live in this situation, I have to work, I have to be active, I have to change things — *try* to change things.

Israeli Peace Activists' Dialogue:
Michel Warschawski, Roni Ben-Efrat, and Stan Cohen
December 1990

Michel "Mikado" Warschawski, Roni Ben-Efrat, and Stan Cohen are all Israeli peace activists, and leftists, with decades of invaluable experience in the military refusal movement, the Israeli women's movement, and working for human rights for Palestinians. Both Roni and Michel recently served prison terms for their activities.

The three of them spoke to our Women's Peace Brigade in East Jerusalem in December 1990, and I was struck by the depth of the perspective they offered us. Perhaps, I thought, by unveiling such complexities — through their willingness to wrestle with contradiction, take on truth, battle for change — in search of their country's moral recovery . . . perhaps Israeli society, as well as my own North American one, can begin to transform. It is in this spirit that this particular dialogue is shared.

Michel: By presenting the case of the Alternative Information Center, I would like not only to give you some specific information about what happened with this Center and with myself, but maybe also to offer some elements for an analysis of the developments in Israeli society itself.

The Alternative Information Center was founded in 1984 in order first to provide, as its name indicates, *alternative information*. This was a time when the Israeli media and the international media were very poor in giving facts and information about the Occupied Territories — repression, resistance, trials, prisons, and so on. We also wanted to create a kind of new space where Israelis and Palestinians could work together, meet together, offer information, take information, and create the first links of an Israeli-

Palestinian cooperation. It was the first institution *ever* where Israelis and Palestinians worked together, were a part of the same framework. It was a kind of a press agency, but we never claimed to be normal journalists. We were people involved in our own communities, involved in the various components of the Israeli peace movement on the one hand, and in the nationalist Palestinian organizations on the other hand, working together.

The Center was closed in February 1987 by an administrative order from the chief commander of the Israeli police. As the Center's director, I was arrested at the same time. The reason for the closing and arrest was explained to me very frankly by the main interrogator of the Shin Bet. He said the following, and I quote almost word for word: "You have been active for almost twenty years with quite radical political views. And except for a few harassments you have been free to do whatever you wanted. Isn't that true?" I answered, "Yes, more or less." "And you know why? Because we are living in democracy. And democracy protects people's right to express whatever they want, including people like you with radical anti-Zionist political positions. Do you agree?" I said, "Yes, more or less." "But *there*," and he pointed in the eastern direction, "*there* is no democracy — it's *occupation*. And we have a problem with you guys and with your Center. It's not clear whether it's in Israel or the Occupied Territories.

"On one hand, *you* are there with other Israelis. On the other hand there are others, political prisoners and people who are active in Palestinian terror organizations, and you have to chose: if you want to be treated as Israelis and protected by Israeli democracy you have to cut off from *them*. If you want to work with *them*, you will be treated exactly the way *they* are." And when I asked, "But as long as we are acting according to the law, what's the problem?" He said, "Don't be a child — you know with these people there is no law. And you have to choose. We don't like this 'no man's

158

land' where it is not clear on which side of the border you belong."

I think he was saying more or less the truth and the content of the *real* Alternative Information Center case. This was what the closure of the Center and my arrest, later my trial and my sentence, was aimed at: to warn the whole of the Israeli peace forces — progressive forces — not to be too close to the border. Not to mix legitimate political life and opposition *in* Israel with the Palestinians. You can do what you want in the family, with Israelis, but in the *family* and not with *"them."*

But by 1987 it was too late to try to scare Israelis away from cooperating with Palestinians. From the doves of the Labor Party to the more radical Israelis, everyone had their own dialogue, contacts, collaboration, cooperation, talks, common work with the Palestinians on many, many levels. In that sense, the aim of the closing of the Alternative Information Center was a failure from the very beginning. We got very large support, and the Center was reopened after six months.

At my trial I was charged with printing material for "illegal organizations" (student's organizations, women's organizations, and union organizations in the Occupied Territories). We claim that these organizations are *legal*; they were never declared *illegal*, they have open activities and public officers, and they participate in public elections and in press conferences. We did what we did, and we will do it again as long as it will not be declared an illegal activity.

One excellent result of our trial is that we were found not guilty of 99% of the charges, except for one pamphlet we typeset about how to withstand interrogations by Shin Bet, which was written by a declared illegal organization — the PFLP (People's Front for the Liberation of Palestine). We claimed that we did not know the connection between these pamphlets and the PFLP. The court said that they believed that we didn't know, but that "we closed our eyes" — that we didn't try to know *exactly* what the connection was between

159

the students who worked with us, and the pamphlet, and the illegal organization behind it.

As the radio stated the same day of the verdict, it was a *tremendous* victory for us — we were found not guilty of supporting terrorist organizations, not guilty of printing all the material we were accused of, except this one pamphlet. The surprise was that after we *won* the trial, we *lost* the sentence, and I got a thirty-month prison sentence, which surprised even the prosecutor. Usually in the Occupied Territories for consciously and willingly printing illegal material, you get a suspended sentence, or two to three months in prison.

This shows again the real political nature of the trial, to try to threaten the whole of the peace movement. Here again the reaction was exactly the opposite — tremendous support through the media, a lot of interviews in the press, a lot of big articles, and many, many expressions of solidarity coming deep from the center of the Israeli map, so much so that the prosecution itself decided not to send me to prison until the end of my appeal to the Supreme Court. Ultimately, the ruling of the Supreme Court confirmed the charge of "closing eyes" to the printing of illegal material, but reduced the sentence to eight months in prison, which I just finished serving one month ago. Now, I am back working at the Center again.

I believe that what characterizes the difference between the last three or four years of the peace movement and the situation ten or fifteen years ago is that now we've achieved a point of no return. The capacity of the Israeli ruling class to recreate a line where Israelis and Palestinians never meet except when meeting a waiter in a restaurant, or one who is working in your garden, or the woman who is selling fruit cheap in the street — this kind of relationship cannot be rebuilt again.

Something has been strengthened through the intifada — a new kind of relationship between the Israelis and Palestinians. Even if I did have to spend a few months in prison and pay some fines, I will say that I've come out of it much stronger and with better feelings than before. I have a real feeling of a political victory, especially when I look at the broad spectrum of people who are doing today what only a few dozen of us were doing five years ago.

• • •

Roni Ben-Efrat: Whoever had their finger on the pulse of what was happening on the West Bank in 1987 could predict that something was going to happen. Our group was very close to it because we had been publishing a biweekly newspaper in Hebrew and Arabic since 1986. Much of the focus of the paper was about the repression and the difficulties in the Occupied Territories on the one hand, and on the other hand, the rise of popular organizations in the West Bank and Gaza. This was something that no one else, apart from the alternative press, would focus on.

When the intifada broke out on December 9, 1987, we were in a good position to be in the center of what was going on. Our organization had a joint board of Palestinians and Israelis, producing and distributing three to five thousand copies of a paper in Arabic. This was something that the authorities didn't like at all.

In our case, their first step was to try and scare us. We got a letter saying that our paper had links with a Palestinian organization, the Democratic Front for the Liberation of Palestine, and that the Israeli authorities were planning to close it down. At that time, they wanted us to drop the Arabic paper, and they would let us go on with the Hebrew paper, but we decided to go on publishing.

After a month we got the letter of closure of the paper — the first time that a Hebrew language paper was closed down. It was a kind of test that they were showing us: "Okay, if you want to go on with your position, you will start tasting what it is to be in opposition here, what it is to be like Palestinians here." Another warning was the arrest of our

Palestinian editor in February, a hint they wanted to give us before starting to treat [the rest of] us the same way. We continued publishing under other names, and the whole case was getting a lot of publicity. The question of freedom of the press was for the first time brought to the public with a very strong debate within Israeli public opinion. Seeing that we continued to publish, they started to arrest us one by one in a kind of domino system. Between the fifteenth of April and the sixth of May, five of our main editors were arrested.

We went through I would say quite severe interrogation in the Shabak department of the Petach Tikvah prison. We were completely in the hands of the secret security, and the only thing that was not allowed was physical beatings, although one of our members went through quite a rough time. It so happened that we were three women and two men, and they used a lot of psychological torture, prevention of sleep, and sexual humiliation, using private information about our lives and children and problems to pressure us and to squeeze out confessions.

In the meantime, the whole thing continued to get a lot of publicity. In the Israeli press, it was called "the trial of the year." The secret security told us once that they were planning to rehabilitate their name on our backs: they were undergoing a lot of problems and accusations against them — Palestinians were dying under their hands — and they thought that our case should be a "clean" case to show how they "uncovered a spy net," and so on.

But in fact what happened was quite the opposite: the Israeli society went through a very big radicalization. The question of having a kind of dialogue with PLO people was becoming an issue for the day. A few months after we were arrested, Knesset members Schulamit Aloni and Oran Amir were talking publicly to PLO people, to Abu Ayad and others.

Meanwhile, we were not allowed to see a lawyer for fifteen days after the arrest. The case was not allowed to be published in the papers at all, so the secret security was leaking information to the press and we were prevented from reacting. All these methods were quite natural when it comes to Palestinians. But it was a new issue for Israelis. It cost them a big price because they could not wage a campaign of demonization against us like they wanted to.

We started another battle, which was the battle to stick together with Palestinian political prisoners, and this was something that was completely intolerable in the eyes of the authorities. They were completely unprepared for this demand: What the hell could they do with four prisoners — Jewish from "good families" — who were demanding to be with the Palestinians? How could they ever explain that to the Jewish public? How could they grant our request? It would have violated a very essential part of what Zionism is all about, which is the principle of racism and the claim that Jews and Arabs don't merge, that we can't live together. This is what the whole story is about.

Because of our request, we were put in isolation. Our last member, Yakov, was just released this past October (1990). He was in complete isolation for a whole year, after his cell-mate Assaf Adiv was released. In the long run, we didn't manage to serve our sentence among Palestinian prisoners, but we still feel that it was an important issue to put on the table, and it was the first time that this issue was addressed at all. I want to add that every time we went on a hunger strike, the Palestinians joined us. This was something new and very important to demonstrate: that Palestinians are seeking dialogue, and that they feel brotherhood towards people who share the same principles. I think it was an important lesson for the Israeli society as a whole.

Now that we are all out of prison, I would like to say that the trial ended in a plea bargain. The plea bargain was applicable because the authorities felt that they had climbed a tree that was too high, and they themselves were willing to come down. So, although they predicted five or six years each, the trial ended more or less on our conditions: that I would be released immediately on the day of the trial (so I sat nine months). Another two comrades, Michal Schwartz and Assaf Adiv, sat eighteen months, and Yakov sat thirty months. He was the only one not to give any confession. So obviously they were eager to give him a very bad time as a kind of revenge.

Now that we are out of prison, of course we are all back in the activities of the peace movement, the soldiers' committee against serving in the Occupied Territories (Yesh G'vul), and the women's movement. We are publishing a newsletter on freedom of the press, and we are working together with other people in the peace movement to publish *Challenge/Etgar* magazine in Hebrew and in English. In general we are working quite freely today — but still we know that the authorities are after everyone who is serious about collaboration and about a genuine solution to the Palestinian issue.

So we are still doing our best to make our positions clear and to change the ideas of the vast majority of the people. I think on the whole we are gaining, not so much from our courage and our determination, but from the fact that historically we are in a process that can't go back. And this is the reason that even though we were arrested and harassed and treated very much as an opposition, we can continue working and publishing and saying what we have to say.

• • •

Stan Cohen: My full-time work is being a professor of criminology and sociology at Hebrew University. My political work is in the area of support for the Palestinian universities, which have been closed for the last three years, and with the Public Committee Against Torture in Israel, which is part of the human rights movement.

I think the three wings of the active fighting Israeli peace movement which are in good shape are the women's movement, the human rights movement, and the campaign against army service in the Territories. Because of the particular vulnerability of the military organization of

Israeli society to that kind of attack, the "refusal" movement seems to me to be the most radical front. Most of the people who are providing the backbone of these three movements are refugees from the Left, rather than people who have been drawn in from liberal activities.

The Public Committee Against Torture was founded at the beginning of 1989 in response to a number of allegations made by Palestinians and some Israeli Jews about psychological and physical torture, ill treatment, and pressure during interrogation. The other thing which forced the question of torture onto the public agenda was the Landau Committee. This was a public commission, which I think says a great deal about the nature of Israeli society and the ways in which the establishment protects itself.

In 1982, an Israeli Caucasian army officer, a man called Nafsu — Caucasians are a small minority sect who serve in the Israeli army — was found guilty of treason for selling military secrets to the Syrians. He had alleged all the way through his trial that his confession had been forced out of him. But in the course of what's called a mini-trial, where the admissibility of the evidence is discussed by the court, a successive layer of military courts and appeal courts threw his claims out and believed his Shin Bet interrogators, that this man had just willingly given this information.

Eventually, through his persistence and through good lawyers, the case came to the regular civilian High Court, and they found that indeed the confession had been obtained by force. The case caused a certain degree of scandal because there had been a number of other public activities by the Shin Bet which had been criticized, and the government was pushed into appointing a commission of inquiry. This was headed by a former president of the Israeli Supreme Court, Justice Landau.

After a period of three or four months, they came out with a report which is an extraordinarily rich document. I think anyone who wants to understand Israeli society should read this report word for word, because it really gives a great deal of insight into the way the security, legal, and military establishments think — into the way in which anything which passes for liberal legal ideas, due process, and the rule of law and democracy is subverted in Israeli society to the demands for security.

The Commission, in very brief terms, concluded on a factual level that over a period of sixteen years the Shin Bet interrogators had indeed lied to the Court, and that they'd been extracting confessions by coercion. When faced with allegations in court, they had systematically lied; indeed, it was their policy to lie. The Commission actually traced documents showing that at various levels of the Shin Bet they'd been told to deliberately lie in court when the accused claimed that their testimonies were obtained by force.

The Commission went on to say that it wouldn't be in the best interest of Israeli society if these people were prosecuted for perjury. It was best to just "leave it" because they were after all "ideological criminals": they were doing their duty to the state of Israel; they were fulfilling a noble mission to save their society from its terrorist enemies. It then described what forms of interrogation were justified in relation to what the Commission calls HTA, which stands for Hostile Terrorist Activity. Virtually every form of Palestinian opposition, and every other form of opposition, becomes labeled under the term "terror," and through a series of extraordinary legal arguments the Commission eventually justified the use of force as an interrogation method.

They said that on the one hand they could just simply condemn it and say, "Well, we don't approve these methods." They could also let the Secret Service do what they like. But, they said, "Instead of that what we will do is lay down guidelines" for the use of what the Commission euphemistically called "moderate physical pressure," which has become a famous phrase in Israel. It's a phrase which the Commission uses deliberately in order to evade international laws which very clearly define torture. Torture, by all international laws, Amnesty declarations, and United

Nations definitions, includes the "deliberate use of force or violence to extract confessions." The Commission didn't want to be branded as evading human rights laws, and because Israel is such a nice democratic society, Israel cannot be seen as condoning torture, so the Commission eventually said it is justified in using "moderate physical pressure."

The Commission, in fact, gave a kind of judicial legitimization for what the Shin Bet had been doing anyway all these years, and in a secret part of the report which has never been published, they established guidelines for what actually constitutes "moderate physical pressure." Within one month of its being published, the intifada started, which made mass interrogations of Palestinian activists routine. Of course the people who were being picked up weren't people who were involved in anything that remotely could be called "Hostile Terrorist Activity." Often they were just attending a demonstration, throwing stones, or raising a Palestinian flag. From our evidence, even people who've been pulled in on mild charges like that have been subjected to "moderate physical pressure."

So we started as a small group of people who had been active doing Palestinian solidarity work for years but who saw that the traditional civil rights organizations in Israel weren't really taking up issues as sensitive as this. I think this is something that is important to understand — the liberal sector represented in Israel by the Association of Civil Rights in Israel (which is our equivalent of the ACLU in the U.S.) has always been reluctant to get involved with anything that might sound like taking sides politically. This is the dilemma of traditional civil liberties work: you work with individual cases; you don't even think of collective national rights.

So we started as a group of lawyers, psychiatrists, and academics to work on three fronts: collecting educational material on this issue and getting it to schools, youth groups, law schools, and any others who might be interested; trying to bring action in the High Court of Justice to make public the secret part of the Landau Commission Report; and working on individual cases which are referred to us. We're also working on issues like the collusion of the medical profession in the whole process of torture and interrogation. This is a very serious issue indeed with very clear international rules which totally forbid doctors from having any part in this procedure: they're not allowed to check people before, during, or after interrogation without reporting on injuries. And from our information, doctors are violating this code in a fairly routine way at the military detention centers in Israel now.

• • •

The following are questions from various members of the Women's Peace Brigade.

• *Roni, can you explain to us why some of the radical activists aren't taking more concrete measures, such as civil disobedience, in protest against the Israeli government's brutality on the West Bank?*

Roni: During the beginning of the intifada, many committees sprang up inside the peace movement to deal with this question of violation of human rights, regarding the bombing of houses, deportations, and things like that. There was the phenomenon of Israelis going out to camps, monitoring the situation, and really making a hard time for the armies in the Occupied Territories. Many times they would be thrown out immediately, but still it was a kind of menace against the army. It built what today we call the peace camp; it's those people who at the beginning of the intifada started to open their eyes.

The second phase was from November 1988 when the peace process started and the PLO opened a peace initiative. [This peace initiative recognized the state of Israel, declared the existence of the Palestinian state, and renounced terrorism as a tactic]. The peace camp sort of let the high politicians do the work, and there was a phase where the political issue became very important and the question of human rights took second place. I think that's one of the problems we're facing today — that the peace process and the belief that soon there may be negotiations with the PLO made the peace camp go to sleep and leave things in the hands of the politicians.

Personally I think that today we must go back to the human rights issues and to the day-to-day problems of the people in the intifada — the harassment, the issue of the green cards. So the point you're raising is very important. I think we drifted away from it, and we should start thinking that this is a way to get the peace camp to see that the solution is not going to come next week or next month, and in the meantime the oppression is going on very strongly.

Stan: I just want to add one thing. We must understand the reasons that the peace camp has "drifted." You know the favorite parlor game of Israeli liberals is called "Waiting for the United States:" there's nothing we can do; we can go out and protest, but we need a political solution which will come from the United States — surely they have the goodwill to do that, so we'll sit back and wait. Now I'm caricaturing slightly, but I think that's what did happen.

At the same time, two other things happened. One was that desensitization to the atrocities took place over a period of time. The print media has been very good over the last five years, and this has been one of the extraordinary things: we've got good investigative journalism, people follow up stories, and nobody can use the excuse "We didn't know what was happening." They *know* what is happening. But somehow now the stories are relegated to the second or third page, and they have dropped off television (which is under much more direct government control), and people became desensitized. They'd heard enough. You couldn't mobilize people with yet another atrocity story. And it's very difficult to revive that feeling, especially given recent events since the Gulf crisis. People have just gone into what is known here as "internal exile" — they're here, but they're not really here. You can't pull people out into the streets and you can't get people involved if their frame of mind says, "There's nothing we can do." So I think you have a deeper sense of powerlessness and alienation.

The second reason is that I just don't think there's any tradition here, even in the radical edge of the peace movement, of civil disobedience or deliberate willingness to break the law. The only area now where that limit is really being pushed is the army refusal area.

Michel: In order to understand the Israeli peace movement, we have to understand what "national unity" is in Israel and how difficult it is to break with this national unity, even for those who are already in a *process* of breaking. It is a matter of fifty years of total identification with the state, with the society. To break with this "family" is one thing — and it's very difficult, not on the ideological level, but on the emotional level. It is to break with the people who have been with you in school and in the army, and you have been twenty or thirty years with them. It's like breaking with your own brother. So to break is one thing. But to *identify* with the *enemy* of your family — the *other* family — is tremendous. *And what the intifada is asking today from the Israeli peace forces is precisely to make a choice.*

For many years even the Left in Israel adopted a third camp position: (1) there was the government that was wrong; (2) there were the Arabs, we don't identify with them at all; and (3) we are a third camp — we are neither with them nor against them, but *not* with them. "They have their struggle, we have ours." Now I think the intifada is making the third camp position much more narrow. There is a war here, and you have to identify with one of two camps, and it's a very difficult thing.

Now I want to talk about the question of refusal to serve in the army, which is the only sector of Israeli society where there is this act of clear civil disobedience. It seems on the one hand very radical — and it is — and it provokes a deep division in the peace camp in Israel. But on the other hand it's *easy,* because by being a soldier and saying "No," you still are saying, "I am part of the family, and I revolt." You react as a soldier and you affirm that you're being part of Israel. It is even hard to say that you are a traitor in such a situation.

And while it is true that the human rights movement is composed mainly of refugees from the radical wing, in the soldiers' movement that is not the case at all. Most of the soldiers who refuse to serve in the Occupied Territories, and most of the soldiers who have been in jail during the last three years (around 150 to 160) are part of the *broad* peace camp of the Zionist Left: the Labor Party, the kibbutznikim, Mapam, and so on. Last week a major and a captain of the same unit refused to serve, the highest rank until now refusing to serve. The second major who refused a few months ago was a right-wing Labor Party supporter of Rabin, he told us, but by his own experience he understood that he can't go on performing his duties in the Occupied Territories.

• *I'm puzzled about one thing you say. If the Israeli peace movement is looking to the United States government for direction, don't they have enough information about what the U.S. does around the world that might cause them to think a little differently about what the United States government is doing vis-à-vis Israel and Palestine?*

Michel: For 99% of the Israelis, including Israeli intellectuals and progressives, we are still a ghetto, and the world is divided between Jews and non-Jews. Nothing else matters, unless it's related to the relationship between "the Jews" and "the others." This is true even in the left-wing. It is not that the press distorts what's happening in the world. I think the average level of the Israeli press is much higher than most of the press in Europe. What is between the United States and

Panama and the United States and Nicaragua doesn't even interest most of the Left.

• Do activists in Israel ever talk about anti-Semitism — not in the context of Zionism, but about the experience of the Jews?

Michel: The main reason I became a radical and an anti-Zionist many years ago was precisely this question, when I discovered how the Israeli propaganda machine exploited anti-Semitism, and mainly the Holocaust. They distorted it in order to serve certain aims — not as something that exists in itself and has to be fought, but as a *means*. It was my first rebellion here, I must admit, and I could speak about this issue for hours because it is something that is moving me every day in my struggle.

I think the idea of comparing or relating the present situation to the Holocaust is a day-to-day practice of the official spokesperson of the Israeli government. From Begin we heard that Arafat is Hitler, or that the PLO is worse than the Nazis. Or the other way around, to say that everything the Israeli government is doing is nothing because the Holocaust was ten times worse.

The second thing I would like to say is that the radical Left has been trying for years to unmask the tremendous hypocrisy in the dealing of the state of Israel with anti-Semitism. For example, the excellent relationship between Israel and a dictatorship like Argentina was a matter of common knowledge — everyone knew it — but certainly there was no anti-Semitism. But when the Israeli government wants a change in alliances, suddenly the only and the main reason to fight against a certain government is not because they have killed hundreds and imprisoned thousands, but because there has been some anti-Semitic declaration by the heads of the government, or that there were some Jews among the Leftists arrested or killed.

• *What future do you see for the state of Israel?*

Stan: I think that the whole issue of withdrawing aid, and the difficulty of American Jews calling for that, and the even greater difficulty of trying to find any support for that within the mainstream Israeli peace movement, is just the other side of the loyalty issue that Michel raised. That is the issue that you don't want to break ranks, you want to stay in the family. And the worst thing you can do is to cut your ties with that favorite uncle [the U.S.] who bails you out every time and signs the check. This is the next step which any kind of serious peace movement must take, but I see very little chance of us having the forces here to get anywhere with it.

Just a comparison with South Africa for a minute. Having grown up in South Africa and having watched it over the twenty-five or thirty years I have been out, I think there has been one key thing in the last ten years that has made the difference between South Africa and Israel. Ten years ago the average white South African — because of the economic pressure, not because of any change of heart — began to realize that the party was over, that they couldn't continue indefinitely with that system. They had to begin to think in terms of what the society would be like after apartheid. Ten years ago they acted as if apartheid was over already, in culture and theater and literature, poetry, universities — all these areas of cultural life were already anticipating that. This hasn't happened in Israel yet — the average Israeli has not paid the price of maintaining the Occupation, has not paid the price of repressing the intifada.

This is difficult for the outsider to understand, because you see all the news and you think, "How can people not be affected?" Well, they are not affected. They see, but they don't see. Daily life can continue — you're here in Jerusalem, but in Tel Aviv, Haifa, and Eilat, life continues even more normally than it did before. It's hard to imagine, but it does. It's only when the price comes in economic form or the

"Lebanon effect," in terms of bodies being brought back in sacks, that people will have a sense that the party is over.

In comparison to South Africa, things here have been relatively easy for liberals. Compared to more totalitarian societies, we've had a lot more room for maneuvering, for example, in our publications and universities and demonstrations. But precisely because South Africa was more repressive, liberals understood very quickly that it was pointless to fight traditional civil liberties struggles because you are living in a society with such gross inequality and gross injustice that the only solution is a political solution. Here the liberals have got the illusion that because the formal structures are intact for them, they can still carry on and keep up with the pretense. Nobody in South Africa ever pretended that the courts or the police or the prisons were anything like fair, whereas here liberals still say, "Well, in Israel everything's fine; over there in the Occupation is where the trouble is."

• *Roni, you said to us earlier that you thought the women's movement was the most radical movement in Israel. Could you elaborate?*

Roni: What happened to the women's movement is really a puzzle to the women themselves, I think. You know that the feminist movement was a terrible flop in Israel, and I'm talking as someone who was active in the feminist movement in the 70s.

Even today, the women's movement is *not* a feminist movement in the conventional sense of the word. It's a *peace* movement, all of whose members are *women*. I don't know if there's such a phenomenon anywhere else in the world. The phenomenon is that suddenly, when the intifada began, it seemed to affect women more than men. So women started to create organizations of their own on *peace* issues, and the percentage of women in other peace groups also became very high.

174

Why did it happen? I feel it happened because women are more sensitive to the oppression, and it was easier for them to have an insight into what is going on and to change it. It also seems the women have a better capability to stick to their goals. The case of Women In Black is proof of it: standing week after week for one hour, being harassed, and so on, without anything really spectacular coming out of it. Without becoming members of Knesset because of it. Without climbing the ladder of success. You have women who are doing it week after week, and when you ask them "What do you do it for?" they will tell you, "It's my way to express my opinion, and to say that I don't go along with this oppression."

I think there's another reason for the strength of the women's organization, and this is the fact that potentially many of them have their husbands, sons, or brothers going into the army. Deep inside, they can't imagine what must be happening to them through the oppression they do in the Occupied Territories. You might say, "Well, men are the ones who are doing it — it should affect them even more." But here we have the problem — for men to refuse to serve in the Occupied Territories is a terrible internal battle having to do with themselves and with society, and this is something they may go through, but it is not developed yet. Women are not part of the army in the Occupied Territories, and maybe it is easier for them to stand at a distance and look at things in a more objective way and say, "We are not ready to have anything to do with this."

As a leftist activist, I really don't know 80% of the women who stand with me in Women in Black. This means these are women who are new to the movement, who come from no political background, but who share an understanding that this can't go on and we must have a change.

• *I don't disagree with what you're saying, but a part of me also feels like there are many women who stand at this vigil on Friday from one to two p.m., and that's all they do. They feel better because they've done that, but they don't want to do more than that — they don't want to come to this East Jerusalem hotel at night.*

Roni: If you could stand there with them and hear the cursing at them and see the spitting at them, you would know that it's very, very difficult for these women you're talking about. For a woman who will not come to a hotel at night in East Jerusalem, to stand there is very, very difficult. I agree with you that we want to radicalize them more, but if you look at what they were before the intifada, and you look at them today, there is a very big step. Today we have a base we can work with. We didn't have a base before, and it's a big achievement.

Palestinian/Israeli Leadership:
Faisal Husseini and Tamar Gozansky
December 1990

*In December 1990, our Women's Peace Brigade had the great
honor of meeting with Faisal Husseini and Tamar Gozansky,
significant personages representing the Palestinian and the Israeli
peoples. Their roles, histories, and levels of responsibility as peace
activists are not parallel — but both have consistently stood for
integrity and breadth of vision.*

*Faisal Husseini is considered to be one of the most prominent
Palestinians in the Occupied Territories and is often quoted in the
international press. Israeli authorities accuse him of being one of
the masterminds of the intifada, and they jail him periodically.
Squeezing time from his incessant schedule to meet us at the New
Regent Hotel in East Jerusalem, Husseini, wearing a neatly pressed
gray suit, spoke directly and clearly. His presence projected
strength and quiet dignity. He began by referring to "international
legitimacy," meaning living under the rule of international law (the
U.N. resolutions and international conventions) and showing
respect for human rights.*

Faisal Husseini: "The neglect of the international legitimacy
to our rights by the Israeli government, and the double
standard used by the United States and other states, are
causing our people to be convinced that we are not living
within the framework of international legitimacy, but that
we are living in a jungle. And then we will start acting like in
a jungle.

"All of these years, we have tried to reach the hearts of
the people here and everywhere. We have tried to convince
the people in Israel and outside that our struggle and message
is that we would like to liberate our people and not to enslave
any other people. We are struggling to build our own state and
not to destroy any other state. We are fighting to secure the

future of our next generations and not to endanger the security of the next generation of any other people.

"Unfortunately the 'other side' [the Israeli government] has not heard this message. Instead of responding positively to our demands, to our new strategy, the only thing that we've gotten from the other side is a more rightist government. This government uses only one kind of language, and the most important word in it is 'no': NO to a Palestinian state, NO to talking to the PLO, NO to talking about Jerusalem, NO to talking with people from Jerusalem about all these things which we have suffered during the last year.

"We Palestinians are not talking about international legitimacy *only* within our borders; we are looking forward to implementing international legitimacy everywhere in the world and in the Middle East. When Iraq invaded Kuwait, within three days the PLO came with the first initiative, calling for four points: the first point was to demand the withdrawal of the Iraqi forces from Kuwait by the tenth of August of that year. Second, to start negotiations between the government of Kuwait and the government of Iraq. Third, to allow the Kuwaiti people to choose their own government without any interference from Arab or foreign forces or governments. And the fourth point was to rediscuss the policy of oil in the Gulf.

"We were for all of these points within the framework of international legitimacy. But when the matter started taking another direction, which was only in the interest of oil, when the American government and other states decided to send their armies there, no one could convince us that those forces were there to protect the great democracy in Saudi Arabia or that they were there because Saddam Hussein used chemical weapons.

"They said that Saddam Hussein used chemical weapons against Iran. And they went on supporting him. Then they said that he was using them against the Kurds, and they went on supporting him. This time he didn't use chemical weapons, but everyone started to attack him and tried to control the situation there. We are convinced that it is not because of chemical weapons, not because of democracy, but because of oil interests. Unfortunately, until now, the value of a tank of oil is more important than the value of a human being.

"But we understand this world, and we know that there is a place for interest. And the language of interest we can understand. But if the Americans and the Europeans have an interest in oil, *we* have an interest in getting rid of the Occupation. And because of that, we are ready to support the side that will help us get rid of the Occupation. Saddam Hussein said that he was ready to implement international legitimacy in Kuwait and withdraw from there, if the same international legitimacy were implemented also in the Middle East and the Israelis withdrew from the Occupied Territories. We find ourselves supporters of the withdrawal of Iraq from Kuwait under this condition. We were not at all, and we will not be in the future, supporters of the occupation of Kuwait.

"Unfortunately, we have not been understood well by the world, and everyone has started to think that we are supporting the occupation of Kuwait. We can't support the occupation, we can't support *any* kind of occupation, even between brothers. We believe that the only way to save not only the Middle East but the world is by solving the problem between Kuwait and Iraq by *political* means and not by *military* ones. In the same way that we are asking for a solution with Israel by political means, we are asking also for a solution in Iraq by political means.

"And we can do nothing but this because it is part of our principles, and because it is the right thing that we must do and we must work for. We hope that the world will understand more and more that there is no way to solve problems in this world by military means, and we must stop dealing with everything 'due to the force that I have.' Because if we are building our security in the future on the balance of force, this means the balance of fears — and I can't understand any kind of peace or security which will be built on the balance of fear. The only way to build a real future is to think about building this future on the balance of *common interests*; and I believe between the people of this world there are a lot of ways to reach this if we can just put aside for a while thinking about who has more force than who. Thank you."

• • •

The home of the Israeli Parliament, or Knesset, is in a well-guarded compound hugging a low hill in West Jerusalem. To reach KM Tamar Gozansky, our Women's Peace Brigade of seventeen had to undergo a comprehensive security check that included a body search and the depositing of all but one of our cameras. We were then ushered across a spacious courtyard through the imposing modern walls, down many halls and stairways, and finally into a large comfortable meeting room.

Gozansky joined the Knesset in 1990 from the Chadash, or Democratic Front for Peace and Equality (the Communist Party). She is one of eight women in the Knesset, out of a membership of 120. Her unaffected manner, humility and warmth contrasted sharply with the formal atmosphere of our surroundings.

Tamar Gozansky: ". . . We are now facing a very unusual and complicated situation. Although we are used to living in conditions of tension and insecurity, now the situation is deteriorating in the Occupied Territories and in Israel even more. Somehow in Israeli society and in the Knesset the danger of war is being overlooked, and it's very difficult here even to convince people that such a war could be the hardest and the most violent war we ever had.

"It is clear now that the Palestinian people are strongly striving for their independence, but since Shamir has been Prime Minister, there has not been one single step taken by the government towards the Palestinians. So the problem of finding any kind of negotiating process is now in a kind of deadlock. This kind of official Israeli policy leads to the violation of human rights in the Territories and at the same time to [Palestinian] despair and to such bloody results.

"Inside the Knesset, the Labor Party is still searching for an alternative policy to the policy of Likud. The suggestions of the Labor Party are full of contradictions, and if the Labor Party refuses to speak with the PLO or to recognize the PLO, we have quite a problem here.

"I would say in conclusion, international pressure on Israel is very useful. Any kind of international pressure. The national and human rights of the Palestinians and their economic development in the Territories, for example, are the subject of international concern, and we are now living in a time when the international community is more important to any kind of effort to solve regional or other conflicts. I would like to welcome you, because your group is a kind of pressure also, as I see it, on Israeli public opinion, and it is very important for us. Thank you."

The following questions are from various members of the Women's Peace Brigade.

• *Do you think that pressuring Israel by withdrawing U.S. aid for the Israeli occupation of the West Bank and Gaza is a correct strategy?*

Tamar: It seems to me that as Americans, it is a correct idea because without this aid Israel would be unable to continue its policy of occupation of the Territories. I personally think that without this aid we would live better, and peacefully. So I think it's a good idea.

• *It seems the main defense by many Israelis for maintaining the Occupation is that it's necessary for Israeli security. How do you respond to that argument?*

Tamar: If anyone in Israel is willing to find security in occupation, it means that there will always be a great threat

181

to the existence of Israel. So my way of dealing with this question is to say that it is not a problem of security, but of whether Israel will continue to *exist*.

Last week Professor Leibovich was honored by the municipality of Jerusalem, and they asked him what his thoughts were on this very important day. He said, "I am very afraid, I am very concerned about the future of Israel." I asked him, "Are you feeling yourself secure now? We have the Territories, we have the best army in the Middle East, we have the nuclear and chemical weapons — are you feeling secure?" "No," he said, "no, of course I'm not feeling secure." "Then what do you think we can do? We can occupy another country, and another country, and a third country — and then what? Because even after occupying two or three more countries, our neighbors will still be Arab or Muslim countries." So the problem is to show that the situation *now* is the source of insecurity, and to convince people that there is another choice.

Last week a meeting of Likud in the Knesset was broadcast on TV. One after another of the Likud Party were saying, "What will the future be like if we are feeling so insecure *now?*" So they were admitting that they were insecure. But they want to convince the Israeli people that there is no choice — and the problem is to show that there *is* an alternative, there *is* a choice. And it's very difficult because the same policy has now been going on for forty-two years even though the government has changed.

• *What is your perspective on the problems being created by the massive immigration into Israel of Soviet Jews?*

Tamar: The problem of the Soviet Jews is now one of the crucial problems for Israel. It's a tragedy because they felt they had to leave their homeland; it's a tragedy for us because it's very difficult to absorb them here. And nowadays, we are beginning to feel the results of the so-called *aliyah* [the Law of Return — that any Jew can make

Israel his or her home]. Israel is based on a kind of nationalist law idea, as an "exclusive" Jewish state. It's very difficult to argue against *aliyah*, because it would mean changing the law of Israel. So we are trying to organize our work so that the one to be blamed will be the government and not the immigrants themselves. The problem with the Israeli government policy is that they want to hold the stick on both sides; one side is to continue the old policy of occupation with a very high military budget, and so on. And at the same time, they want to create jobs for the Soviet Jews, to facilitate their well-being and absorption here in Israel. So where will the money come from?

The emphasis of the government now is on cutting the salaries of the Israeli workers, and cutting any kind of state help to the unemployed, to poor people, to educational and medical services. It was said yesterday very clearly in the Parliament that the price will be a lower living standard for Israel. The government for many years had a policy against involvement in investments and economic development. So now we are paying the price: there are no jobs, there are no flats.

• *Do you feel that the economic burden that's being placed on Israelis by Soviet immigration might move people towards seeing the need to negotiate?*

Tamar: From historical experience, it is well known that an economic crisis by itself doesn't mean that the Left parties will win. It depends on the balance of forces and the actual historical moment. Because economic difficulties can be used very dangerously by the extreme right-wing. If the peace forces in Israel are able to convince more people that there is an alternative to the present Israeli policy, then some economic or social problems can force people to work or to struggle even more. But if someone is fascist and chauvinistic and anti-Arab — and he has no work — then the very natural solution for him is to demand the dismissal of the Arab worker and to go to work *instead* of him. We have a situation now where Arab workers are fired only because they are Arabs, in the name of immigration, in the name of "Jewish Labor." So, for the time being, economic difficulties will not help us. On the contrary, I think they will be used against us.

• *What is your opinion about the existence of racial discrimination in Israel?*

Tamar: Racial discrimination is part and parcel of the basic Israeli policy. Ever since the establishment of the State of Israel, we have had all kinds of segregation and racial discrimination against the Arabs. And I'm sure we cannot deal really deeply with this prejudice against Arabs without peace. Peace is the key to our moral recovery. And the question is much more difficult among young people. Students of secondary schools, of high schools, are much more chauvinistic, much more against the Arabs, than the older generation — because they are young and have no experience, because they are influenced by the situation. The Israeli society is going to the right all the time, so the young generation is usually the first.

• *What do you feel is the women's role in all this? They are the mothers of these children, so they must be somewhat responsible for this, but on the other hand, women are often more empathetic to peace and justice — so how do they fit in?*

Tamar: One of my relatives, a woman a bit younger than me — before her son was enlisted in the army, she was usually talking with me about peace and against occupation and "Who needs these Territories?" and "How long can we live with such a fear?" She wasn't especially active, but at least she showed a very sincere attitude towards this question. Then her son was enlisted and sent to the Golan Heights. After a while I met her, and she had changed completely: she was talking about how strong we must be and how we must work harder for our army, and so on. What I'm trying to say is that women can help to bring peace only when they are actively working on it. You must defeat all the propaganda and all the pressure you are under as an Israeli citizen.

I'm also very proud that so many Israeli women are now engaged in the peace movement, but of course we're still a minority. What is very important is that this peace movement is now, I would say, the *heart* of the peace movement in Israel. I remember after the beginning of the Gulf crisis all other movements became silent, more or less. Only the Women in Black continue to stand in the demonstration, and it is very, very important.

• *I've heard some Israelis talk about a mutual economy between Israel and Palestine, while others talk about a need for two independent economies and that there's a need to create an independent Palestinian infrastructure. What is your opinion?*

Tamar: For the past twenty-three years, the Israeli government has very successfully uprooted all beginnings of economic development in the Territories, so nowadays they are very dependent on the Israeli economy. They are buying products in Israel, and they are working in Israel.[1] The idea was that this kind of economic connection will make the Green Line a piece of history — there will be no more Green Line.[2] But it changed because of the intifada. The intifada showed very clearly where the Green Line is, even inside Jerusalem: on this street you *have* intifada, and on the neighboring street there is *no* intifada, because this is the Green Line.

Now to say that Israel will develop the Occupied Territories is to demand that Israeli authorities become more liberal occupiers, as the British did in India. But this is 1990,

[1] However, since the war, the number of Palestinians allowed to work in Israel has been cut in half.
[2] The Green Line is the border which now delineates Israel from Palestine.

185

and it's impossible to follow the example of the old colonial system.

I am not against investments in the Territories; I am all for developing their minimal rights, their living conditions — we need to do anything necessary to keep there from being hungry people in the camps. But economic development as we understand it can only happen when there is an independent state, and *they* can decide what *they* want to do, what *they* want to develop, and how *they* want to live — *they* can develop *their* country. I hope also that it will be achieved by a peaceful solution, and then there can be economic cooperation. I am for economic cooperation — but cooperation between equal sides, not cooperation when one side is under occupation.

Tamar Gozansky was one of approximately six Knesset members to oppose the Gulf War once it had begun. In late January 1991, Shamir admitted Rechavam Ze'evi of the ultra-right Moledet Party to his Likud Cabinet, a strong advocate of the mass transfer of Palestinians from the West Bank and Gaza to Jordan. During the Knesset session when Ze'evi was being welcomed into the Cabinet, Gozansky and Mohammed Nafa (an Arab KM) held up pictures of yellow stars of David — the symbols Jews were forced to wear in Nazi Europe. Gozansky and Nafa were formally censored by the Knesset for this action and were barred from attending general sessions for two weeks.

Gulf War Chronicle
February-March 1991

"Since neither man [Bush nor Hussein] is restrained
by his people, the ruling force is still macho pride . . ."
— Carl Rowan, *The Washington Post*

*January 16, 1991, was a day of great grief and shame for many
Americans, when George Bush, with the acquiescence of a
Congressional majority, initiated six weeks of incessant bombing
attacks on the people of Iraq. Although over thirty Iraqi scud
missiles landed in Israel, killing or injuring several people,
destroying homes, and terrifying millions, the Palestinian people —
along with the Iraqi and Kurdish peoples — were among the major
victims of this war. Israeli Simona Sharoni aptly describes it: "They
were sealed in the West Bank and Gaza, with no food and medicine,
and no one to bear witness."*

*I originally intended to present in this volume my interviews
conducted through December 1990. I hoped they held a certain
form and flow, an aesthetic melded with message. History
intervened, however, and sculpted this material more harshly; and
these "Conversations" would be incomplete without the interviews
which follow. Nothing is as it was. All our lives are changed.*

*The following excerpts are from radio interviews conducted
from Berkeley, California, to East and West Jerusalem, via
telephone, between February and March 1991.*

*Eileen Kuttab is a youthful university professor who is active with
the Union of Palestinian Women's Associations in East Jerusalem.
This interview was conducted on February 4, 1991.*

• *Eileen, can you describe the situation now in the West Bank
and Gaza?*

Eileen: The whole West Bank and Gaza Strip, nearly two
million people, have been under curfew for the last nineteen

187

days. All normal activity has ceased. Schools have been closed. Workers cannot go to their work to earn their daily living, especially those who work inside the Green Line [West Jerusalem and Israel]. Hospitals lack sufficient staff and medicine. Even daily operations for sick people have been postponed — people are really in prison, confined in their homes.

• *How often are people allowed out to get food?*

Eileen: Mainly every three days the authorities try to lift the curfew for three hours, but it doesn't always work out. Sometimes, as in Gaza, only women are allowed to be on the streets during the lifting of the curfew. And in the West Bank, anyone under twenty-five years old is not allowed to be out in the streets at all. For example, three or four days ago in Ramallah, they arrested fifty people in the main center of town, because they were men above twenty-five years old, and they didn't know about the new law.

• *So how long will this go on?*

Eileen: Today the Israeli civil administrator said that "for security reasons" — this is the magic word — they're going to keep it on as long as the war is on and as long as the Palestinians are supporting Saddam Hussein. That's the official statement.

• *But how can people live like that for an indefinite period of time, under lock and key?*

Eileen: I have no idea what the consequences will be because the majority of the workers in the refugee camps and the villages have no money, no income at all. This means that even if the shops are open they cannot buy their basic needs.

• *How are people supposed to survive without money to buy food?*

Eileen: I don't really know. This is part of the policy — starving the people because of their support for Saddam Hussein and pressuring them to really give up and say, "Of course we don't want to deal with Saddam Hussein anymore." It doesn't seem that the Palestinian people are going to surrender because of these practices. On the contrary, they're trying to be more and more organized, and the leadership has called for new popular structures to emerge to be able to help in the continuation of steadfastness.

• *So they're continuing to support Hussein?*

Eileen: Well, he's an Arab leader who has been able to seriously challenge the U.S for the first time, even by devastating his own country and his own people. And at the same time he has been able to link his issue, the Gulf issue, with the Palestinian issue. More and more this has made the Palestinians feel that he is somebody who is really doing something; he's not just giving lip service as other Arab leaders, and other leaders, have done before.

• *Eileen, there were reports here that when the Iraqi missiles landed in Israel, Palestinians were cheering. What is your response to that?*

Eileen: I feel that our misery as Palestinians had never been felt by the international community until the intifada started. The intifada has been symbolic for the whole world, that the Palestinians as people still are struggling for their own national rights. In terms of the missiles, of course no one wants to see people injured, Israelis or Arabs, but we feel that for the first time the Israeli society is tasting the medicine that we have been subjected to by them. Because of the Israelis, we have also been devastated for the last forty-three years: tear-gassed, shot, beaten, our land expropriated, our homes demolished. Maybe at this moment these Israelis will start to think what they are doing with the Palestinians too.

• Eileen, you're staying right now in East Jerusalem — do you have a gas mask?

Eileen: Yes, all Jerusalem people have gas masks.

• Do you have any idea how many Palestinians have them in the West Bank and Gaza?

Eileen: Only the UNRWA (U.N. Relief Works Agency) workers and the health workers in different organizations were offered gas masks. The other very important thing is that gas masks in the West Bank and Gaza Strip are offered only to people over fifteen years old, *which means that they exclude the children.* This also means this is a misery for the parents, because they cannot take these gas masks themselves and watch their children not have them. The Israelis have been promising all the time that they will be distributing them, but they haven't up until now, and at the same time some of the officials have said, "We will not be distributing to the West Bank because they are not the targets. All the nuclear weapons are going to be targeted towards Israel." But of course we never know, and it's a war; the missiles can go anywhere.

• Do you have any other message for the American people right now, Eileen?

Eileen: Yes, I just want to say to the Americans, why should you accept what's happening, and why should you accept the deaths of your children, the new generation? I wish that you could be more effective in changing the strategy of Bush because what I see now is only an arrogant . . . I don't even want to define him as a leader because a leader is a person who abides by his people's will. He's not doing that — that's how I see it — I see the demonstrations against this war. And I hope these demonstrations will grow and grow, be more and more effective and stop this war. What's happening is a crime — they're bombarding civilians, hospitals, preventing medicine from reaching children, and that's a crime.

190

• • •

Tikva Honig Parnas is an Israeli who works with the Alternative Information Center in Jerusalem. This interview was conducted on February 4, 1991. As we spoke, I heard her exhaustion and felt her voice charged with grief.

• *Tikva, what information do you have right now about the blanket curfew in the Occupied Territories?*

Tikva: The Israeli authorities are imposing the curfew in different places at different times so people won't be able to contact each other. Even villages adjacent to cities, their curfew is not lifted at the same times as in the towns nearby. This stops the whole distribution and supply system from working. But the most serious thing is that all the workers who worked daily can't go out to their work, so people right now lack the cash to buy food.

The second thing is the whole economic system, the production system, is collapsing because only a very, very few can work the fields and take care of the crops and market them.[1] Industry, most of it, is frozen, and the Civil Administration gives permits only to those they choose to.[2] The medical system is collapsing because doctors can't move without special permits, and only one third of the doctors receive these permits. So they can't come to the clinics, they can't come to the hospitals. Patients with very serious diseases can't get to a hospital from a refugee camp without special permits, which take hours to receive. So you find children with serious cancer who were in the middle of their medical treatment in Hadassah Hospital in West Jerusalem who had to stop their treatment, because they are not given permits to get there.

• *What are Israelis in the peace movement doing about this?*

---

[1]As of March '91, losses in agriculture, crops, and livestock were estimated at $5-20 million in the short term, more in the long term. ("From the Field," Vol. 1, No. 7, March 91, Palestinian Human Rights Information Center)
[2]As of March '91, local economists estimated $10-12 million in lost industrial production during the first month of the curfew (Ibid.).

Tikva: We are organizing a trip to bring food to the refugee camps, but generally the peace camp is paralyzed. Most of it joined the "national consensus" that supports the war, and they condemn the peace movements all over the world, calling them "innocent," "naive," or "hypocritical." They regret their previous support (although it was very hesitant) for the rights of the Palestinian people. It's very, very discouraging. There are here and there attempts to sign petitions, but not one has come out yet.[1]

Even the whole struggle against occupation is pushed into a corner, and most of the Women in Black, for instance, who come from the Left organizations, are refusing to go on standing against occupation, claiming that this is not the right time, that it's a very complex issue. We haven't been standing for three weeks, all over the country. In Jerusalem, part of us are going to start standing again next Friday.

• *Clearly, Tikva, from what you're saying, you are one of the people in the peace movement who opposed this war . . .*

Tikva: Yes, of course! We are calling for a cease-fire. When we talk to the Israeli public, we say that we don't believe that this war is going to advance the security of Israel and the peace in this area.

• *How many people in Israel do you think agree with you right now?*

Tikva: Maybe 200. Some of the women from the Left think that there is no one to listen to them, and they don't want to be in this small minority which thinks that there is a linkage — and there *is* a linkage between the war and the situation of the Palestinian people.

---

[1] On January 25, several dozen Israeli peace activists gathered, with gas masks strapped to their shoulders, opposite the U.S. Embassy in Tel Aviv to protest the Gulf War. On February 15, an antiwar petition was published in *Ha'aretz* ("the *New York Times* of Israel"), signed by more than 200.

- *We've heard here that when the missiles dropped on Israel, Palestinians cheered. I know that you have relatives in Tel Aviv, and I'm wondering how you felt . . .*

Tikva: I can't blame them. After more than twenty years of being repressed, of being killed, of being arrested, of being uprooted, of course they are happy that missiles are being sent to Tel Aviv. Although I am against killing citizens, I can't accuse them because Israelis are not only calling for abolishing the whole Iraqi people, they are right now not even lifting one finger against what's going on every day in the Occupied Territories.

- *Personally, Tikva, how do you feel when you hear the air raid sirens going off?*

Tikva: I am tense, I am tense. I go with my family to the sealed room. But being afraid doesn't affect my political attitude.

February 21-24, 1991[1]

- *Tikva, we've heard that mobility in the Occupied Territories continues to be drastically limited. Do you have any new information on that?*

Tikva: The entire Occupied Territories are divided now into military zones — the Northern West Bank, the Southern West Bank, and Gaza — where people need permits to move from one area to the other. The dependence of the inhabitants on a pass to get through a checkpoint to reach a hospital or to go to another city — this is a new situation which, according to the Israeli plans, is meant to crush any indigenous effort to establish any economic or medical or educational infrastructure. And this is a precedent which we haven't

[1] In this interview I was assisted by Howard Levine, Associate Director of the Middle East Children's Alliance.

witnessed before. So the Americans gave the green light to Israel to do this in the Occupied Territories.

I attended a press meeting of international NGO's which are involved here in development projects, and they declared that all their budgets — which were meant for economic and educational development in terms of working together with the Palestinian organizations — are going now to feed the populations who are starving, who don't have the cash money to buy food.[1] Everything that was in the process of developing is now destroyed.

• *Tikva, are any Israeli peace activists still working to get food into the Occupied Territories?*

Tikva: Yes, last Friday we brought food to one of the camps. The Arab population in Israel is doing it daily. The Women and Peace Coalition is taking a convoy of food this Saturday. But these are drops in the ocean. And as much as it is important, these are not real indications of what's going on in the majority of the peace camp.

• *Do you have a sense if any more women in the peace movement are against the war than in the peace movement in general?*

Tikva: No, but the "hard core" of the Women and Peace Coalition, in contrast to the Women's Network *(Reshet)* which is more at the center of the political map, is mostly against the war and openly calls for stopping the curfew. The women are still the only organization in the peace movement who speak explicitly against the war and for the PLO and for ending the occupation and the curfew.

• *Tikva, how much influence do you think the U.S. government could have if it decided to pressure the Israeli government to end the curfew?*

---

[1] Estimates of losses by 304,000 Palestinian wage laborers employed in Israel or the Occupied Territories as a result of the curfew between January 17 and February 10 were calculated at $130 million (*B'Tselem*: Israeli Information Center for Human Rights in the Occupied Territories).

Tikva: The United States? It can do anything. That's why I say it's a kind of green light which the American government gave to Israel to try again to crush the intifada. This is the payment the U.S. gave Israel for not intervening in the war.

But on second thought, it's not only payment: it's part of an entire plan in which Israel has its role. In the new map of the Middle East, Israel has an important role — although it has lost much of its exclusive role in the military, because now there are the other Arab countries supporting the United States. But in the American plan, Israel has its role in looking to help establish a kind of stable regime in the Occupied Territories. So there is no question the United States could stop the curfew. But it doesn't, because of the Israeli cooperation.

● ● ●

Chaya Shalom is an Israeli-born Sephardic Jew and an organizer with the Women and Peace Coalition. She's been active in the Israeli lesbian-feminist community for over 12 years. We spoke in early February 1991.

● *Chaya, can you tell us what it feels like in West Jerusalem now?*

Well, it's now 7:30 pm, the time when you're wondering when you'll hear the siren ... Jerusalem is supposed to be safe — but for how long? How can I feel safe when sixty kilometers from here people are losing their homes, their belongings, their lives? Saddam said today that he has more surprises for us — a secret weapon — what does he mean? Men invent these awful weapons and use them with such enthusiasm. They say they produce and distribute them to prevent war; we know this is nonsense. The weapons are made to be used, and the men are only looking for the "right time" when public opinion will be ready. You can't stop the war machine now.

• *How is the women's peace movement responding?*

We know that now the Palestinian question is more urgent than ever, with the curfew, no gas masks, losing their jobs here, and so on. But when people are losing their lives and property *here*, the peace movement doesn't have any support. That's why Women in Black won't have their vigil for a while; only a few women would participate. And if only a small number stand, there is a chance to lose the rest. To me, it seems that we can't have the vigil, not only because of low participation, but because it's not tactical to do it in these days. On the other hand, we have to let people know that although we stopped, it's only a break; the occupation must be stopped.

• *How are you doing personally, Chaya?*

I never ever remember myself as frightened as when I hear the air raid. It is like a punch in my stomach that continues to dominate my whole body. The first time, my mouth was so dry with fear I drank half the water bottle with my mask on. People who know how small my bathroom is find it hard to believe that I can stay here. Well, I prepare it so that I have everything I need: radio, sleeping bag, cushions, food, water, clock, books, letters, paper, flashlight, of course the mask, and tape to seal the door.

Life here stops when darkness comes. We don't want to be away from home, because we don't know when the missiles will fall. So the days are very short, and the evenings and nights very long.

Only a few minutes ago, I talked to a friend in Tel Aviv who told me if she survives tonight, she'll come tomorrow to Jerusalem. She's leaving her job and apartment. People there are in terror. I would feel the same. I want to be an optimist, but it's hard these days. My dog Choco keeps me sane.

And I've heard about the racism in America against the Arab people — how awful so much evil gets out these days!

196

• • •

Suha Hindiyeh is Director of the Palestinian Women's Research and Training Society in East Jerusalem. She graciously agreed to talk with me and Howard Levine at 3 a.m., Jerusalem time, during the third week in February 1991.

• *Suha, can you give us an update from your perspective on what's happening right now with the curfew?*

Suha: Two weeks ago, we thought that the curfew was going to be lifted, that things were going to be eased. However, it was just for a couple of days, and then the curfew began all over again twenty-four hours a day. Almost 4,000 Palestinians have been arrested and detained since the start of the war.[1] And a large number of people have run out of money. Just yesterday I heard in a press conference that in one of the villages near Ramallah, fifty families are literally penniless, and these families have been given some relief money by some NGO's (Non-Governmental Organizations).

We've been hearing that the Israeli soldiers have been committing many atrocities in certain refugee camps. For example, the Israelis raided the Kalandia refugee camp just a couple of days ago and asked all men to get out of their homes. They were beaten, and four were arrested. Actually, the Israeli Defense Forces might be taking the Gulf War as an excuse to do whatever they want.

• *So what do you think is going to happen?*

Suha: The Gulf crisis is now understood as not concerning the liberation of Kuwait but the interests of the Allied Forces, and in particular the American government. When the U.S. has a strong military government in the area, eventually they can control the area for hundreds of years to come — and

---

[1] The Israeli Center for Human Rights in the Occupied Territories, B'Tselem, confirms that from the beginning of the Gulf War to the end of February, 3600 Palestinians were arrested for breaking curfew.

197

bring about a "new world order," which is America being Number One.

We would like to see this war stopped and a political solution found because peace cannot be brought about by killing hundreds, thousands, millions of people. It can only be brought about by sitting together and talking to find the best solution. It's a pity that billions of dollars are being spent on this crazy war, when millions of people in Africa, Latin America, Asia are going through starvation.

• • •

Zahira Kamal is the Chairperson of the Palestinian Federation of Women's Action Committees; she participated in the first post-War delegation of ten Palestinians to meet with Secretary of State Baker in Jerusalem. This interview took place on March 20, 1991.

• *Zahira, how did you feel about the meeting with Secretary of State Baker last week?*

Zahira: The meeting was held under the umbrella of international legitimacy and the Security Council resolutions. The major issue we had to discuss is the need to apply the same measures, the same enthusiasm, the same emphasis in dealing with the Security Council resolutions concerning the Palestinian problem, as in the resolutions against Iraq — because in our point of view there are no resolutions to be applied while others are kept on the shelf.

Second, in that meeting we affirmed that the PLO is our sole legitimate representative. After the Gulf War, because of the stand of the PLO, some tried to bypass this and to find alternatives — and here we confirmed that any solution to the problem is impossible without the PLO. The Palestinian problem is the core of the problem in the region, and any solution should acknowledge the political and national rights of the Palestinians.

Third, we discussed the Israeli settlements in the Occupied Territories. We affirmed that these settlements are obstacles on the road to peace, that the Israelis are using them to establish a new reality in the Occupied Territories, and that the U.S. could play a role in stopping the build-up of the new settlements in the West Bank, Gaza, and East Jerusalem.

• *What will your strategy be now for the intifada and for trying to get a Palestinian state?*

Zahira: There is a Palestinian peace initiative, and we are committed to it. What we are working for is to find a mechanism to push this peace initiative forward.

• *I recently read in the paper that Israeli General Dan Shomron said, "Israeli force cannot stop the Palestinian uprising, and a peace settlement is worth more than territory." Does that give you any cause for hope?*

Zahira: The message from the Gulf War is that neither weapons nor power can bring peace to the region and security to Israel — because the missiles can reach everywhere. Annexing new territories is not bringing peace or security to Israel; peace and security can only come by making peace with the Palestinians themselves because they are the closest neighbors to Israel.

• *Zahira, what do you see as the priority struggles right now for Palestinian women?*

Zahira: We have a lot of problems as a result of the long curfews and the green cards so a lot of workers can no longer go to work inside Israel. This has meant that women have to find work, and now they are participating in what we call the "home economy," becoming self-sufficient on a subsistence level. It is done outside the house, a kind of workshop in the area where women come according to their time, and they are independent in a way, and they are helping earn income for the family.

Zakaria Khoury
April 1991

Although I had heard his name often, I didn't meet Zakaria until he agreed to be one of the Palestinian guides for our U.S. Women's Peace Brigade in December 1990. All of us quickly came to appreciate his quiet wit and finely tuned intelligence, blended with a boyish charm, that consistently and passionately worked to serve his people's struggle for self-determination.

It was hard to absorb how much could change in only four months. When Zakaria visited the United States in the spring, to collect humanitarian aid for his tremendously traumatized postwar society, I felt deeply the impact that the Israeli-imposed curfew was having on the people of the West Bank and Gaza, along with the subsequent closing of the Israeli borders to most Palestinians.

Zakaria's handsome Semitic face that so easily broke into a mocking smile was now strangely drawn and pale. The smile was still there, but the strain behind it was clear, and a dark tragedy seemed to lurk in the depths of his eyes. Middle East Children's Alliance Director Barbara Lubin and I spoke with Zakaria in early April.

• *I just read in the L.A.* Times *that the Israeli government is passing laws essentially to legitimize the additional repressive measures against the Palestinians that they were using during the war. One of these includes deporting any Palestinian activist that the government suspects of encouraging actions against the Israeli state. Do you know anything more about this?*

Zakaria: In fact, since the first day of the war, the Israeli authorities have imposed martial law, and they considered the state of Israel in a state of war. What does this imply? That any action by the Palestinian population which might be against the movement of the army or the "security" of

Israel would be faced with harsh punishment. The soldiers have been given permission to shoot anybody who commits any action during the period of war.

And all these restrictions which have been imposed by the Israeli government, like disconnecting towns from each other, not allowing people from the West Bank to get into Israel or the other way around — there has been a lot of talk about establishing this as permanent. This has really affected the situation of our people and stopped their movement, so they can't get to their jobs, and you have to consider that more than 130,000 Palestinians had jobs inside Israel.

Deportation is one of the collective punishments which have been used during the Occupation, and in a more intensive way during the last three years in the intifada. The Israeli authorities have been trying to establish a new situation where, if somebody commits any violation against the Israeli state or the Occupation, the Israelis will pick him up and deport him. This is just a matter of expanding the right of the Israeli authorities to deport as many people as they can. It's their way of trying to suppress the intifada.

• *What kind of mobility do people have at this point?*

Zakaria: They must get permission from the military governor or the civil administration. The way the government does it is that workers are not allowed to move by themselves but have to be picked up by their employers at one or two spots in Gaza, and be taken by bus to their jobs and returned at the end of the day, nearly two hours each way. This makes life very difficult for our people, leaving nearly 100,000 Palestinian workers without jobs.

• *We heard a lot about how the entire economic infrastructure of Palestine was destroyed because people couldn't get out to harvest their crops. Are they being allowed out now to work in the fields, to harvest, to plant?*

Zakaria: The period of the war was during the main season for some of the products — mainly citrus oranges and other fruits. So farmers were not able to collect their produce. Even if they managed to do this, they had no permission to market it. So the restrictions that were imposed really stopped any economic activity — with farming and other industries. For example, the Israeli authorities allowed the medical factories to open, but most of the workers were from various villages and towns and were not permitted to reach the factories. So in practice the factories were not running.

• *From what you're saying, it sounds like it hasn't gotten much better since the war "ended."*

Zakaria: Not much. The whole thing goes on in order to serve the interest of the Israeli economy, under the line of "linking the Palestinian economy to the Israeli one." Only the industries or small factories which can help support the Israeli economy have been given permission to operate. For example, the dairy factories in the Hebron area were allowed to open but not to collect the milk from the surrounding villages. They have to buy Israeli milk in order to run the factory, so in a way it serves the Israeli economy.

• *So, Zakaria, where do we go from here?*

Zakaria: Well, as we said, the situation has been going very badly. This is unprecedented — it has never been as bad as it is these days.

• *Even before the intifada?*

Zakaria: Even during the last twenty-four years of occupation of the West Bank and Gaza, our people have never had to go through the kind of situation that we've seen during the past few months since the war started. Taking into consideration

Palestinians who came back from the Gulf — who were employed in the Gulf states and had to quit. Thousands of Palestinians were forced to leave Kuwait, and many of them are residents of the West Bank and Gaza. They came back, and they are unemployed. This adds even more economic difficulty and deterioration for the general situation of our people.

As we mentioned, immigration is another factor which has been threatening the future of our economy and the future of our people. Because as more immigrants arrive in Israel, more land is confiscated, more settlements are made, more water resources are confiscated, and more jobs are lost for the Palestinians. So the immigration issue is really a threat to our future, especially in the Green Line and in the West Bank, since more than 30% of the Soviet immigrants have been settled in the West Bank so far, and more are coming in the future.

We had been hearing a lot about a campaign, which is led by the United States, trying to disqualify the PLO as the legitimate representative of our people, while *our* people are thinking that it is their *only* representative.

We think it's very important, as a first step, to call for United Nations protection for our people in the West Bank and Gaza, who have been facing an escalation in harassment and oppression at all levels by the Israeli authorities. And the second step that we feel is very important is for European countries to push for the implementation of the United Nations resolutions which are relevant to the Arab-Israeli conflict in order to achieve the establishment of an independent Palestinian state. Our people have been suffering from this occupation for twenty-four years, and the Americans have not been listening. We feel that it is time to deal with it in a more realistic and logical way.

• *How are people feeling? What is their spirit like?*

Zakaria: Of course the war has had a lot of impact on the emotions and the feelings of our people. Especially now, after the war, seeing the waste, the killing, all the massive destruction which was caused by the Allies against the Iraqi people. The attitude against the Palestinians — the campaign led by the United States against our people as a punishment for the position taken by the PLO regarding the Gulf crisis — has some negative effect on our people, of course. But we have a hope in our intifada continuing until we achieve our right to self-determination and establishment of our state in the West Bank and Gaza Strip.

Roni Ben-Efrat
March 1991

Roni Ben-Efrat is striking in her commitment, her warmth, her sense of purpose. Although we had met briefly in Jerusalem several months earlier, it was at the Middle East Justice Network Conference in Albuquerque, New Mexico (March 1991), where we really had a chance to connect and talk. I was grateful for the opportunity to delve a bit more deeply into the status of the Israeli peace movement with someone I so respected from that movement, so soon after the war's "end." Roni and I are close in age, and I clearly felt how our positions could have been reversed — how I might have been the one destined to struggle within Israel for a just and lasting peace. I wondered if I'd have had Roni's quiet stamina, steady principles and tireless fortitude . . .

Currently, Roni is an editor of the magazine Challenge *(or* Etgar), *which is written by and for Israeli peace activists.*

• *Roni, you have been active in the Israeli peace movement and the Israeli women's movement for many years, and you recently served nine months in prison for publishing a journal about the atrocities in the Occupied Territories. I was hoping you could talk about where the Israeli peace movement and the women's peace movement are today?*

Roni: I think the peace movement has a lot of thinking to do about what happened during the war, so it can strengthen its principles and establish a new basis for its activity. Because the collapse during the Gulf War was really very difficult. Throughout the three years of the intifada we were working on the issue that if a peace process doesn't go on, then there will be a war. The funny thing was that once the war started, suddenly the people who understood this all along, backed off and said, "Okay, we're not playing the game anymore; we are supporting our own government."

I was part of a very small minority inside the Israeli peace movement that did stand firm, and said all along the way that this war could have been prevented if there had been a willingness to go for a solution in the Middle East, and if the Israeli government were engaged in a peace process. What has been revealed in this war is that it's too dangerous to let our destiny be handled by people like Bush and Shamir.

• *So do you think women are going to come back into the peace movement?*

Roni: Well, women did come back. At the beginning of the war, the vigil of the Women in Black stopped for two weeks because women were confused and felt very shaken by what was happening. The interesting thing was that none of them wanted to call the vigils off completely. Some of them, though, thought that it would be a better idea to delay the demonstrations until after the war. My personal position, and this was the position that in the long run won the vote, was that we must continue demonstrating by all means. We don't have to have a common position on the war, but we must have a common position about fighting the occupation. It's quite obvious that the occupation didn't stop during the war, so why should we stop our vigils during the war?

Another reason for continuing the vigils was that we said this was a time of a test. What did three years of standing in vigils mean, if in a time of crisis we are going to back off? We decided that if we didn't stand during the war, we wouldn't have any moral justification to stand once the war was over. I'm very glad to say that we won the vote and we convinced many women who were hesitant beforehand to join us.[1]

The first time we stood during the war, we had forty women, and the second time we had sixty women. I am sure

[1] In fact they immediately put on their black clothes, walked to the square and stood for one hour in the biting rain amidst cries from passing cars of "whores of Saddam!" (*Jewish Women's Peace Bulletin*, May 1991, Nos. 8-9, Jewish Women's Committee to End the Occupation.)

that we are now back to our normal size of 120 women per week. I think this says something about the women's movement and its inner force, its conviction, and its power.

• *When I was there in December, a lot of the Palestinians were frustrated with Israeli peace activists who had abandoned their support of the Palestinians. Since so many more peace activists came out in favor of the war, what do you think this has done to the cooperation that was going on between the Israeli peace movement and the Palestinians in general — especially between the women, in terms of breaking trust?*

Roni: The situation that you are talking about did happen, and we cannot evade it even if we would like to. You simply cannot build a movement on the basis of always taking and never giving. I think that what Palestinian women felt was that while they were making many concessions, they didn't really get many concessions from the Israeli side.

But on the other hand, I think that the Israeli women's movement as a whole understands this very well. This is because of the special character of the women's movement. It's not just a feminist movement that deals with issues of women, it's a movement of women for peace. Therefore, whether they like it or not, they must be connected to the struggle of the Palestinian women; there is an awful lot that binds them together.

• *Do you think the Palestinian women will continue to be willing to work with you?*

Roni: We had a very important experience just before I came over here, in the Women and Peace Coalition. In the middle of the war, we called a meeting with the Palestinian women's organizations, and all of the women from the Palestinian side came, each one representing a different faction within their women's movement. We told them that we would like to make an initiative of going into a refugee camp and bringing aid to the women. We wanted to call it for the eighth of March, International Women's Day.

We were quite hesitant because we didn't know what their approach would be. The fact that they all came to the meeting was very encouraging. They were willing to go on working with us. We didn't know how to go about it because we didn't want it to seem as if we — the white, intellectual, educated Jewish women — are going into a camp and giving humanitarian aid, when our government is going on with this curfew. We asked them, "What do you think about the idea of our writing a leaflet which stresses our political beliefs and our support for you, written in Arabic, for us to give to the women?" They thought that was a very good idea, and this is what we did.

We asked them, "What would be the most useful thing for you in the camps right now?" And they said, "Well, because women are very short of money, we think it would be a good idea if you brought hygiene materials, like sanitary pads and things like that." So this is exactly what we did, and we raised a lot of money. I think this shows that if we are willing to continue on a principled basis of *political* support, and not just humanitarian support, it will be easier for them to convince their women to continue this kind of dialogue.

• *I heard that when Women in Black stood in Jerusalem on International Women's Day one of the signs they had was "No to the Curfew." Have the demands, the slogans, been changing in terms of the Israeli women's peace movement?*

Roni: I'm sure it's not going to change. A two-state solution is very deep-based in the consciousness of all the peace activists, and even people who supported the war are still accepting this solution.

There is also the question of negotiating with the PLO, although we are not getting too much help from the American administration with this. The way Baker tried to divide the

Palestinian people and its leadership is really unheard of. It's not helping the peace movement in Israel get along in the peace process. But nevertheless, we are determined about this issue, and we will just tell Mr. Baker and Mr. Bush and Mr. Shamir that whatever comes, they will have to deal with the leadership of the Palestinian people. Just like when de Klerk wanted to make a genuine change he knew he had to talk to the African National Congress leaders — he didn't go around saying that he would talk to the United Democratic Front leaders.

• *I was just talking to a peace activist who recently moved here from Israel and has been working as a part of the Israeli Left for about fourteen years. When I asked him about the diminishing of the peace movement since August, he told me that those people were only "pseudo peace activists," and that while they may have supported "land for peace,"[1] they weren't really in support of Palestinian self-determination. Do you think that's true? And if so, what do you think are the implications for the future of the peace movement at large?*

Roni: I think that what he said is basically right. In the Israeli peace movement we have two kinds of peace activists. One group, I call the pragmatists. The others are the principled peace people. The principled peace people are those who for years have held the position of two states for two peoples. The pragmatists are all the people who during the intifada changed their minds about accepting a two-state solution, and we are welcoming them. I think it's positive and very good. But we are aware of the fact that if the intifada diminishes or if the PLO gets weaker, they would be willing to back off from their recognition of the PLO and the two-state solution.

---

[1] "Land for peace" is a commonly used term referring to the proposal that the Israeli Government trade "land" (the West Bank and Gaza) for "peace" (a two-state solution).

Personally I am not too worried about them, because they really get their motivation from the intifada. As long as the intifada is going strong and as long as the Palestinian people know what they want, the whole peace movement will have to support it. Since I have a lot of faith in the Palestinian uprising, I think the peace movement will just have to rally behind it.

• *Since you brought up having a lot of faith in the uprising, how do you see it recovering from the incredible economic devastation that's happened as a result of the curfew, not just economic but socially, too?*

Roni: I think it will not recover. I think what will happen is it will make the struggle more intense because the situation is so bad and so desperate and it needs such a big push. All this business with the green cards that are being issued against any people who were involved in any political activity . . .

• *Not just being in prison?*

Roni: No, no. *Anyone* who has been politically active is being issued a green card. We are talking about tens of thousands of people. These people are not allowed to enter Israel to work, and they are also prevented from traveling. Because if someone gets a green card and he is living in Nablus, for instance, and he can't enter Israel, then he can't go to Bethlehem — because he has to pass through Jerusalem to get there. And he can't go to Gaza, because he has to pass through Jerusalem.

• *In this period of the last few months, have any clear lessons emerged for you — given how the struggle has changed?*

Roni: I think the main lesson that has been learned is the *gravity* of the situation — that we can't play around anymore, it's too dangerous. We were on the verge of nuclear war; we saw that we can be hit also. It's not always that we are hitting the Arab world. We are *vulnerable*. It means that we have to adopt a new way of thinking. And living in a world which is dominated by one power means that we will have to rely on ourselves and on the efforts of peace movements all around the world. This puts an awful lot of responsibility on forces which were inclined to let the governments do the work. But the governments are damaging us, sacrificing our lives, and we just cannot afford to put our lives and security in their hands. We must take more responsibility.

• *In terms of the mood of the people in Israel right now, I read in a poll last week that 49% of Israelis supported "land for peace." Yet Shamir is remaining as intransigent as ever. Bush is hemming and hawing but is still going ahead with millions of dollars of additional military aid. What do you think the prospects are for peace with justice coming any time soon?*

Roni: Although one should sometimes be doubtful of polls, I believe the results of that poll, because at the beginning of the intifada 54% supported talking to the PLO. The vast majority of Israelis during the Gulf War were for restraint. This means that the Israeli population is not ideologically motivated to the Right; the majority is willing to do anything its government is doing.

What I mean is, if tomorrow morning Shamir would come to his people, to us, and say, "Okay guys, we have to change our direction" — something like what de Klerk said to the white South Africans — I am positive that the vast majority, apart from a very small minority of ideological right-wing people, would support him totally. If he had the courage and the vision to tell them what peace can offer them — in the sense of economic welfare, in the sense of security, in the sense of being able to use the resources of the Middle East to benefit all the people — they would just rally behind him.

• *It's so hard to imagine Shamir doing what you're saying. What would it take for the Israeli people to pressure their government to change? Is that even a possibility?*

Roni: I think the main pressure would come from the American administration. It's absurd when you think about it, the amount of aid Israel gets without really doing anything for it. If the Americans would just put a little bit of pressure on Israel, you would see this whole balloon emptied of its air. Israel could not survive one day without the aid of the American administration and the American taxpayers.

• *Before we go on with that, let me backtrack a minute. If Shamir were to go to his people — to your people — and say, conversely, that it's time to transfer all the Palestinians from the West Bank and Gaza into Jordan, do you think they would support that as well?*

Roni: I think that many would support it, but he can't do it now.

• *Why not?*

Roni: Because half the population would go against it, and Israel is the kind of state that has to work in a consensus. This was the problem in the Lebanon War. When half the country said, "Let's pull out," it was unable to go on occupying Lebanon. I think that half of the population would not go along with the transfer plan. This is one point. The other is that I don't think that, internationally, Israel is in a position today to do such a thing. It doesn't have the backing, and it will not have the backing. The third issue is that the Palestinians will resist very forcefully. It's out of the question.

• *To pick up on what you were talking about earlier — about the aid — were you saying that the American people need to pressure our government to stop funding the Occupation?*

Roni: Exactly.

• *Is there anything else we should be doing to help support you?*

Roni: I think the American people have to be more aware of the situation, be more courageous — support Israel by supporting the *peace* people in Israel. This is a real change of state of mind, to really support the people who want peace. You want to fund Israel? Okay — fund projects that are going to the welfare of the poor people in Israel. We have 700,000 Arabs in Israel who are suffering a terrible situation of discrimination and inequality. If all the aid could go to these issues and not to the military, it would be a real breakthrough.

• *Roni, you spent nine months in an Israeli prison. What were some of the most powerful experiences you went through there?*

Roni: Well, it made me much stronger, in the sense that I was more aware of my ability to not give in. Our main demand was to be with Palestinians, since we were political prisoners and so were they, and we share so many of the same values. We wanted to share prison life with them, because it would have helped us survive the experience, but we were denied this. Although I was convicted of the same crimes as the Palestinian women, I was not allowed to be in prison with them due to unofficial apartheid. Whatever comes, you are a Jew in the government's eyes, and they are scared stiff of any kind of dialogue between Jews and Palestinians, even if it is going on behind the bars.

• *Earlier, you were telling me about the Palestinians you met in prison who did not talk about all the things they had done?*

Roni: I was talking in general about people I've met after prison who don't talk about their experience and all the tortures they have gone through — people who have sat in prison for ten years, but when you talk to them they don't even mention it. I think this is real heroism, for someone to come out of prison after ten years and continue the struggle and go on.

But my whole work is connected with working together with Palestinians. I know the way they act, I know the way they behave, I know their motivation — and you really feel the force that they have as a collective. It's incredible the way they stick up for each other. If somebody's house is demolished, they will immediately be invited to live with their neighbor.

I was devastated seeing the homeless people in New York, because I can't imagine this happening in a Palestinian society — someone just being left out to sleep in the streets. There is such a sense of communal help and solidarity that this couldn't be possible. When you see the Palestinians struggling, although they are struggling under terrible conditions, they are doing it *together*, they are united. They help each other. You don't have the situation where a person is left to struggle against the whole world alone. I don't know how American people can go by seeing these homeless people without screaming. For me it was a terrible shock. I just can't imagine it.

• *You mentioned "real heroism" a minute ago — who are your heroines or heroes?*

Roni: Many Palestinian friends, whose names I cannot just say. I think the people who especially motivate me are those people who are very modest, who are behind the scenes, not

214

in the spotlight, and who are doing this courageous work of changing the world for the benefit of others, without looking for a kind of prize that comes with it. Every time I see them, it teaches me a lesson to be more modest and to do the hard work and not to look for the glory. I always feel that I learn something from them.

• *When I was in the airport yesterday I was sitting next to a woman who was wearing a jeweled pin of the American flag . . . My question is, how do you keep from demonizing the people who disagree with you — or do you?*

Roni: Can you elaborate?

• *I was sitting there, and there was a conversation among the people around me. One woman said to the other, "What a lovely pin you have there." And the other woman said, "Yes, my husband saw it and said 'you must get that.'" Well, of course I turned to look at the pin — it was this American flag that's all in jewels which really alienated me, given what this flag had just done to Iraqi children.*
Then I remembered the words of people like Veronika Cohen, who said that we have to understand the point of view that the other side has, so that we can try to work together. There are definitely a lot of people here in the United States who have this approach, and I can see the value of that approach, to break down the "us and them" mentality. But it's not easy for me. So I'm just asking if you have any experience with that? Is that relevant to the way you're working?

Roni: Well, I think in our peace movements, we lack the values and the tolerance to deal with people who do not share the same values that we do, or who are not as fortunate as ourselves to have a critical viewpoint of these things, and who are very easily misled. I think that if you had been able to sit down and talk to this woman, you would have been able to at least raise a few doubts in her mind, as I would be able to do if I were to talk to people in my country who walk around with the Israeli flag.

I think it's a weakness that we are all suffering from, and we have to get over it. In this sense, people in the church and religious people have the patience and the tolerance to talk to the unconvinced, and this is something that is *very* important. And that's why I admire people like Veronika Cohen.

• *So Roni, you've been doing this a long time. What keeps you going?*

Roni: What keeps me going? I think it's the fact that I simply wouldn't be able to get up in the morning and look at myself in the mirror, without doing the things that I'm doing. I'm serious about it. Living so close to the atrocities and the injustice that is being practiced against the Palestinians, it makes me feel that I don't have the right to be here if I am not doing something to change it. I think this is what is motivating me.

Sometimes I ask myself, if there *were* to be a Palestinian state — if this problem were to be solved — then what would happen? I'm just leaving this question open . . .

Rihab Essawi
July 1991

I caught up with Rihab Essawi in Palo Alto, California, when she was with a Palestinian delegation in a "Beyond War" Conference. A Professor of Education at Hebron University in the West Bank, Rihab comes from a family of political activists. Since I knew she had faced great sadness in her life, I was expecting a somewhat "tragic figure." Instead, I found a lively, fresh, and energetic spirit — poised, down-to-earth, easy to relate to. As the Friday rush-hour traffic whizzed by, we spoke in my car outside the restaurant.

• *Rihab, I actually know very little about you — except that you're a Palestinian woman whose life has been strongly affected by the struggle for a Palestinian homeland. We all make such different choices in our lives, and I wondered what experiences motivated you to work for peace?*

Rihab: You're starting a big issue with me; I don't know where to begin. I think what 'motivated me really is the suffering we started going through when my father became very active in the revolution in 1936. Toward the end he was a political refugee in Iraq, and he was sentenced to death by the British three times. In 1970 I had a brother who was arrested and he spent twelve years in jail. I have another brother who was murdered in 1982 during the Lebanon invasion, and during the intifada other brothers have been arrested, as well as nephews. And I have been arrested three times.

• *Why were you arrested?*

Rihab: The first time, I came back from the United States after I got my master's degree, and my brother was in Iraq and he couldn't come back home. So after five years of being away, I decided to go and visit him. I was then tried for getting in touch with an illegal organization, meaning my brother, because he was active with the PLO at that time. I was sentenced to three months for being in touch with my own brother, and I was given a one-year "withholding" sentence for three years — if I did anything during the three years, I would get in trouble.

• *And how about the other arrests?*

Rihab: The other times — exactly a year after I was released, I think it was done to tell me "Hey, we're here, be careful." I was taken for twenty-one days of interrogation, and then I was freed without charges. I was taken again about two years later, they say because of "being active." They took my father with me, and he was put in a jail cell for ten days; they don't even ask him one question.

• *Can you tell me what it was like for you the different times you were in jail — what the conditions were like?*

Rihab: During interrogation it was the worst, because I was denied sleep, denied food, tortured anytime day or night, whenever they felt like it. And I was threatened sexually during the investigation. During one of the interrogations — it was about midnight — they tried to get me to sign a confession that I belonged to the PLO. They especially tried to pinpoint that I had been in touch with some people and gotten some information back and forth for them, which I denied — and I refused to sign the paper. So finally, they told me, "We know what kind of woman you are. You've been in the States, and you've been working in prostitution, and you're *bad*, and we're going to tell your father you've been running around there." I told them, "This is my business with

218

my father, it's not your business." And they said, "Okay, we want to find out."

I just sat there and then they made a phone call, and they invited some Druze guy.[1] When he came, they told me, "Okay, you know what this guy is here for? This guy wants to make love to you, so we can find out if you are a virgin or not." Imagine! I had been standing at that time for about three hours on my feet; they wouldn't let me sit. And the interrogator told me, "Get undressed." I looked at them and there were three people sitting there, including a policewoman. I decided, well, what can I do now, there are three of them, and I wanted to go ahead and see what would happen. So I started getting undressed, and I unbuttoned the first three buttons of my blouse, and the interrogator asked me what I was doing. I said, "Just what you asked me to do." He was so furious — he was drinking a can of beer at the time — that he threw the can of beer at me and said to the people around him, "Take her away from here or I'll kill her. Most Arab girls, when we tell them we want to do *this*, they confess, and this one's *definitely* a prostitute because she doesn't mind."

They sent me away, and then brought me back again for interrogation the next day. When he asked me "Why did you agree to get undressed?" I told him, "I'd be crazy to resist." He said "What will happen if you get pregnant?" I answered, "Nothing will happen." He said, "Won't you go and have an abortion?" I said "No, I would keep it. And I would wait until the baby grew up, and I would tour the whole world with this baby and say to the whole world, 'This is the kid I was forced to have, not by my own choice.' I would use this for propaganda for my country." And he was really furious; he smacked me a couple of times when I said that.

[1] The Druze split off from the Shiite Moslems in the eleventh century. They now live mainly in the mountains between Syria and Israel and are used extensively in Israel as border police.

Even now I have two nephews who are in jail, and I have two sisters and both their husbands are in jail. So we have to go to visit the prison all the time, and we have to go through lots of hard things. When you see all these things done to you and to your people, you have to do something, you really have to do something. And I don't think there's anything more now that we can do, especially after the Gulf War, except look for peace.

• *So what are you doing right now — and what do you think needs to be done?*

Rihab: I don't think that we by ourselves can really do too much, because we have been trying all this time. I think negotiating with the Israelis, with a third party involved, would be the right thing to do. I could see the involvement of the United States, and the Soviet Union, and the European community, too. That would bring something to an end, especially after we saw that within six months of the whole crisis starting in the Gulf, there was a solution. Yet in our case it's been twenty-four years. I am talking about just since the '67 war — forget what happened before. It seems the whole world judges us Palestinians in a different way than it judges other places. When we saw what happened in the Gulf, we thought: it's time to move and pressure the world to do something for us.

• *What was it like for you during the War? How were you affected by it?*

Rihab: It was a terrifying feeling, for us and the Israelis alike. I don't know if you know this or not, but Scuds fell on Arab villages too. It's not easy for anybody to live in a condition like this, especially when you are not allowed to go anywhere, and you are under a curfew and waiting . . . it's really terrifying, but you have to keep brave to keep going, to encourage the little ones to stay alive.

• *As you know, around the world (including in the Israeli peace movement) there was a lot of negative response to the fact that Palestinians supported Saddam Hussein. When people ask you about that, what's your response?*

Rihab: I think this is the hardest question we face. I was in Helsinki last month at a United Nations conference, and after that I was in Rome for another conference which was on Women and Peace — and they always ask about the support for Saddam Hussein. Well, if you are somebody who is sinking, and somebody comes and says, "All right, I'm going to save you" — without knowing if this guy is able to save you or not, yet he offered to help you — definitely you're going to say, "Oh, all right." You jump at the opportunity, and you take it.

But still, our support — what support do we have? Not one Palestinian went and fought in the war. Arafat did not send anybody there. What kind of support, except to say, "Okay." What did we do? Nothing! We have no planes to send, we have no fighters to send there, so what kind of support are people talking about?

• *Do you work with any of the Israeli women in the peace movement?*

Rihab: Yes, I do, and I've been in conferences together with them. These women, they really move from their hearts in what they are doing. They suffer, like Palestinian women too, when their kids go to the army and they get killed. I think they've had enough of all that too, and they want to live to see a peaceful settlement.

• *Some of my Israeli friends in the peace movement are discouraged, because during the Gulf crisis some women dropped out. Have you felt frustrated by that at all?*

Rihab: Maybe they are discouraged for a little while, but I am sure they are picking up again. Because when you work from the inside, if you believe in what you are doing, you might get discouraged, but you won't turn your back on the whole movement. That's my experience with my Israeli friends.

• *What message do you have for American women? What do you want us to know about you and what do you want to make sure to tell us?*

Rihab: Not just for American women, but for all women in the whole world: I want them to know that we are like everybody else; we are the same. We have the same hearts. We have families. But we are denied the most important things — our homeland, to feel free, to be like every other woman, to enjoy life, to think about raising our kids in an independent way, have our own institutions, run our country the way we want. We want the people all over the earth to look at us as humans, as women too — we have rights, and we want them. The intifada is our way of showing the whole world that enough is enough.

• *I wonder if we could backtrack for a minute. You were talking about your family before . . . and I had heard that your fiancé was the longest-held Palestinian political prisoner? Do you feel like telling me about that?*

Rihab: Well . . . you're talking about Omar Kassem. He started to be a friend of my brother's, and they got arrested, and we would visit them at the same time. But I knew Omar when he was a little kid; he was involved with the national movement. I was a little younger, but I was helping him and my brother by taking leaflets and doing things they wanted me to do while I was going to school.

This thing between us began to grow more when I was visiting my brother and visiting Omar, and the commitment took place really when he was in jail. That's why I decided to go to the United States — to study more, to keep myself busy and come back and work. After I got my master's, I worked for the American Friends Service Committee in Palestine for about seven years. Then I went back to get my PhD I was trying to make my life fit with my situation and hoping that someday he would be with the prisoners who were released. Three times that took place, but every time they asked that he be released, the Israelis refused to do it.

You know being twenty-one years in jail and the bad conditions there, this wasn't easy on anybody. I committed myself, that this is my destiny, and I'm going to stick with it. But every day we had hope, both of us, that he would be released and things would work for us. Even the day before he died, he was saying to me he would be released. He was in the hospital, and at that time I knew that he would never leave the hospital, because I knew how bad his condition was. He had kidney failure and hepatitis, and when he was transferred to the hospital, he was *really* beyond help; they couldn't do anything for him. But he was in the emergency room all the time, and I visited him every day. And the sad thing was, he was tied to his bed.

The morning of the day he died, he sent a message to us because we were having a press conference that day at the American Colony Hotel. I went back around one o'clock to tell him what had happened at the press conference. We were not allowed to go in — there were two policemen guarding him. They said, "The doctors are trying to help him, and you can't see him now," so we waited about three hours. Then suddenly the guards came, and I was there with his sister and his mother, and they said, "The doctor wants to see you." I walked into the doctor's room to see what he wanted, and his sister was walking behind me. I just entered the room — the doctor didn't tell me to sit down or anything — he just looked up at me and said, "He just died." Very simple, very easy for for the doctor to do this. I got really upset and said, "Don't tell me he died. You killed him!"

I left immediately and went to see Omar. He was in bed, and I saw that he had really suffered — the way I saw him in the bed, the shape — it's just unbelievable, unbelievable. I tried to put the pillow under his head and stretch out his legs . . . this is the first time I saw a dead body. But I did not feel he was dead; I didn't. I went and hugged him, and I lifted his head, and I said to him, "Did they kill you?" — and you can believe he looked at me. He looked at me at that minute and tears came out of his eyes. And that was the end.

After that the authorities decided they could give him to us so we could bury him in Jerusalem. I called his brother to tell him what had happened and that we were bringing him back. I told him, "Don't come. I'll try to arrange an ambulance and bring him." He called me back and said, "Bring him to the al-Muqassed Hospital." So I went to the al-Muqassed Hospital, and I saw a crowd of people in front of the hospital — people I knew, and people who were in jail with Omar, and most of the leadership. But I also saw lots of army, lots of police, lots of green-beret guys sitting there. I decided I'm not going to stop, because I know they will take him away.

So I told the driver, "Keep going," and we passed this crowd and left. Then they followed us, and they took us to the Russian Compound Detention Center. They made the ambulance stand outside in the yard there, me and his sister and him in the ambulance, for an hour and a half. They came and looked at us, and they lifted the cover from his face; they looked at us and laughed and said, "Look, they are not afraid; they have a dead body with them, and they are not afraid!" That got me really frustrated, so I yelled at them, "This is not a dead body! This is our hero, and we are strong, and we take our strength even from what you call 'dead body.' He is that to you, but to us he's a hero."

After an hour and a half we were able to go back, and by that time they had sent everybody home. We left him at the hospital and his family went to see him. And that's the end of it. But his funeral was the biggest funeral ever in the history of Jerusalem.

• *And when was this?*

Rihab: Two years ago on June 4th, 1989.

• *After going through all this — what keeps you from being bitter?*

Rihab: I don't think I just can forget all of this and say I don't have any other feeling. I would be lying, and I would be not honest with myself. I do feel, when I look at his picture, or at my brother's picture — and I lost my mother, too, just a year ago. . . she suffocated from tear gas — when I see their pictures, I think of being bitter. But then I say to myself, "I have to be rational about it. It's done. What can I do to make life a little easier, and not go through more suffering?" And that's the main thing.

• *By doing this work, it makes it easier for you?*

Rihab: It helps. It helps. At least maybe I feel inside of me that I can spare other people from going through what I went through or what my family went through. I think of the future, of other people's future — why should they suffer? The world should be a better place to live.

Michel "Mikado" Warschawski
July 1991

Michel "Mikado" Warschawski chooses his words with care. With gentle dignity, he speaks clearly, richly, and passionately, his sensitive features emphasizing every thought or innuendo. Here is a human being who has tirelessly confronted and exposed his government's wrongdoing — and whose life's work is bridging the gap, making the connection, crossing the border between Israeli and Palestinian. For this he has been prosecuted and imprisoned. And for this he continues to stand quietly as a paradigm of Israeli conscience, compassion, and courage.

I spoke with Warschawski at length during his summer tour of the U.S. in July 1991, hungry for his perspective, for any slim rays of hope about peace with justice between Palestine and Israel.

• *Michel, when you spoke with our Women's Peace Brigade in Jerusalem this past December, you said that compared to ten or fifteen years ago, the Israeli people's move toward peace had reached a point of no return. And whereas Israeli society had created a line where Israelis and Palestinians rarely met, the intifada had achieved a new kind of relationship between Israelis and Palestinians — that there was a much broader spectrum of people doing the work than five years ago. Since the Israeli peace movement largely supported the Gulf War and some of those people also abandoned the Palestinians, what is your perspective today?*

Michel: I don't think that the Gulf crisis and the Gulf War will have a substantial effect in changing the influence of the intifada on the society. That is, I don't think that there is today in Israel any kind of return to the previous belief that the status quo is bearable. The Occupation is still conceived as something which has to be resolved — by a settlement, or by repression and ultimately deportation — one way or another.

As for the peace movement in Israel, there is no doubt that the war created a framework for a withdrawal from stated positions, and a change in the overall attitude toward the Palestinian question. But here too, I do not believe that the divorce papers the peace movement gave to the Palestinian national movement are real divorce papers. They are more a kind of political statement, oriented to the Israeli political map during a period of war, saying, "You see, when there is a war, we are back home. And we consider the Palestinians our enemies."

The fact is that the same people who before the war said, "Bye-bye, PLO," and closed their doors to the Palestinians they used to meet with are meeting again. Whether it is Yael Dayan who was at the head of the May 1991 Geneva Conference of Palestinian and Israeli women; whether it is Ron Cohen or Dedi Zucker already renewing their meetings with Palestinian representatives in the Occupied Territories.[1] There was a setback, without a doubt; I think we don't have to exaggerate how far-reaching and how deep it was.

• *When you spoke last night you said that during the Gulf War, the Israeli peace camp disqualified itself as a peace movement. What would it take for the general Israeli peace movement to become a real peace movement again?*

Michel: It would have to overcome several of its attitudes to be a true peace movement, a true *human rights* movement. First, I think Israel is the only place in the world where the mainstream peace movement considers the White House as

[1] Yael Dayan is a Peace Now activist and journalist. Her father was Moshe Dayan, former Israeli cabinet minister known for his militaristic stance. Ron Cohen and Dedi Zucker are Zionist liberals who are associated with the Ratz, or Citizen's Rights Party.

the staff of the international peace movement, truly believing that American policy is striving towards peace and justice in the world.

Secondly, the peace movement in Israel, the Zionist Left, accepts that the crucial division is between Jews and Arabs, and not between different ideals and values. "Left" and "Right" have meaning *inside* the Jewish community, but it cannot transcend the division between Jews and Arabs. In that sense, the first loyalty is to the nation, to the tribe. And only in the framework of the tribe is there a meaning in whether you support progressive ideas or other kinds of ideas. The Palestinian who shares the same opinions, the same solutions, as the Israeli peace camp, is still an "enemy." And the Israeli who holds an opposite position is still a brother. From this, comes the attitude of "I feel, in the peace movement, in total solidarity with my state, whatever it may do."

Another point is that the peace movement in Israel, the Zionist Left, competes with the Right around the same values.

• *How do you mean?*

Michel: Human rights, natural rights, self-determination are not values in themselves according to the outlook of the Zionist peace camp. These are *means* to achieve the values in which they really believe, and these are the same as those of the right-wing: security, Zionism, "Jewishness." The competition between Right and Left, according to the peace movement, is how to achieve these common values they share with the right-wing — whether by violence or by peace.

If you don't challenge this conception that Jews and Arabs are enemies — if you don't try to present the relationship between the two peoples completely in another way — if you don't argue that human rights and self-determination are values in themselves which you should fight for, then your

228

debate is only a technical one: which is a more efficient way to provide security?

• *I know you consider yourself part of the anti-Zionist peace camp — what are you pushing as a strategy, and what kind of support do you have for that?*

Michel: Exactly the other way around. I do believe in human rights as values — absolute values. I believe in national rights, or the right to self-determination, as an absolute value. And most of all, I do believe that the situation of the Israeli/Palestinian conflict is not something which has to do with genetics, or anything like that — it's the result of a certain *situation*. I have learned during the many years of my political activity and mainly through the beginning of the intifada, how surprisingly generous the Palestinian people and their leadership are toward Israelis — but not only the leadership, the people in the camps as well. How deep is their will for togetherness and a peaceful relationship . . .

I am among those who gave maybe too much importance to the peace movement in Israel. But it's nothing compared to many Palestinians who were convinced that it was a matter of a few months, maybe a few years until the majority of the Israeli people would be supporting their rights. We are still very far from it. We have to translate this openness, this readiness among the Palestinians for a true community, and their willingness to live together with us side by side, to the Israeli public, and say to the Israeli public: "It's possible — it is the *only* possibility, to live in peace."

• *What kind of support do you have inside Israel now for what you're talking about?*

Michel: In December 1989, you met with all these new projects, new initiatives of solidarity, of common activities, common groups. These were the beginning of a new way — not only to do politics, not only to oppose occupation — but, I

229

believe, a new way to consider and to publicize Israeli/Palestinian relations.

Now hundreds and hundreds of Zionist peace activists are being obliged, in my opinion, to deal with the core of the problem of the Israeli/Palestinian relationship. And therefore, also the core of the problem of what kind of strategy to use.

For the first time, the debate on racism and the debate on Occupation have become one. And this is what it's all about. It's not only a matter of territory which is occupied, where you draw the line, what kind of security measures, disarmament, and all these questions — they are important in themselves, but it's linked also to a relationship. Racism relates to the question of relationships between peoples.

I think it's linked to something else which is also very important, but not sufficiently understood, even in Israel. It's the matter of generations. One of the main structural limits of the Zionist Left is the fact that they share a big part of the responsibility for 1948. It was *Mapam* [one of the Zionist Left parties] that was at the forefront of the conquest of Palestine, the deportation of the Palestinian peoples, and building kibbutzim one after the other on Palestinian land. They had to lie to themselves, to erase their whole history, and to dethrone completely their reality.

And it was not only for foreign consumption that they used to be big liars. The 50s and the 60s were the years of the big lie, denying everything: "there were no Palestinians, it's not true that we expelled them, it's not true that there were Arab villages here, we never began any war, we always were for peace" — all these lies were, first and foremost, lies to themselves. Because on the one hand they believed that they were progressive people, they believed that they were not bad people — but on the other hand, all the reality in which they were active participants was to the contrary. So they had to lie. And they had an unconscious feeling of guilt which made them totally unable to do anything right. They

230

were only looking for justification for when and why they could support the government.

The new generation, which came to political maturity around the end of the 70s, after the trauma of the '73 War and entered into action during the Lebanese War, is not bound by these limits. They didn't participate in '48 — for them it's history. The Israeli state is a reality and the Israeli/Palestinian conflict is a reality, and they don't have to justify by a big lie and a big erasing of the history of the state. I believe that a society which is unable to grasp its past cannot understand who it is and what to do next. It is the same as an individual who would go to an analyst to do it. I think the best analyst for the Israeli society was the Palestinians themselves, who said, "We are here!" in the late 60s and early 70s, and then with the intifada.

And there is the phenomenon of the new generation of historians in Tel Aviv University and other places, who are doing research and publishing books and articles in the mainstream media about '48, about the history of the Israeli army, about the refugee questions — reassessing the reality of the Israeli/Palestinian conflict. They are able to do it because they don't feel the old kind of responsibility. A true look at the history of the Israeli/Palestinian conflict and at the reality of the Palestinian movement is a precondition for dealing with the present reality, which is a direct product of the past reality.

• *I read recently that there was a Peace Now protest at a site where there was going to be a new settlement, and I was wondering why these activists are not just laying their bodies down to keep the settlement from being constructed?*

Michel: Because we have what we call a "luxury peace movement" in Israel where you stand in between: you don't support the government, but the Palestinians are still the enemy. You are simply giving advice, sometimes protesting to the government and saying, "No, it's not good, it's not beautiful," while suggesting to the Palestinians, "You should change your course too, and maybe be more moderate, and make more concessions."

To be an *active* participant — this is precisely what is totally new. Abie Nathan is an example. He is an active participant. He said, "I have to do something, because if I don't, it means that nothing will change." But as a whole, protesting is one thing; trying to change is completely different. We don't have a resistance movement in Israel, we have a protest movement. And this is exactly the same with the settlements. We are unhappy with the settlements; we protest them, but we don't try to stop them.

I have to add, though, that Peace Now just sent a delegation to the United States to influence the American administration to pressure Israel against building new settlements in the Occupied Territories. It's a radical change in Peace Now, because for them it was exactly what is forbidden: You don't go with an enemy, or with an external force, against your government; you can be against your government — between you and your government — but not with the Palestinians, and not even with the Americans.

• *During the war, I know the Palestinian economy lost hundreds of millions of dollars because people couldn't go to their jobs, and they couldn't harvest their crops. Since the war, I heard that tens of thousands of Palestinians have been issued green cards, so they're not allowed inside Jerusalem to work, and consequently almost one third are without support. Given this economic disaster, where is the hope today in the intifada and for the future of a Palestinian state?*

Michel: First, I don't think that the hope for the intifada is on the economic level. But already after the war the building companies were urging the government to change the policy, to allow more and more Palestinians to go back to work, when they became convinced that the Russian immigrants were not really able to do the work the Palestinians were. According to the last figures I have read, 70% of the Palestinians who were working in Israel at the end of December, 1990 are back to work.[1]

But the reason I say that it is not just an economic question, and this is very important, is because it will have an impact on various aspects of the intifada itself. The Palestinians know how important the fact is that they work in Israel, and they know it now better than before. It's not an accident that today, among the many things which are discussed by the Palestinians about the next steps of the intifada, is the question of whether or not to reduce the number of general strikes because they can jeopardize their jobs. It's not easy to answer this question; it's too easy to say "no." Because many workers ask, "Will you give me a source of income if I am again out of a job? Can you guarantee that I will not be expelled from the job once again?" I don't have any answer to this question, but I think the intifada *is* dealing with it on the basis of the real debate which exists now.

There is a second aspect which is very important in order to answer the question "What's next for the intifada?" and this is being considered both within the Occupied Territories and in the PLO outside, too: Is there any room for the Palestinians in the 'New American Order?'" That is, do the Palestinians have *anything* to expect from the many talks about a settlement? Or is it a joke and a way to gain time, which is exactly the Israeli policy — to gain time in order to add more settlements in the Occupied Territories, more land confiscations.

This is important because, in my opinion, one of the big mistakes of the last two years was a mistake for which we all share part of the responsibility. We had big illusions about a quick political achievement, some kind of negotiation and settlement as a direct result of the intifada. You don't

[1] According to Naseer Aruri of the Palestine National Council, as of November 1991, permits to work in Israel were denied to 50% of those Palestinians who were working in Israel in November 1990.

behave the same way as a movement, if it's a two- or three-year struggle, as you do if you understand that it's a long struggle — that it's not an event, but a *state*. Then you organize it in a totally different way.

I believe that today, part of the discussion is precisely that: is the intifada a big and long demonstration, or a new way to be occupied and to fight occupation? These are two completely different frameworks to relate to the intifada, to the rhythms of the intifada, and to many of the initiatives. You don't have the same kind of strikes, you don't relate to arrests the same way if it is something you know you have to keep going two or three or five years as you do if you think of it as a struggle of ten or fifteen years.

• *Related to that . . . I've recently heard that over 70% of the West Bank and over 50% of Gaza has been confiscated for settlements, and that about 80% of the water in the Occupied Territories has been confiscated for Israel. It seems that rather than blatantly transferring Palestinians to Jordan, Shamir's trying to squeeze them out and make life so unbearable, by eroding their human rights and their economy, that they'll be forced to leave. And some of my Palestinian friends living in the West Bank have said that he's being successful — that people are leaving. Is that your sense of what's happening, and how could that be reversed?*

Michel: Yes, it is my sense with only one qualification — I don't think there is any plan behind Shamir's behavior. Shamir never planned anything in relation to the Palestinians. Shamir is planning what is good for the Jews. So we need the land, we take the land. We need the water, we take the water. As a by-product, it is also helping with the permanent dream or hope shared by many people inside Israel and the Israeli establishment — that some day, some time, the Palestinians will disappear. By planning what is good for the Jews, this government is making more of an agenda for what is the most realistic conception of transfer.

I don't believe, and I always oppose in the Israeli peace movement, this kind of cataclysmic idea of transfer: that one day loudspeakers in each village will say, "In five minutes everyone must leave" . . . applying to Palestine the memories of Jews in Eastern Europe. This is very dangerous, because then you wait for D-day, and until then you don't pay attention to the fact that there is another kind of transfer and repression going on. And so you wait, because there is a general agreement among tens of thousands of Israelis that transfer will be opposed by any means. This also happened before the war — many groups held meetings about "What we will do if transfer occurs in the framework of this war?" And I was among those who said, "It's not impossible — it happened in the 40s, it happened in '67 — but I doubt that transfer is the most probable option. And instead of looking only at this very limited expression of transfer, we have to be careful to notice other means of repression." What happened was exactly that: waiting for transfer, no one reacted to the horrible curfew during these times.

But there is today a struggle for life, for survival in the Occupied Territories — on the level of agriculture and on the level of land, food, and so on. So I have the feeling that we will have, in the next few years, an intifada integrated with a very strong element of *samoud* — steadfastness. Intifada was a reaction to *samoud*, which means "we have to *keep on*, to keep our land." This was the strategy of the Palestinians until the intifada. But the intifada was an offensive, not just "keeping on." I believe that now we'll have a kind of mixture of both — it will be the intifada, with a lot of *samoud*.

• *I hear repeatedly that half the Israeli public supports "land for peace." How can Shamir remain oblivious to this much public opinion?*

Michel: Shamir is very peculiar; Shamir can disregard everything. He's an autistic person as a politician, maybe not as an individual. He's someone who is completely cut off from reality. It's the way that, even in his own party, people relate to him. And his last statement that he would never personally give back any of the Territories, but that maybe the one after him would, means "I don't care what happens after me, but *I* will not do it." I believe that, even in the Likud, there are many politicians who are unhappy with this policy. Not that they want to give any rights to the Palestinians, but they understand that not doing anything is not a policy. Housing Minister Ariel Sharon, for example, is an alternative; he *wants* to do things [fill the Occupied Territories with Israeli settlements.] And he knows and understands, and I think he's right, that he has a few years to create new facts, because later there will be an American reassessment of the role of Israel in the area. Israel's main importance has been her location in an area of regimes or popular movements which threaten stability and American interests. Now that we don't have any regime which is trying to mobilize some kind of movement among the Arabs in an anti-American program, Israel will still be a central asset in the American strategy as a threat and a type of military base. In fact, Israel is an American military base today on the level of huge amounts of American armaments inside Israel. But its role will be relativized.

As some in the Labor Party say, "We have a few years to accept a kind of settlement — otherwise, after these two or three years, we'll have a worse one. So let's deal with getting the best settlement possible, because now is the time."

• *Many women in the Israeli peace movement talk about the connection between the Israeli soldiers' violence to the Palestinians in the Occupied Territories, and the violence in their homes. Do have any information about this?*

Michel: In the last two years there has been a dramatic increase in murders of Israeli women by their husbands. Every week last year there was either a murder or very strong aggression in the home. What is no less important is that the courts were very sympathetic towards this phenomenon. The sentences were very light — usually the husband was not accused of murder, but only of manslaughter, and got between four and six years of prison. While a Palestinian who throws a stone at a car, without hitting anyone, can get a one-and-a-half-year prison sentence.

Many professionals dealing with mental health draw the conclusion that it is one side-effect of the intifada, bringing more violence into the society, and more tolerance in the courts of Israeli violence such as in relation to the settlers. Against Palestinians and against women, you have the right to do things. It's part of an overall deterioration in our attitude toward violence, especially among the youth.

A new kind of game in Israel, which has brought about the deaths of several children and the wounding of many more, is "road roulette." The object is to run as close as possible to a moving car. One explanation I heard on TV was that the Israeli Jewish youth were confronted with the bravery of the Palestinians, and they wanted to be brave too. So this is a way to express their virility.

• *Speaking of Israeli youth, I've heard you say that in the first two years of the intifada, young Israeli soldiers were committing suicide at an increasing rate until the army changed its strategy, and those suicides decreased. What did the military authorities do to effect this change?*

Michel: At the beginning of the intifada, the army had two problems. One problem was the need to have many, many military forces to do a job which the reserve units couldn't really do because they were not ready emotionally or professionally. So they started using more active-duty soldiers and fewer reserve units, which is still the case. Today the active-duty soldiers almost exclusively undertake "initiative actions" — actions which are not reactions to demonstrations or something, but which are initiated by the Israeli army.

The second problem was that these young soldiers, who were more efficient in doing this repression, were not prepared mentally and conceptually. There is now a new film based on interviews with active-duty soldiers during this time. It's extraordinary how the soldiers tell the story of these years — how confused and distressed they were. There were sometimes even fights in military units between those who were ready to do everything and were even happy, and those who were uneasy and tried to oppose or to stop them.

So the army changed its policy again and decided on a new approach of presenting the repression of the intifada in terms of *military operations* — to use a new type of vocabulary, to arm and organize the soldiers *as if they were in a battle*. It helped give the soldiers some kind of pride. They felt that they were not soldiers, and they wanted to be soldiers, or at least to behave like soldiers. But they were not even dressed as soldiers. They were given a club, but they wanted a rifle — a soldier feels ashamed with a club. He prefers to kill, to shoot. Then he is acting like a soldier.

And this the army understood, and decided not to use any more terms like "demonstration," "youth," "women," but instead to use words like "target" — to present the day-to-day operational orders in terms of battle. "You go to the target, and 'Force B' will go from the north and attack, and if the enemy reacts . . ." The "enemy" was these children and women.

It succeeded partially — there are fewer problems with the soldiers. But there's this total dehumanization of the "target." It's not "Palestinian children" or "Palestinian women"; it's "the enemy." And that's the reason why it's so easy today for a soldier to shoot.

• *How do you deal with your own military service?*

Michel: When my unit is sent to the Occupied Territories, usually I get a phone call from my liaison officer who says, "Look, we are going now to Ramallah or Tulkaren; I understand you will not go, that you will refuse. So I suggest that you go with another unit somewhere else." This is the way my unit is dealing with me, and nine out of ten soldiers who are not ready to serve in the Occupied Territories obtain these kind of arrangements. Usually when someone has been in prison once or twice for refusing to serve, the officer either behaves the same way as with me — trying to find alternative service — or he expels you from the unit, to another unit, where you may not have to serve in the Occupied Territories.

• *So you also were in prison for refusing to serve?*

Michel: In Lebanon and in the Occupied Territories — I've been in prison three times [for refusing to serve].

• *How is it for you to be part of the military at all? Is that a conflict for you?*

Michel: No, it's not a conflict, because being part of my military unit is the same as being part of Israeli society. And this is the basic choice. I can't understand those among my friends who say at a certain point, "I cannot share anything." Because just *being there* means not only are you paying taxes for repression, but you are living on Palestinian land that's been stolen, you are eating and drinking the blood and sweat of the Palestinians. So I understand some of my friends who decide to quit, and say, "It's not a place to live or to raise and educate my children." But I think I share some kind of responsibility with the people of Israel. It's a decision I made a quarter of a century ago.

And the Lebanon War showed that what seemed to be a very arbitrary bet — that some splits *can* occur in national unity, that some opposition can emerge in Israel — can became a reality. If it happened once, it can happen again, and I would feel like a kind of deserter if I did not go on trying to convince people that, for their sake, another road is possible and should be taken. I am convinced that any substantial crisis in Israel which creates a break in Israeli society will happen around a military something — either the intifada or a war, etc.

But the army is not simply an army. It is the *state*, and it is the main tool for coping with anything in Israel, because the story of the Israeli state is permanent war and dealing with the conflict. Whether there will be peace or war or uprising, the army will be there, and you have to be there.

And I hope that I am driving toward the situation now where I can call to my friends in Peace Now to *go back* to the army. Because then there will be deep splits in our units, and we will be needed there. Not only would I be going to jail, refusing, and saying "This is a bad war," but I would be trying to tell the soldiers in my unit to collectively refuse to do things. And to express a new opinion from the army to the government saying, we, *the Israeli army*, are not ready to do this kind of job. This is the moment we will win the war.

• *Can you tell me how prison has affected you — if there are any significant things that happened to you there that changed you?*

Michel: You are mixing two things. I was in military jail three times, which has nothing to do with the prison. It's a kind of disciplinary measure, and you never got more than thirty-five days. Some of us have done up to three times consecutively. When I was in the military jail, mainly during the Lebanese War, it was a very positive experience. The first time, we were a group of around twelve refuseniks together. We were the kings of the prison because we were all older people, reservists — and there are not a lot of reserve soldiers in prison. We had a lot of support, even within the jail.

At the time when I was there, in 1983, the war was already very unpopular. Even the young prison guards from the military police were very open to our ideas. For the twenty-eight days I served the first time, it was a nonstop political teach-in — for the soldiers, but mainly for the guards. For three years there had always been refuseniks there, and we built a real library; we had places where we hid beer and food, and in fact it was fun. Of course it was jail, and we were not free; but we didn't suffer, because we knew that the fact that we were there was helping a movement which was very active at that time and expressed its solidarity almost every day.

The normal prison, where I went last year, was another kind of experience. Though I must say that I have a lot of good memories. Without trying to romanticize it at all, I discovered a lot of humanity among the criminals, even among the guards, but also a lot of misery. I couldn't imagine the level of illiteracy there, and yet on the other hand how thirsty many of these prisoners were to learn! The Arabs more, the Jews a little bit less. I was a teacher in prison; I asked to try to teach. At the beginning they opposed it, but finally I was allowed to. Not only to teach how to read and write but also, with the younger prisoners, to try to teach some kind of values. And I was never confronted with hate, though everyone knew exactly why I was in prison. There was a lot of respect among these people because, in their eyes, I was ready to fight for my opinions and even to pay the price.

I even made some friends there, and I also promised myself that I would not stop my connections with this new part of my life. I'm still helping them to edit the newspaper, I am still keeping in contact with some of these youths when they are at home on the weekend. They call me and I go to their places and drink beer and discuss things with them, help them look for jobs, etc. And with the Palestinians, it was no surprise; I was considered their brother and they accepted me immediately.

• *You have said, Michel, "I am a person of moderation." Yet from my understanding, you're one of the most articulate and outspoken Israeli peace activists. You're the one the Israeli government chose to prosecute and imprison for eight months. Is that a person of moderation?*

Michel: When I say that I'm a person of moderation, I mean that I try not to antagonize people who do not share my political opinions. I try to help them take their own steps in their own rhythm. And many times when there are conflicts, though I belong to the extreme Left, I am usually considered the one who can help mediate with people. I don't think that *I* can, and I don't think that anyone can change the world. You need masses of people to do things. And masses of people need to pass through their own experiences to do these kinds of things.

The slogan of my life is "It's not enough to be right — you must also convince people to do things." And it's more useful to let many people walk their way and myself to run along forwards. I believe that is one reason why I was targeted. There have been many radicals like me, and I have been radical for many years now, but to be with these kind of ideas and to be efficient at the same time — this is not usual in Israel. To be known, yet not to change anything in the way that I believe, not be cut off from people and to gain more and more trust — this is something which apparently is dangerous to the authorities.

• *You also said "I don't want to be the Jew of the Palestinians — I want to be part of my community, but at the place where the two communities are meeting each other." What does that mean for you?*

Michel: It means many, many things. On the practical level, it means that I'm more useful to the cause of Palestinian rights and able to change something *in* my community, as *part* of my community, coming from a Jewish Israeli background, than if I were to cross the border and be one of them. I think I can contribute more by trying to organize here, like with your

242

question about the army: to have an impact on the army and share the army experience, which means also making a lot of compromises with myself, rather than deserting the army and maybe being without that contradiction anymore.

But I think it's more than that. When my friends invite me to parties and popular celebrations for the Day of Independence of Palestine, or the Day of Land, or even their family events, I can feel very good things — but they're not mine. It's not my language, it's not my culture; I can feel totally at home, but nevertheless it's not mine. And I don't think it's impossible because I was born a Jew. I believe that if I were to live in Ramallah for many years, it would be mine. But I am not living as an Arab inside the Arab community; I am living among the Jewish community. My children are going to Israeli schools, not to Palestinian schools. I am reading Hebrew newspapers and books, and not Arabic ones.

So I belong to something, and this is where I stand. I never chose to change where I belong, because I have a sense of responsibility toward the people I'm living with. It's the same way as with the neighborhood. I decided to live in this neighborhood, and after some years I feel some kind of responsibility as a member of the neighborhood committee, fighting to have another kind of garbage collection system, and so on. I decided to live there, and after a certain moment I became part of it. I would say somehow it's the same.

And also maybe as a father, it's important. Because somehow I decided to become an Israeli, though I was not born an Israeli. But still part of my cultural roots are different, and I could have chosen later another place to live and to identify with, but this is an option which does not exist for my children anymore. They were another component deciding for me who I am and where I stand. This has been their world from the moment they were born, and unless they are taken from this reality — to Palestine, to Canada, to I don't know where — this is their home, and obviously the way I feel

243

responsibility toward them, I have an enlarged feeling of solidarity among people like them.

• *What's the difference for you between talking or arguing in your country with right-wing Zionists, and talking with Jews here in the U.S.A. who support "Israel, right or wrong"?*

Michel: I think it's ten times easier to do it in Israel for one basic reason — because we share the same experiences there, and we are confronted with the same facts. And when the facts are hard facts — like a stone is a hard fact, and a war is a hard fact, and the fact that you cannot enter East Jerusalem for three years now is a hard fact — no one can deny these facts. So we argue and debate on common ground.

Many times when I am speaking with American Jews, we don't speak the same reality, they don't know anything about Israeli reality. For them Israel is a myth — something which never existed, but for sure does not exist in the eyes of any Israeli anymore — something which is pure, beautiful, and without any problems. So I am a troublemaker. I "invent problems," and they argue whether or not the Occupation is good, and whether or not there are Palestinians, and whether or not there are divisions in Israeli society. I don't invent divisions in Israeli society — it's a fact. But here I have to argue that what I say, it's not only me, but hundreds of thousands of Israelis. So this is the big difference between Israel and here.

• *So as a progressive Israeli, what do you see as a priority for American people, both Jews and non-Jews, vis-à-vis pushing forward a real peace process?*

Michel: To stop the direct American involvement in the repression of the Palestinian people's rights. And when I say "direct," I mean *direct*, because without American money it would be impossible to build new settlements in the Occupied Territories, it would be impossible to send new immigrants to these Territories. So stop your involvement. I completely disagree with this opinion in Israel that "we don't have to ask the Americans to intervene by cutting the aid to Israel." It's absurd — this aid *is* intervention, *is* active participation. When I give money to my son, and I know that he's going to buy beer with it and get drunk, I actively participate in it. I cannot say that I give him money and he decides what he wants to do with it. It's *my* responsibility, and I think that your duty here is to complain about that issue very strongly. Even though it's very unpopular, this is your duty for yourself as an American.

There are many ways to do it. You are closer to American reality, and you should condition aid to Israel to respect the Fourth Geneva Convention [which "bars an occupying power from transferring its own civilian population into territory it occupies"]. This is one of the few decisions of the Security Council that the Americans supported. You need to *condition the support to Israel by insisting that not one single house is built in the Occupied Territories.* Condition support by applying to Israel the various international resolutions and international conventions.

• *You said before that Russian immigration will be as explosive to Israeli society as the intifada. How so?*

Michel: The massive Soviet immigration into Israel is presented to local and international public opinion as one of the main achievements of Late Zionism. Some use the term "The Second Zionist Revolution." It was not spontaneous like immigration is supposed to be for Zionism — people deciding to come to Zion because of anti-Semitism or other reasons. They were transferred, by force almost, to Israel by agreements with both the Soviet authorities and the American authorities, obliging direct flights to Israel.

When they were free to choose, until 1988, most chose to go everywhere *except* Israel. 90% chose — in 1987 and 1988, and a little bit less in '85-'86 — to stay in Europe or to emigrate to North America or Australia. This one is not motivated whatsoever by Jewish reasons, not even by anti-Semitism, according to the last Report to the Commission of Immigration of the Knesset. It is motivated by the dramatic economic situation and by political instability.

The problem, which is very typically Israeli, is that they are very efficient on the first move, but they do not plan the second one. They are very bad chess players in Israel. And there is no plan whatsoever how to integrate one million people — which is what is expected as a minimum — into a society of four and a half million, including the Palestinians, inside Israel. It is a huge number of people into a society which had an unemployment rate of more than 10% *before* the mass of Soviet immigrants began to enter the labor market.

So how did the government resolve the problem? Using the new liberal fashion in the world, they say that they do not have to intervene. They used to decide where immigrants should live and help them look for jobs — but now the immigrants are free of *any* bureaucracy. *Which means free of any responsibility by the state.* The state is giving a certain allocation for a year, providing a school to learn Hebrew — and now the first day the Soviets must decide where they want to be, and they have to look for an apartment, for a job, and so on. And there are very few apartments. Sharon is building at a very rapid rate, but even if they have apartments, which is not yet the case for 300,000, they will not have any jobs.

Already now, when less than one third of these immigrants have arrived in Israel, there is 80% unemployment among the Soviets — this is the official figure of the mayors of the development towns. In most of the development towns, there are no single apartments for them. In many places, like in Jerusalem, they are living three families in two-room apartments and are accepting any kind of job for almost no money. And I'm speaking about concrete cases everywhere. There are full-page reports in every daily newspaper.

There's a new phenomenon of beggars, which hasn't existed in Israel for many years. You have soup kitchens in Jerusalem for the first time since '48 — four soup kitchens, full from morning to evening with Soviet immigrants, and there is streetside prostitution, among women students in particular. It's *misery*.

I think that the Russian immigration is, in a nutshell, the whole history of Zionism. Intending at the beginning to be an answer for the Jewish people, the Israeli state became an aim in itself, *using* the Jewish people and the suffering of Jews in order to fulfill the interests of the state of Israel, without taking into account whatsoever what the needs of the people are. In a purely cynical and manipulative attitude, I will say that, instead of the Jewish state being a means to resolve their problems, the Soviet immigrants are being used to gain other achievements for the state of Israel. They are *victims* of Zionism.

• *And then connected to this are the 15,000 Ethiopian Jews that were just transferred in?*

Michel: The same, and worse qualitatively. Quantitatively it's marginal, when compared to the hundreds of thousands of Soviet immigrants. But it's worse because they are not considered completely Jewish by the religious authorities who decide who is a *real* Jew, and also because they are Blacks. Obviously it's easier for a white to cope with Israeli reality and to be accepted than it is for a Black Ethiopian.

• *They're not considered real Jews because . . .*

Michel: . . . because their tradition did not take into account an important part of the Orthodox tradition. I don't know all the details, but the way they practice Judaism is different. And the Orthodox Jews decide who's a Jew in Israel, so the

Ethiopians are not considered exactly Jewish — their marriage traditions, their circumcisions, are not exactly the same or something — I don't know.

• *I almost forgot to ask you this question, but I want to ask it now — because it was such a big issue in this country during the war, especially for some of the American Jewish community. How do you respond to the fact that parts of the American Jewish community expressed such horror when they heard that Palestinians were dancing on rooftops after the Scuds landed in Israel?*

Michel: I saw the Palestinians dancing on their roofs. I was able to cross their curfew on a few occasions, and once when we heard on the radio that there were missiles in Tel Aviv, I saw a whole village out, during the curfew, as if it was the Day of Independence, with drums and flags. I was not surprised; I would have been surprised if they hadn't expressed joy because Israel was hit.

And I don't know if, without these Scuds on Tel Aviv — the real ones, and mostly the imaginary ones which fell on the Knesset and everywhere else they heard rumors about — if they would have managed to keep on during this terrible curfew. The joy they got from these illusions was what gave them enough strength to keep on during this time. Otherwise there would have been nothing but total despair.

I think if the American peace movement had not felt any kind of sensitivity to the suffering of Israeli children and innocent people, I would have been angry. Looking at the TV footage of the bomb damage (which was less than what it looked like on TV), if they had not felt any kind of empathy towards the people of Tel Aviv, I would have been angry. But I do not expect the same thing from the Palestinians. I don't feel any kind of anger or surprise. Their enemy was hit — *so what!*

I was more surprised by a telephone call I got the second time the missiles fell on Tel Aviv, and it was on the radio and the TV. My family was in the sealed room, but I was out. I got a call from a friend in Am´ari refugee camp asking if I had any news of Marcello and Asiah and Hannah in Tel Aviv, because he heard that the missiles had hit there and he was afraid that maybe something happened to them. *This* was a surprise to me. I am not sure that during a war, when I am under curfew and at the total mercy of the army which could shoot at any moment, when I am not allowed to move or do anything, closed in my unsealed apartment without masks, without anything, with my wife and five children — that I would be worrying at that moment about what may happen to my friends on the other side!

This was my real surprise — and it was a good one. I almost cried on the telephone. You phone me and ask what is happening with my Jewish friends in Tel Aviv, when we are the enemies? *This* is what you're thinking at this moment? You don't have gas masks for your children; tomorrow you could be transferred, tomorrow one of your kids could be shot! And you call me during an alert to ask about our common Jewish friends in Tel Aviv? I think this is what I would say to your American friends.

• *Thanks, Michel. . . Any final thoughts?*

Just that we are seeking a peace based on *cooperation* and *solidarity*. It's something women will do much quicker than men; it's a fact. The kind of relationship which exists between women — they're doing things now that the men of Peace Now will not do for another five years.

• *Why do you think that is?*

Michel: I believe that there is something like sisterhood. I do believe in it . . . That many of these women are sensing another way to relate to politics, and to power politics. I believe that it's easier for women to relate to the "other" women and see dimensions other than simply "ally/enemy,"

249

and "my tribe/your tribe" — because of the experience of woman in the society. She's part of the tribe, but she's a very special part of the tribe, and therefore she shares something with the women of the other tribe. And in that sense, it's not an accident that there is a human dimension between women more easily than between the men, who will keep their distance from each other.

Epilogue
November 1991

"What has been done in Madrid is the first step
in a thousand miles." — Suha Hindiyeh

*The world held its breath as dignitaries and delegates from
Palestine and Israel, Jordan and Syria, Egypt and Lebanon
gathered in Madrid, Spain in mid-fall 1991.* Accompanying
them were observers from Saudi Arabia, the European
Economic Council and the United Nations. The Middle East
Peace Conference was officially convened by the United
States and the Soviet Union from October 30 to November 3.
In part, it was a response to international pressure on the
United States by numerous governments and peace movements
who felt an international conference could begin to resolve
regional conflicts, prior to the U.S. bombing of Iraq. It was
also intended to merge neatly with U.S. plans for domination
in the region. The gathering itself bulged with dissonant
agendas, many of them hidden.

For the Palestinian people, it was not the international
conference that they (or the U.N.) had called for with
formal recognition of the Palestine Liberation Organization
as their representative. But it was an opportunity they could
not pass up, a desperate effort to stop the building of new
Israeli settlements and save their homeland, to articulate
before the Israeli leadership and the world, on prime-time
television, their struggle for an independent state.

Although the Palestinians were forced to participate as
part of a joint delegation with Jordan, their clear
intelligence, calm logic, flexibility, and dignified desire for
peace shone through, illuminating them as a distinct and
principled people. For the first time in recorded history,
Palestinians and Israelis officially sat down at the table
together. For the first time in memory, they shook hands.

251

In the keynote address of the Palestinian delegation, Dr. Abed al-Shafi implored, "The settlements must stop now. . . The status of the Occupied Territories is being decided each day by Israeli bulldozers and barbed wire. . . We are willing to live side by side on the land with Israelis and the promise of the future. Sharing, however, requires two partners willing to share as equals. Mutuality and reciprocity replace domination and hostility. . . Your security and ours are mutually dependent, as entwined as the fears and nightmares of our children. . . Set us free to re-engage as neighbors and as equals on our holy land."

The Palestinian delegates returned home to demonstrators waving olive branches on the West Bank, and to a dramatic reduction in clashes on the Gaza Strip — yet the Israeli government's broadcasting authority ordered that "peace songs" not be played "so as not to create euphoria." Meanwhile, a spokesperson for the Israeli settlers, Aharon Domb, claimed, "What we are talking about is playing for time. I need another three years in order to settle 200,000 people in Judea and Samaria, and then they can give as many conferences as they want. No power in the world will evacuate that many people."[1]

The real work lies ahead — that of struggling point for point for real peace with justice. What will be the outcome? Is there *any* willingness by the Shamir government to move? Will this be essentially a settlement of "limited autonomy" which grants Palestinians the right to supervise their own garbage collection and delays indefinitely the question of Palestinian independence? Is there any chance that the "promise" of this land can actually be realized — for *both* peoples? Whatever the results of the current peace process, this question remains.

* * *

1 "News From Within," Vol. VII, No. 11, November 9, 1991; Alternative Information Center in Jerusalem.

• *What is your personal feeling about what happened in Madrid?*

Suha: I'll start with the positive. I would say the Madrid Conference brought the Palestinian issue back onto the scene. It brought back into every foreign house all over the world that a Palestinian people does exist — and the fallacy that used to be stated by the Israelis, that we came into a "land without people," is not there anymore. We have proved to the world that we are looking for peace; our presence actually was very strong.

Here at home we do call the three days of the Conference "ceremonial." Now we face the difficult task of bringing peace into reality. What has been done in Madrid is the first step in a thousand miles. It's going to take years — and it might be halted at any stage.

Those who have come back from Madrid are now going into the Occupied Territories, the camps and villages. They are giving talks to the people about the conference, explaining what to expect, and answering their questions.

Palestinians have made clear that they will not be dictated to. There are Palestinian demands that we have been reiterating all through the intifada, and long before the intifada as well, and these demands and rights should be met. My personal feeling, as well as the people's feeling, is that we are for the bilateral talks, but with caution. We're not placing too high hopes on this — irrespective of the fact that on television you might have seen Palestinians in the streets giving olive branches to the Israeli soldiers. Even *this* was met by the Israeli soldiers with shootings.

• *In Madrid, Hanan Ashrawi became known around the world as the leading Palestinian spokesperson and as the most prominent figure at that conference. Do you feel there's any special significance in the fact that a Palestinian woman emerged in this role?*

Suha: Hanan is really qualified to have this position. I look at her as a woman and a human being who has been put in the right place, and she has proven herself.

• *The Israeli government considered prosecuting Dr. Ashrawi, claiming that she met with the PLO, which they said was illegal. What's your response to that?*

Suha: I think all the members of the delegation, in one way or another, mentioned the PLO in their talks. Even in the Palestinian speech that was given at the Conference, they referred to "our leadership" and the Palestine National Council, which is the PLO governing body. It has been made clear in their interviews that we are receiving guidance from the PLO. And I think deep in their hearts, the Israelis know that these Palestinians represent the PLO.

Hanan is not going to be prosecuted because of the international and local pressure that has been put on the Israeli government. They said, "Well, we do not have enough evidence against her," changing their attitude in just one day — that means a lot.

• *We keep hearing that at best the Israeli government may propose an autonomy plan, under which Israel would still control the land and the water of the West Bank and Gaza. What would a plan like that give the Palestinians?*

Suha: Israelis are not only saying this, they are still building settlements. And we do say that if settlements are going to go on we're going to withdraw from the bilateral talks.

It has been reiterated by the Palestinian delegation that we are not going to accept the autonomy *they* want to apply here. What they call "autonomy" we call a "transition period." We're hoping for it to be a very short transition period. During this period we are determined to be in control of our resources and our destiny, and eventually to have our own Palestinian state.

• *Does that also mean that the military should leave?*

Suha: Yes, even during the transitional period, any military presence should be removed from the country. According to our demands, international forces should be in the area.

• *Have the conditions in Palestine improved much since the war's end? Or are they about the same?*

Suha: Actually, I would say nothing has changed since the war — except that there's no more blanket curfew over the Occupied Territories. But oppression is still there: house demolitions, arrests, shootings, women and children being deported because they do not have "residence visas." Occupation is occupation, whether during the war or at any other time.

• *I know a lot of Palestinians were issued Green Cards and have been refused work permits in Israel. Do you know what the unemployment rate is right now in Palestine?*

Suha: I don't know exact numbers. It might have become easier for workers to go back to their work, but still unemployment is very high. When there are special occasions, such as the Madrid Conference, or our Independence Day on the 15th of November, or even when Baker is around, no one is allowed to come from the Occupied Territories into Jerusalem. This means that workers cannot go to their work.

255

Just yesterday in fact Ramallah was under curfew; Nablus is under curfew now and then.

• *Earlier you spoke of the settlements, Suha — and here we're very aware how serious the situation is in terms of the increasing number of these settlements. How can there actually be two states now, given how many Israeli settlers are already in Palestine, especially in the West Bank? How would that work?*

Suha: I don't know about the future. However, we do say that settlements should stop, and even all lands that have been occupied, from 1967 up until now, should be returned back to the Palestinians.

Now when negoiating the issue, the reference should be international law. International law, the Fourth Geneva Convention, says that these settlements are illegal; the occupation itself is illegal.

• *But realistically, do you think it's going to be possible to get those thousands of Israeli settlers to leave their new homes?*

Suha: If they actually are for peace, then they should do something about it.

• *What do you think the significance of the intifada has been in the initiation of the peace talks?*

Suha: The intifada was the impetus for what is going on now. I don't want to say "if it wasn't for the intifada . . ." However, the intifada is the outcome of twenty-two years of occupation, and the intifada has brought the attention of the whole world to the Palestinian people, who had been forgotten for two decades under occupation and oppression.

• *As a Palestinian, what would you like to communicate to the American people right now?*

Suha: We are a people who deserve a state, like any other people all over the world. We have historical and cultural roots in our land. That was proven at the Madrid Conference, and the time has come for this state to be materialized. And the intifada is going to go on as long as our demands are not met.

The Madrid Conference is a stage, but not a final stage in our struggle. Now it is a political struggle that we are going through and, as has been said, political struggle is even harder than going to war. Because in a war, there will be a clear loser and winner. But a political struggle is more difficult — there's no loser, there's no winner.

* * *

As Palestinian and Israeli peace activists continue to wage peace, whatever the outcome from Madrid, I hear the soft voice of Ellias Rishmawi from Beit Sahour: "Palestinians and Israelis each have their dreams about the land of this area. As Palestinians, now we've stopped dreaming and started to be a realistic nation . . . This doesn't mean that we gave up the dreams, but I cannot continue living only on dreams. I can only continue to live on realistic attitudes . . . I hope the Israelis won't wait another 40 years to stop dreaming."

APPENDIX
Resource Groups

Following is a partial *listing of resources and groups working for peace in Palestine and Israel, with a special focus on women's organizations. The list is by no means comprehensive; it is only a place from which to begin. Thanks to* Jewish Women's Call For Peace/*Firebrand Books and* Travel & Resource Guide to Palestine/*Patricia Gardiner for invaluable assistance.*

Palestine/Israel

Acre Arab Women's Association, Ha'Atzma'ut Street 21/23, Acre, Israel. Provides teacher training and day care for Arab women and preschoolers in villages near Galilee.

Al-Fajr Newspaper, tel. 283-791, English: 281-035.

Al Haq (Justice), P.O. Box 1413, Ramallah, West Bank via Israel, tel. 952-421. Law in the Service of Man.

Alternative Information Centre, P.O. Box 24278, Jerusalem, tel. 241-159. Israelis and Palestinians gather and disseminate information about the situation in the Occupied Territories. Publishes "News From Within" (monthly) and "The Other Front" (weekly).

American Near East Refugee Aid, P.O. Box 19982, Jerusalem, tel. 288-449.

Association of Israeli and Palestinian Physicians for Human Rights, P.O. Box 10235, Tel Aviv 61101.

B'Tselem (In the Image), Keren Hayesod 18, Jerusalem 92149. Israeli Information Center for Human Rights in the Occupied Territories. Has newsletter.

East For Peace, 37 Bar Yehuda St., Bat Yam, Israel. Oriental Jewish group.

Gesher L'Shalom (Bridge to Peace), P.O. Box 11567, Tel Aviv.

Ha'Gesher (The Bridge), P.O. Box 9401, Haifa. Strengthens existing ties and forges new links between Jewish and Arab women.

In Defense of Children Under the Occupation, P.O. Box 44984, Haifa.

Isha I'Isha (Woman to Woman), 88 Arlozorov St., Haifa. Haifa Women's Center — brings Palestinian and Jewish women together.

Jerusalem Media and Communication Center, P.O. Box 25047, East Jerusalem, tel. 827-478.

Palestine Human Rights Information Center, P.O. Box 20479, Jerusalem, tel. 287-077.

Palestinian Center for the Study of Nonviolence, Nuzha Building, P.O. Box 20317, East Jerusalem via Israel.

Palestinian Women's Research and Training Society, P.O. Box 19591, East Jerusalem via Israel, tel. 824-757.

Palestinians & Israelis for Nonviolence, P.O. Box 8343, Jerusalem 91083, tel. 710-892. Branch of the International Fellowship of Reconciliation.

Peace Now, 177 Ben Yehuda St., Tel Aviv 63472, tel. 03-546-227.

Peace Quilt, P.O. Box 36448, Tel Aviv, 61363. Women's project; to contribute, send 20x20 cm squares of peace designs on fabric.

Public Committee Against Torture in Israel, P.O. Box 8588, Jerusalem, Israel 91083, tel. 630-073.

Rabbinic Human Rights Watch, P.O. Box 32225, Jerusalem 91999, tel. 710-892. Rabbis protesting human rights abuses against Palestinians.

Red Crescent Society, West Bank: tel. 282-116. Gaza: tel. 860-642.

Red Line: Jews and Arabs Against the Occupation, P.O. Box 207, Nahariya.

Reshet, P.O. Box 9668, Jerusalem 91090, tel. 410-002. Women's Network for the Advancement of Peace.

Runners for Peace, 19 Kfar Etzion St., Jerusalem, tel. 732-936. Israeli-Palestinian running club sponsored by *Runners World* magazine.

Save the Children Federation, Jerusalem, Tel. 02-894-343.

Shalom Akhshav (Peace Now), 6 Lloyd George St., Jerusalem 93108.
Mainstream Israeli peace organization and the largest in Israel,
closely aligned with the Labor Party.

*Shani (Israeli Women's Alliance Against the Occupation), P.O. Box
4319, Jerusalem, tel. 699-870.* Organizes house meetings and
lectures by Jews and Palestinians, pays solidarity visits to
Occupied Territories.

Shutafut (Partnership), P.O. Box 9577, Haifa 31095, tel. 660-281.

*Tandi (Movement of Democratic Women in Israel), P.O. Box 29501,
Tel Aviv.* Palestinians and Jews working for peace and equal
rights for women and children.

*Union of Palestinian Medical Relief Committees, P.O. Box 51483,
East Jerusalem via Israel, tel. 850-021.*

*Women & Peace Coalition, P.O. Box 61128, Jerusalem 91060 tel.
255-984.* Umbrella organization for other Israeli women's groups.

Women in Black, P.O. Box 61128, Jerusalem 91060, tel. 255-984.
Stand in vigils every Friday afternoon against the occupation.

*Women for Women Political Prisoners, P.O. Box 8537, Jerusalem
91083, tel. 241-159.* Provides legal, medical, and emotional
assistance to (mostly Palestinian) women prisoners. Has
booklet and newsletter.

*Women's International League for Peace and Freedom, P.O. Box
11567, Tel Aviv 64373.*

Yated, P.O. Box 559, Kiryat Ata 2800, Israel. Oriental Jewish Group.

*Yesh G'vul (There is a Limit), P.O. Box 6953, Jerusalem 91068, tel.
637-201.*

Palestinian Women's Committees:

*Federation of Working Women's Committees, East Jerusalem, tel.
271-917.*

*Federation of Palestinian Women's Committees, P.O. Box 1250,
Ramallah, West Bank via Israel, tel. 953-420.*

*Palestinian Federation of Women's Action Committees, P.O. Box
20576, East Jerusalem via Israel, tel. 824-757.*

*Palestinian Women's Committees for Social Work. P.O. Box 1306,
Ramallah, West Bank via Israel, tel. 952-904.*

Union of Palestinian Women's Committees, P.O. Box 20076, East Jerusalem.

United States

America-Israel Council for Israel-Palestinian Peace, 4816 Cornell Ave., Downers Grove, IL 60515, tel. (708) 969-7584.

American Federation of Ramallah-Palestine, P.O. Box 2422, Livonia, MI 48150.

American Friends Service Committee, 1501 Cherry St., Philadelphia, PA 19102, tel. (215) 241 -7000.

American-Israeli Civil Liberties Coalition, 275 7th Ave. #1776, New York, NY 10001, tel. (212) 696-9603. Has newsletter.

Arab-American Anti-Discrimination Committee, 4201 Connecticut Ave., NW #500, Washington, DC 20008, tel. (202) 244-2990.

Arab American Democratic Federation, 918 16th St., NW #501, Washington, DC 20006. Lobby in Democratic Party to get Arab-Americans into office.

Arab-American Institute, 918 16th St., NW #501, Washington, DC 20006 tel. (202) 429-9210.

Association of Arab American University Graduates, 556 Trapelo Rd., Belmont, MA 02178.

Family Sponsorship Program, c/o UPWA, P.O. Box 25881, Chicago, IL 60625.

Foundation for Middle East Peace, 555 13th St., NW #800, Washington, DC 20004, tel. (202) 637-6558. Publishes "Report on Israeli Settlements in the Occupied Territories. "

Friends of Yesh G'vul, 1678 Shattuck Ave., Box 6, Berkeley, CA 94709, tel. (510) 848-9391. Has newsletter.

General Union of Palestinian Students, P.O. Box 57, FDR Station, New York, NY 10150.

International Jewish Peace Union, P.O. Box 20854, Tompkins Square Station, New York, NY 10009, tel. (212) 979-8754 or P.O. Box 5672, Berkeley CA 94705, tel. (510) 527-5003.

Jerusalem Fund, 2435 Virginia Ave., NW Washington, DC 20037, tel. (202) 338-1958. Serves the West Bank & Gaza.

Jewish Peace Fellowship & Fellowship of Reconciliation, P.O. Box 271, Nyack, NY 10960, (914) 358-4601.

Jewish Peace Lobby, 8401 Colesville Rd. #317, Silver Spring, MD
20910 tel. (301) 589-8764 .

*Jewish Women's Committee to End the Occupation of the West
Bank and Gaza*, 64 Fulton St. Suite 11, New York, NY, 10038,
tel. (212) 227-5912. Organizes regionally against the occupation
and publishes peace bulletin which lists Women In Black
groups nationwide.

Labor Committee on the Middle East, P.O. Box 421429, San
Francisco, CA 94142. Publishes Middle East Labor Bulletin.

Middle East Children's Alliance, 2140 Shattuck Ave,#207, Berkeley,
CA 94704 tel. (510) 548-0542. Sends humanitarian aid to children
in Palestine and Iraq; leads delegations to Palestine and Israel.
Has newsletter.

Middle East Cultural and Information Center, P.O. Box 3481, San
Diego, CA 92163 tel. (619) 293-0167.

Middle East Justice Network, P.O. Box 558, Cambridge, MA 02138
tel. (617) 666-8061.

Middle East Witness, 515 Broadway, Santa Cruz, CA 95060 tel. (408)
423-1626. Sends delegations to Palestine.

Najda (Relief), Women Concerned About the Middle East, P.O. Box
7152, Berkeley, CA 94707, tel. (510) 969-7584. Provides
information on the Arab world and assistance to Palestinian
women and children.

New Israel Fund, 111 West 40th St. #2300, New York, NY 10018 tel.
(212) 302-0066.

New Jewish Agenda, 64 Fulton St. #1100, New York, NY 10038 tel.
(212) 227-5885.

Palestine Aid Society, 2025 "I" St. NW #1020, Washington, DC 20006
tel. (202) 728-9425.

Palestine Human Rights Campaign, 220 South State St. #1308,
Chicago, IL 60604 tel. (312) 987-1830.

Palestine Human Rights Information Center, 4753 N. Broadway
#930, Chicago, IL 60640 tel. (312) 271-4492. Publishes "From the
Field."

Palestine Solidarity Committee, P.O. Box 27462, San Francisco, CA
94127 tel. (415) 861-1552 or P.O. Box 372, Peck Slip Station, New
York, NY 10272 tel. (212) 964-7299.

Palestinian American Women's Action Committee, P.O. Box 3068, Daly City, CA 94015, tel. (415) 755-2640.

Union of Palestinian Women's Associations, P.O. Box 25656, Chicago, IL 60625 tel. (312) 436-6060.

United Holy Land Fund, P.O. Box 1981, Chicago, IL 60690 tel. (312) 332-3131

United Nations Relief Works Agency Liaison Office, DC2-550, United Nations, New York, NY 10017 tel. (212) 963-2255. Provides assistance to Palestinian refugees.

United Palestine Appeal, 2100 M St., NW #409, Washington, DC 20037 tel. (202) 659-5007.

U.S. Interreligious Committee for Peace in the Middle East, Green &Westview, 3rd fl., Philadelphia, PA 19119 tel. (215) 438-4142.

U.S. Omen, P.O. Box 16308, San Francisco CA 94116. Provides aid and educational needs.

Women's International League for Peace and Freedom, 743 Spruce St., Berkeley, CA 94707.

Handbooks/Magazines/Newspapers

Al Fajr, English weekly translated from Arabic version issued in East Jerusalem. 2025 "I" St., NW #902, Washington, DC 20006.

Arabic Book Center, 791 Valencia, San Francisco, CA 94110, tel. (415) 864-1585.

Arab World and Islamic Resources, 1400 Shattuck Ave. #9, Berkeley, CA 94709 tel. (510) 704-0517.

"Beg, Borrow or Steal: Israeli Settlements in the Occupied Palestine Territories" (Sept. 1991). Jerusalem Media and Communication Center, tel. 827-478.

Bridges, P.O. Box 18437, Seattle, WA 98118. Writing by Jewish feminists and others which "recognizes and honors difference."

Challenge/Etgar. P.O. Box 2760, Tel Aviv 61026. English language magazine written by and for Israeli peace activists.

Jerusalem, Palestine Committee for NGOs, B.P. 554, Tunis Cedex 1080, Tunis, Tunisia, tel. 787-266/286.887. Excellent source of information from the Territories.

Jewish Women's Call for Peace, A Handbook for Jewish Women on the Israeli/Palestinian Conflict, edited by Rita Falbel, Irena

Klepfisz and Donna Nevel (1990), Firebrand Books, 141 The Commons, Ithaca, NY 14850 tel. (607) 272-0000.

MERIP Middle East Report, 1500 Massachusetts Ave. NW, Washington, DC 20005 tel. (202) 223-3677.

New Outlook, 9 Gordon St., Tel Aviv 63458. Publishes a guide to peace networking.

Palestine Focus, P.O. Box 27462, San Francisco, CA 94127 tel. (415) 861-1552. Newspaper published by Palestine Solidarity Committee.

The Other Israel, Newsletter of the Israeli Council for Israeli-Palestinian Peace, P.O. Box 956, Tel Aviv 61008.

The Washington Report on Middle East Affairs, P.O. Box 53062, Washington, DC 20009 tel. (202) 939-6050.

Tikkun, 5100 Leona St., Oakland, CA 94719 tel. (415)482-0805.

Travel & Resource Guide to Palestine, Patricia Gardiner, P.O. Box 3481, San Diego, CA 92163, tel. (619) 293-0167.

HUMAN RIGHTS VIOLATIONS SUMMARY DATA
The Month of May and Uprising Totals from
DECEMBER 9, 1987 THROUGH MAY 31, 1991

VIOLATION	MAY 1991	UPRISING TO DATE
DEATHS		
TOTAL	| | **14 (3)**	| | **956 (247)**
Shot	| | 13 (3)	| | 802 (202)
Non-Bullet Cause	| | 1	| | 64 (9)
Tear-Gas Related	| | 0	| | 90 (36)
INJURIES*	| | **1621** (prelim)	| | **113,150** (est)
EXPULSIONS (Emergency Defense Reg.)	| | **4**	| | **66**
ADMINISTRATIVE DETENTION		
New	| | 85	| | 15,100 est. total
Current	| | 731	
CURFEWS (days) [excluding war]	| | **127**	| | **10,072**
West Bank	| | 99	| | 5628
Gaza	| | 28	| | 4444 (*59)
(*all Gaza Strip)		

January 16-February 25: Blanket curfew or military closure orders on entire West Bank and Gaza Strip. These were gradually lifted at the end of February.

TREES UPROOTED	| | **3195**	| | **110,646**
LAND CONFISCATION** (dunums)	| | **88**	| |373,651
DEMOLITIONS & SEALINGS		
House and other Structures	| | 41	| | 1951
•"For Security Reasons"		
Demolished	| | 6	| | 460
Sealed	| | 6	| | 321
•Unlicensed/Demolished	| | 29	| | 1097
•Demolished by Settlers	| | 0	| | 3
•Indirect Demolitions	| | 0	| | 70

* Injury estimate based on total PHRIC figures for Gaza plus live ammunition injuries and double the preliminary PHRIC figures for all other injuries in the West Bank.
** Land confiscations data must be periodically revised; some orders are given only verbally, while some written orders city incorrect number of dunums.
() Figures in parentheses = number of children killed. See comprehensive chart in *The Cost of Freedom: 1989 Annual Report of The Palestine Human Rights Information Center*, for notes and other categories.

from "From the Field", The Palestine Human Rights Information Center of the Arab Studies Society, May 1991.

UN Resolution 242 *[22 November 1967]*

The Security Council,

Expressing its continuing concern with the grave situation in the Middle East,

Emphasizing the inadmissibility of the acquisition of territory by war and the need to work for a just and lasting peace in which every State in the area can live in security,

Emphasizing further that all Member States in their acceptance of the Charter of the United Nations have undertaken a commitment to act in accordance with Article 2 of the Charter,

1. *Affirms that the fulfillment of Charter principles requires the establishment of a just and lasting peace in the Middle East which should include the application of both the following principles:*

    i. *Withdrawal of Israel armed forces from territories occupied in the recent conflict;*

    ii. *Termination of all claims or states of belligerency and respect for and acknowledgement of the sovereignty, territorial integrity and political independence of every State in the area and their right to live in peace within secure and recognized boundaries free from threats or acts of force;*

2. *Affirms further the necessity*

    (a) *For guaranteeing freedom of navigation through international waterways in the area;*

    (b) *For achieving a just settlement of the refugee problem;*

    (c) *For guaranteeing the territorial inviolability and political independence of every State in the area, through measures including the establishment of demilitarized zones;*

3. *Requests the Secretary-General to designate a Special Representative to proceed to the Middle East to establish and maintain contacts with the States concerned in order to promote agreement and assist efforts to achieve a peaceful and accepted settlement in accordance with the provisions and principles in this resolution;*

4. *Requests the Secretary-General to report to the Security Council on.the progress of the efforts of the Special Representative as soon as possible.*

Adopted unanimously at the 1382nd meeting.

UN Resolution 338 *[21 October 1973]*

The Security Council,

1. *Calls upon all parties to the present fighting to cease all firing and terminate all military activity immediately, no later than 12 hours after the moment of the adoption of this decision, in the positions they now occupy;*

2. *Calls upon the parties concerned to start immediately after the cease-fire the implementation of Security Council Resolution 242 (1967) in all of its parts;*

3. *Decides that, immediately and concurrently with the cease-fire, negotiations start between the parties concerned under appropriate auspices aimed at establishing a just and durable peace in the Middle East.*

MEMORANDUM

The Honorable U.S. Secretary of State James Baker III
The U.S. Consulate General
Jerusalem

In the aftermath of the Gulf War, neither regional nor global politics can afford procrastination or evasion. As Palestinians who have been made to endure prolonged occupation and dispossession, we are heartened by verbal commitments and statements of intent to solve the Palestinian Question on the basis of the principle of land for peace and the implementation of all pertinent U.N. resolutions. From our experience, however, resolve and application hold the fate of our whole nation in sway. We maintain that in spite of the painful and traumatic experience of the Gulf War, the time has come for embarking on decisive and future-oriented action rather than indulging in recrimination and retrospection.

It has thus become imperative that the activation of the U.N. as the expression of the will of the international community be impartially maintained in the non-selective implementation of legality and the values of justice and moral politics. If a new global vision is emerging, it must be solidly based on the objective will and consent of the international community and must protect the inviolable rights of peoples as enshrined in the U.N. Charter and all other international conventions and agreements. Such a vision of justice, peace and stability cannot admit the subjective criteria of power, wealth, land acquisition, strength of arms, natural resources, ethnic origins, religious affiliation, cultural perspectives or national identity as factors in the intransigence of the violator in relation to the victim or to the manipulation of the powerful in relation to the weak. The will of the international community must be maintained as a firm and uniform reference for equitable arbitration not subject to selective alteration or deferment.

We, the Palestinians of the Intifada, the portion of the Palestinian nation who bear the yoke of occupation rather than exile and dispersion, on the strength of our commitment to this new vision affirm the following:
1. The PLO is our sole legitimate leadership and interlocutors, embodying the national identity and expressing the will of the

Palestinian people everywhere. As such, it is empowered to represent us in all political negotiations and endeavors, having the democratic legitimacy of a popular base and enjoying the overwhelming support of its constituency. The Palestinian people alone have the right to choose their leadership and will not tolerate any attempt at interference or control in this vital issue.

2. We confirm our commitment to the Palestinian peace initiative and political program as articulated in the 19th PNC (Palestine National Council) of November 1988, and maintain our resolve to pursue a just political settlement of the Palestinian-Israeli conflict on that basis. Our objective remains to establish the independent Palestinian state on the national soil of Palestine, next to the state of Israel and within the framework of the two-state solution.

3. Our adherence to international legitimacy remains unwavering, and we uphold the rule of international law in accepting and supporting all U.N. resolutions pertaining to the question of Palestine, and thus call for their immediate and full implementation.

4. The national rights of the Palestinian people must be recognized, safeguarded and upheld — foremost among which is our right to self-determination, freedom and statehood.

5. No state must be singled out for preferential treatment by the international community or considered above the norms and laws that govern the behavior of or relations among nations. Thus Israel must not be allowed to continue pre-empting, rejecting or violating U.N. resolutions vis-à-vis the Palestinians especially in the annexation of East Jerusalem, the establishment of settlements, and the confiscation of land and resources. Of particular relevance and urgency is the imperative necessity of applying the Fourth Geneva Conventions of 1949 to protect the defenseless and civilian Palestinian population from the brutality of the occupation, particularly in its persistent violations of our most basic human rights and all forms of collective punishments such as house demolitions, closure of universities and schools, curfews, military sieges and economic strangulation.

6. The de facto sovereignty which Israel illegally practices over occupied Palestine must cease immediately, and a system of protection for Palestinians and accountability for Israel must be established and applied within the mandate of the U.N. with the Security Council exercising its right of enforcement.

7. The peace process must be advanced with the momentum generated by the will of the international community, and not made subject to Israeli concurrence and rejection.

8. The most suitable mechanism for advancing the peace process is the International Conference which is capable of producing concrete results. Any transitional steps or arrangements will have to be structured within a comprehensive, interconnected and coherent plan with a specified time frame for implementation and leading to Palestinian statehood.

9. The peace process cannot be further undermined by Israel's policy of creating facts to alter the geopolitical, demographic or social realities of our area. The political decapitation of the Palestinian people through the arrest and detention of our political activists and peace advocates must stop and the detainees be released. The Iron Fist policy and the escalation of all forms of repression and harassment not only create intolerable conditions for Palestinians but also generate feelings of hostility and bitterness which are capable of sabotaging the peace process.

10. Security for the whole region will be ensured only through a genuine and internationally guaranteed peace, not through the acquisition of arms and territory or through violence. Genuine peace and stability will result from addressing the central causes of conflicts in a serious and comprehensive manner, the Palestinian question being the key to regional stability. Only by solving the Palestinian-Israeli conflict can the Arab-Israeli conflict be solved in a durable and just manner.

11. The stability and prosperity of the region can be achieved through future cooperation based on mutuality, reciprocity and the recognition and pursuit of joint interests and rights.

As Palestinians under occupation, we are able to transcend the inequities and oppression of the present and to project a future image of peace and stability. In doing so, we affirm our national rights, adhere to international legitimacy and envisage the prospects of a new world based on the politics of justice and morality.

East Jerusalem
March 12, 1991

Israeli Settlements on the West Bank
as of March 1991

Most of the interviews included in this volume are available on audio tape from Pacifica Program Service. For ordering information contact:

Pacifica Program Service
3729 Cahuenga Blvd. West
North Hollywood, CA 91604
(818) 506-1077 or 1-800-735-0232